For more than three centuries the criminal law has given rise to a divergent set of approaches to the crime of homicide. Whereas the law of murder has not conceptually changed, the crime of manslaughter has resulted in some forms of homicide being visited with relatively minor penalties. These various categories of unlawful killing present considerable problems relating to intention, or lack of it, and the culpability of those whose behaviour, while lacking in evident malice, is characterised by the grossest recklessness. The reaction of the relatives of victims is generally simpler. They frequently find it impossible to understand how those who kill by dangerous or drunken driving may receive comparatively lenient sentences, while those convicted of manslaughter following a drunken brawl may be dealt with more severely, and yet others, convicted of so-called 'mercy killings', are subject to the mandatory penalty of life imprisonment.

This book addresses the powerful and controversial arguments for the current distinctions between murder, manslaughter and other specific categories of crime to be abolished and subsumed within a single crime of culpable homicide. In the course of this analysis the authors consider a number of issues of great contemporary importance, including the presentation of expert evidence in cases involving unexplained infant death, corporate killing, and the question of the defences available to the accused, including self-defence and provocation, where popular notions of what is reasonable or justifiable may be at variance with legal precedent.

While this book aims to consider criminal homicide in its social, historical and legal setting, it also goes far beyond in setting out the case for radical reform.

With Malice Aforethought
A Study of the Crime and Punishment for Homicide

LOUIS BLOM-COOPER QC
and
PROFESSOR TERENCE MORRIS

·HART·
PUBLISHING

OXFORD – PORTLAND OREGON
2004

Hart Publishing
Oxford and Portland, Oregon

Published in North America (US and Canada) by
Hart Publishing c/o
International Specialized Book Services
5804 NE Hassalo Street
Portland, Oregon
97213-3644
USA

Hart Publishing is a specialist legal publisher based in Oxford, England.
To order further copies of this book or to request a list of other
publications please write to:

Hart Publishing, Salter's Boatyard, Folly Bridge,
Abingdon Road, Oxford OX1 4LB
Telephone: +44 (0)1865 245533 or Fax: +44 (0)1865 794882
e-mail: mail@hartpub.co.uk
WEBSITE: http//www.hartpub.co.uk

British Library Cataloguing in Publication Data
Data Available
ISBN 1–84113–485–6 (hardback)

Typeset by Hope Services (Abingdon) Ltd.
Printed and bound in Great Britain on acid-free paper by
MPG Books Ltd, Bodmin, Cornwall.

Contents

Table of Cases

Whenever the usual form of citation would be 'R *v* D' signifying prosecution by the Crown, cases are listed under the name of the accused.

Table of Statutes

Medieval and Tudor Legislation

1

Prologue and Apologia

————

WHAT THIS BOOK IS ABOUT

Lord Mustill in his judgment delivered in the House of Lords in July 1997 used these words:

> Murder is widely thought to be the gravest of crimes. One could expect a developed system to embody a law of murder clear enough to yield an unequivocal result on a given set of facts, a result which conforms with apparent justice and has a sound intellectual base. This is not so in England, where the law of homicide is permeated by anomaly, fiction, misnomer and obsolete reasoning. One conspicuous anomaly is the rule which identifies the "malice aforethought" (a doubly misleading expression) required for the crime of murder not only with a conscious intention to kill but also with an intention to cause grievous bodily harm. It is, therefore, possible to commit a murder not only without wishing the death of the victim but without the least thought that this might be the result of the assault. Many would doubt the justice of this rule, which is not the popular conception of murder and (as I shall suggest) no longer rests on any intellectual foundation. The law of Scotland does very well without it, and England could perhaps do the same.[1]

This is as devastating a comment upon the state of the law in England as it governs the prosecution and punishment of criminal homicide as has been heard in recent years. Yet, for all the notice that has been taken of it in the ensuing years, whether in government or the media, his trenchant observations might have been little more than a dialogue with the deaf. Although the instant matter involved fatal violence towards a child *in utero*, the exploration of the law upon which the Court was obliged to embark revealed the shortcomings upon which it was necessary to comment at the outset.

Murder is, indeed, widely thought to be the gravest of crimes[2]. Irrespective of how the idea is expressed, it is impossible to escape from the fact that for

---

[1] Judgment of Lord Mustill in *Attorney General's Reference* [No.3 of 1994], [1998] AC 245, at 250 D2F. The Law Commission, in its report *Partial Defences to Murder* (Law Com No 290, 2004) was more sparing in its language. It called the law of murder 'a mess'.

[2] In an earlier work, we observed:

> Murder produces a sense of profound social shock—heightened in our society by the dissemination of the details through modern mass media. It can normally be relieved only by some highly dramatic act on the part of the community towards the offender, Terence Morris and Louis Blom-Cooper, *A Calendar of Murder* (London, Michael Joseph, 1964) at 272.

society at large, no less than for the individuals who are affected directly by it, the killing of a human being by another, in whatever circumstances, is an awesomely dreadful happening. Accident is bad enough, but when the killing constitutes a criminal event it moves to the foreground of individual and public consciousness. One might not unreasonably expect the law to provide 'apparent justice' founded upon a 'sound intellectual base'. Is such a thing so much to ask? Clearly, it is otherwise. This being so, we consider how things have reached this point after a long traverse of the centuries since the times of de Bracton, Fleta, Coke and those other legal luminaries who have contributed to the development of the law of homicide. It will quickly become clear to the reader that our view is that the time for further amending the law of murder is over and that the time has come for fundamental reform; in short, our case is that all the offences presently identified as murder, together with all the various categories of manslaughter, be brought together into a single offence of criminal homicide in a process of amalgamation or consolidation.

As far as the penalty for this new offence of criminal homicide is concerned, it follows that the mandatory sentence of life imprisonment for murder would disappear with the crime of murder itself. Amalgamation aside, we are unequivocally of the view that mandatory penalties without any possibility of mitigation have always been, and remain, wholly without merit, whether they relate to death or imprisonment for life, or are inflicted as a penalty for a particular category of offence irrespective of the individual circumstances of the criminal event. No army could effectively march if its soldiers' boots were issued on the principle of 'one size fits all'; any system of criminal justice employing such a maxim is similarly hobbled.

The quality of justice is contingent upon balance in more than one dimension; between responsibility and harm done, and between the interests of society and the rights of those accused of crime. A consequence of this, which follows from our proposal for a single offence of criminal homicide, is that those defences which currently function as a means for reducing the crime of murder to that of manslaughter would cease to have any forensic purpose, becoming matters to be put in mitigation. Since each criminal event must be individually assessed the proper place for such assessment is not the bear pit of politics, often echoing with calls for rhadamanthine punishments to be inflicted whether they fit or no, but the ordered atmosphere of the courtroom. Politicians are nothing if not ephemeral and the immediate attention span of the media seldom exceeds 24 hours. Historically, there was a time when judges were as prone to do the will of their political masters no less eagerly than some of them took bribes, but those days are long gone. While there are occasions when we may not approve of their judgment, there is never a time when their reasoning is so arbitrary or opaque that it cannot be subjected to critical analysis with intellectual rigour. And, in the absence of a written constitution, a judiciary whose probity is above reproach can alone be the ultimate guarantor of individual liberty. Indeed, if we cannot trust the judges, not least in imposing sentence, we can trust no one.

It is a particularly irony that at a time when the intellectual quality and independence of thought characterising the higher judiciary approaches an excellence hitherto unknown, that there should be a tension between executive and judiciary. There seems little doubt but that it has developed since the powers of the Home Secretary in the setting of tariffs for mandatory life sentence prisoners have been successfully challenged in the courts.

While we would not expect to succeed in persuading every reader to our viewpoint, our hope is to promote debate. Scrutiny of the law of homicide is not new, even if the resultant changes have been limited and slow to emerge. As a preliminary, we present a selection of various opinions, each in its own way authoritative, which have been expressed in various *fora* of debate at different times.

VOICES FROM OLYMPUS

1874

If there is any case in which the law should speak plainly, without sophism or evasion, it is where life is at stake; and it is on this very occasion that the law is most evasive and most sophistical[3].

1993

. . . before any such prisoner (*serving a mandatory sentence of life imprisonment*) is released on licence, I will consider not only (a) whether the period served is adequate to satisfy the requirement of retribution and deterrence and (b) whether it is safe to release the prisoner, but also (c) the public acceptability of early release. This means I will exercise my discretion to release only if I am satisfied that to do so will not threaten the maintenance of public confidence in the system of criminal justice[4].

1995

. . . it may be said that to abandon the mandatory life sentence would betray those who voted to abolish the death penalty in 1965 and 1969, as well as those who vote against its re-introduction on the understanding that the life sentence for murder will continue to be mandatory[5].

---

[3] Select Committee of the House of Commons, *Special Report from the Select Committee on the Homicide Law Amendment Bill* (315) 1874. *Parliamentary Papers*, (1874) Vol 9, at p 471.

[4] The Rt Hon Michael Howard, QC, MP, Secretary of State for Home Affairs, *Hansard*, HC, Written Answers 863–65, 27 July 1993. In answer to a Question tabled by Sir Ivan Lawrence QC, MP respecting the House of Lords judgment in *R v Secretary of State for the Home Department ex parte Smart, Pegg, Doody and Pierson* [1994] 1 AC 531.

[5] House of Commons. Session 1995–96, Home Affairs Committee, (Chairman, Sir Ivan Lawrence QC, MP.) *First Report, Murder: The Mandatory Life Sentence*, 13 December 1995, xx 54.

1996

The present government has . . . made it clear, in the face of a continuous barrage of well-informed pressure, that it sees no reason to alter the present constituents of the law of murder, nor, indeed, to alter the mandatory sentence for murder . . .[6].

2000

In my view the arguments advanced by Mr Howard[7] comprised all the major points that need to be made in favour of retention of the mandatory penalty and the setting of tariffs by the Home Secretary.

I remain unconvinced that change to the current system is either necessary or appropriate[8].

2003

The noble and learned Lord [Ackner] is right to say that the Committee[9] held the view that the mandatory life sentence should be replaced with a maximum sentence of discretionary life. The government of the day did not accept the recommendation, and neither do we[10].

It (*the life sentence*) is not a 'dishonest fiction'. There is a misunderstanding of what 'life' means[11].

THE TASK UNFINISHED

Those who persevered upon the long and difficult road that led from the Parliamentary debates of 1948 to the passing of the Murder (Abolition of the Death Penalty) Act of 1965 and its final ratification in 1969 undoubtedly believed that their task was finally accomplished. The office of hangman had become redundant; the condemned cells and their adjacent gallows in the prisons where, mostly unremembered, scores of those convicted of murder—often rightly but not infrequently wrongly—had met death; these would be employed for another purpose. No more would the crowds—deprived since 1868 of the spectacle of public executions—gather at the prison gate; on occasion angry at perceived injustice though often no more than morbidly curious. The sentence

---

[6] Law Commission, *Report on Involuntary Manslaughter*, 229 (1996) para 1.28.

[7] In his response to the report of an independent inquiry into the mandatory life sentence for murder commissioned by the Prison Reform Trust, *Report* (London, PRT, 1993).

[8] The Rt Hon Jack Straw MP Secretary of State for Home Affairs, (private communication, 23 June 2000).

[9] Select Committee of the House of Lords on Murder and Life Imprisonment. (*Chairman, Lord Nathan*) *Report*, HL 78–1, (HMSO, 1989).

[10] The Baroness Scotland of Asthal speaking in the debate on Amendment No 73 to the Criminal Justice Bill on 17 November 2003, Hansard HL, Vol 654, No 171, Col 1807.

[11] *Ibid.*

of death, executed by means of hanging the prisoner by the neck until he or she be dead, was at last, like the even more frightful ways in which the condemned suffered death in former times, consigned to the museum of the penal system.

As far as the future of the new mandatory penalty for murder was concerned, matters were not to be so straightforward and it would subsequently prove to have been a mistake to think that the problem had been boxed and put away in the attic of the political past. But this was a discovery yet to be made. Abolition had been accomplished during the tenure of the Wilson government in a decade that was exceptional in being characterised by what might in some sense be described as a torrent of reform across the whole spectrum of the law. While one ought not to over-indulge in speculation bordering upon a naive historicism, it is impossible to avoid wondering how things would have gone but for the involvement of Gerald Gardiner, QC, elevated in 1964 as Baron Gardiner of Kittisford to the status of Lord Chancellor. Gardiner had a reputation as an advocate that was second to none[12]. Whether he ever developed political skills is a matter for debate; whether he was wholly comfortable in the world of politics is equally open to question. His one attempt to enter Parliament at the general election of 1951[13] was a failure but a decade later he had clearly become Wilson's first choice for Lord Chancellor. His great enthusiasm lay in the field of penal reform and, above all, with the abolition of the death penalty. It had become his great project and he was determined that the window of legislative opportunity which presented itself should not be missed. His private papers reveal that as the abolition Bill went through its various Parliamentary stages, his concerns fastened increasingly upon abolition alone; they provide an explanation of why he was opposed to the constructively innovative amendment of the Lord Chief Justice, Lord Parker of Waddington[14] that would have given the judges discretion in sentencing, lest it imperil the safe passage of the legislation and its precious cargo, abolition. Had the Parker amendment been enshrined in the Act it is likely that much of the subsequent controversy that has centred on the propriety of the executive being involved in the setting of tariffs would have not arisen. After all the debates, and those in the Lords had been of high quality, there remained at the end two fatal omissions.

Firstly, there was no serious consideration given to the definition of life imprisonment and what conflicts of interpretation such an omission would

---

[12] He had represented the author of *Exodus*, Leon Uris, who was sued for libel by one Dr Dering who had been a doctor in one of the most notorious of the Nazi concentration camps, in an action in which the Royal Courts of Justice in the Strand seemed to have become the setting less for a civil suit than a war crimes trial.

[13] He was selected as the Labour party candidate for Croydon West but roundly defeated by his Conservative opponent at a point when the national political tide was ebbing rapidly away from the party still led by Clement Attlee.

[14] It is an irony of history that the Parker amendment was so widely supported on all sides, not least by the former Conservative Lord Chancellor, Lord Dilhorne, who was a an enthusiastic supporter of the death penalty.

engender. There was a simplistic assumption that the penalty of 'life' having been substituted for that of 'death', the management of life sentence prisoners, including their release by executive action, would assume the same pattern as that in respect of those reprieved from the gallows and sentenced to 'life' as an alternative. Secondly, there was not the least awareness that so fundamental a change in the penalty for murder might bring in its train a whole series of wider issues leading inexorably to the conclusion that something would need to be done about the substantive law of murder. The reformers, perhaps unwisely, were content to rest upon their laurels, unaware that what lay in the not so distant future would not only change the whole climate of criminal justice policy, but also ensure that these fatal omissions would become the source of a new and in some senses, more intractable problem than that of the death penalty.

CLIMATE CHANGE IN THE POLITICS OF CRIMINAL JUSTICE;
A TRANS-ATLANTIC CHILL

Few of those involved in the promotion of law reform in the 1960s remotely imagined the possibility of such a dramatic change in the political climate that so many of their cherished assumptions would within a few short years be regarded as no more than suitable material to be thrown upon a bonfire of liberal shibboleths. The ideal of rehabilitation was to be subordinate to the use of the penal system as a mechanism of social control in which the function of incarceration was primarily that of social incapacitation. The rise and rise of what might be termed the 'new right' challenged the traditions of humane conservatism throughout the western industrial world, but notably in the United States, Britain and the larger countries of mainland Europe. Penal policies that saw the protection of the public as best assured by the reformation of the offender were rejected along with welfare systems predicated upon the direct involvement of the state. Through its imputed rationality, perfection in all things was to be sought nowhere but in the market. And in an uncanny echo of the rationalist psychology of the Enlightenment, it was assumed as axiomatic that human behaviour was motivated by self-interest alone. The evangelists of the new penology readily embraced not only this psychology but also much of the rhetorical baggage of homespun philosophies of the God-fearing and self-reliant variety.

The chill wind of change was first felt in the United States. Capital punishment having been in abeyance, rejected as unconstitutional on the grounds of its cruel and unusual character, was re-enacted by many State legislatures. Electric chair, gas chamber, gallows and firing squad were overtaken by the technology of the lethal injection, while the prison population began inexorably to grow in consequence of laws providing for longer and mandatory sentences. As the policy of 'getting tough' on crime was skilfully moulded into compelling political slogans,[15] it became a powerful card in the hand of those seeking office. The Reagan years in America were mirrored, albeit imperfectly, by the era of Margaret Thatcher. There were numerous Parliamentary attempts to re-introduce the death penalty by clauses that were 'piggy-backed'—though without success—on other criminal justice legislation.

THE RESURRECTION OF 'CIVIL DEATH': CONFINEMENT IN THE 'IRON CAGE OF VENGEANCE'

For the last 20 years successive governments, both Conservative and New Labour, have pursued penal policies, which, although they claim to be distinct, and may indeed differ in detail, nevertheless present to the objective observer a broader picture of seamless continuity. From Leon Brittan, *via* Michael Howard and Jack Straw to the present incumbent, David Blunkett, there has been a consistency of approach towards the penalty for murder; a consistency, moreover, which has been consonant with the expressions of opinion in those sections of the media which claim, and with some justification, to represent public opinion. The question is; how far is that opinion informed by fact rather than popular belief and moderated by reason rather than prejudice? The public in the United States needed little persuasion that it would be a good thing if capital punishment were to be restored and while in this country recognition that unsafe convictions can result in irremediable injustice may be one reason for Parliamentary reluctance to re-introduce it here, there is undoubtedly a great enthusiasm for the idea of incarceration for life, or something very like it.[16] But this reluctance was not matched by any concern that the mandatory sentence of life imprisonment had been uncritically elevated to the status of its substitute. The question of the setting of the tariff of time to be served by lifers in order to satisfy the requirements of retribution and deterrence—itself an executive construct—became increasingly vexed. Through the mechanism of judicial review, Strasbourg jurisprudence and latterly, the application of human rights law in a domestic context, the role of the judiciary has been clarified and the powers of the executive severely curbed. It is not impossible that the genesis of those parts of the Criminal Justice Act 2003 dealing with this issue arose from dissatisfaction on the part of the executive with the results of these earlier legal decisions.

Another thread in the fabric has emerged; that of the 'whole life' tariff. It is not that incarceration for life is entirely novel; dangerous offenders have

---

[15] In this country slogans of the type known in the United States as 'bumper stickers' emerged from both Conservative and New Labour spokesmen in the early 1990s, promising to be 'tough on crime and the causes of crime' or admonishing 'If you don't want to do the time, don't do the crime.' This was also the era of the slogan *'Prison works!'*

[16] Notorious crimes, particularly the killings of children which are often the subject of sensational reporting in the media, almost always result in expressions of outrage accompanied by demands for condign punishment for those responsible.

frequently been detained indefinitely in the past in the interests of public safety (though generally in special hospitals) and in past ages political prisoners have languished in prison for the remainder of their natural lives. The contemporary 'whole life' tariff—recalling that the tariff has been defined as that part of the life sentence considered proportionate to the requirements of retribution and deterrence—is imposed in order to underwrite what is often described as 'public confidence' in the criminal justice system. It is not difficult to appreciate how the term may be read, perhaps more sceptically, as a euphemism for satisfying the demands of the more vocal expressions of public sentiment. Even if this should be, as some assert, the clear will of the ordinary citizen, this, in itself, is no compelling reason for compliantly bending to it. If there were no process that ensured public policy was not uncritically driven by populist demand there could be little decency in civil society. Children might still be hanged for murder, sex offenders castrated or put to death, and persistent thieves branded with hot irons. None of these penal practices would need to be re-invented and some of the apparatus survives in the form of museum exhibits.

'Whole life' tariffs apart, the policy of maintaining a mandatory sentence of life imprisonment for murder, undifferentiated in any way save for the *quantum* of the tariff, imperils on the one hand the principle of proportional justice and on the other, the no less noble ideal of rehabilitating the offender; it would seem to have as its objective, or so it would appear, only to keep secure the prison gate and, in the case of those condemned to a 'whole life' tariff, to weld up what has in another context been termed the 'iron cage of vengeance'.[17]

TOWARDS THE ABOLITION OF THE PENALTY OF CIVIL DEATH

The current political climate in which the retributivism that characterises so much of what might be described as the penology of New Labour is, to say the least, dispiriting as far as constructive debate is concerned. The dominant resonances are authoritarian in tone and those of control rather than rehabilitation. They sound against a background in which, contrary to the evidence, there is widespread public belief that crime, far from having diminished in the last decade, has increased remorselessly, year on year. It is likely that this firmly held belief is related to a greater social awareness of disorder in public places involving crimes of violence and criminal damage as well as more general incivility. These phenomena are undoubtedly in turn related to the problems connected with the patterns of alcohol consumption that now form an integral element of popular entertainment in town and city centres. Though victims and offenders are predominantly young, this does little to dissuade many law-abiding citizens

---

[17] A term employed by Simon Jenkins in an article inspired by the sentence of imprisonment for five years passed upon the disgraced London head teacher Colleen McCabe for serious financial irregularities with money not her own. *The Times*, 3 September 2003.

of more sober habits that the mechanisms of law enforcement are diminishingly effective in controlling crime and that they, themselves, are not exempt from becoming victims. The general effect can be to stimulate the belief that crime can only be controlled by 'tough' as opposed to 'tender' penalties and that where homicide is concerned it is a folly to be liberally indulgent.

Successive Home Secretaries in recent years have indicated, unequivocally, their support for the mandatory sentence of life imprisonment for murder. A reform of the law which would amalgamate murder and all varieties of manslaughter is not an issue which has been seriously considered; when it has been suggested it has for the most part been summarily dismissed out of hand.

As to the question of the mandatory penalty, we already have what pass for reasoned answers on the part of government, spelled out in 2003 during the debates on the Criminal Justice Bill, which has now reached the statute book. We shall consider that in greater detail in Chapter 7, but suffice it to say that ministers currently, no less than their immediate predecessors, remain unmoved on the issue and wholly dismissive of the contrary opinion.

Why this should be can only be the subject of speculation. Is it that government goes in daily fear of the sometimes stridently expressed demands of what might be termed the 'tabloid constituency' in contemporary society? Only those privy to its workings can supply the answer. Perhaps among government managers there are those who caution against going against the tide of public opinion—assuming that its strength has been reliably estimated.[18]

Whether the current approach to criminal justice generally, and the mandatory penalty for murder in particular, stems from an independently simplistic and authoritarian perspective on the part of government, or whether it is intended to serve, instrumentally, as an emollient for the demands of a populist penology, is not a question for this book. Suffice it to say that as an approach to the crime and punishment of homicide, given legislative substance in the Criminal Justice Act 2003, it is scarcely a good omen for constructive improvement in the law.

In sum, it is our view that the need for a reform of the law is long overdue and that in the course of such reform much that is hallowed, by the usage of long years rather than by illuminating the matter from a 'sound intellectual base', will need to be swept away. In this we share, enthusiastically, in the 'passion', which the Baroness Scotland of Asthal[19] so succinctly identified in the contributions to the debate on the mandatory penalty made by Lord Lloyd of Berwick and Lord Ackner.

---

[18] In 1948, the powerful influence of Herbert Morrison helped to dissuade the Attlee government from including an amendment to abolish capital punishment in its Criminal Justice Bill, though it was a more general disenchantment with the austerity of the immediate post-war years, rather than any progressive approach to penal policy that was fatally to wound the government in 1950 and ensure its downfall the following year.

[19] The Minister of State at the Home Office responsible for the guidance of the Criminal Justice Bill 2003 in its passage through the Lords.

The very concept of the 'whole life' tariff applied to the mandatory sentence casts a dark shadow over that reasonable expectation which even an offender guilty of the most appalling crime ought to enjoy, contingent upon his or her genuine reform and contrition, of rehabilitation on licence in the community. We recognise life-long incarceration as a regrettable necessity in exceptional circumstances, but its sole justification can only be an overriding requirement to ensure public safety. It follows that we regard this as an issue in every way as important, though clearly different in character, as the abolition of the death penalty itself. That was an endeavour of previous generations that was uphill until the very last, but that did not mean that eventually reason and humanity were unable to triumph.

As with capital punishment, events may yet force the pace of legislative change with regard to the penalty for homicide and it is not without significance that the present population of life sentence prisoners is not only greater than that in the remainder of the European Union combined, but that it increases year on year. The incarceration of offenders when it is measured neither in months, nor in years, but in decades, must at some point be questioned if they no longer pose any discernible public risk; if not as an expensively indulgent form of retributive justice then at least in terms of its value for public money.

The arguments against the mandatory penalty of life imprisonment for murder (or, as we would prefer, criminal homicide) are compelling and ought to be persuasive for those who approach the subject with open minds; we advance them in common with others. But more than that, the substantive law (of homicide in general and of murder in particular) is in urgent need of review for the purposes of rational application in the 21st century. That much is incontestable. Its defects have been identified judicially and the ordinary citizen is only too aware of those of its glaring inconsistencies that are not only intellectually indefensible, but not infrequently the source of an imbalance that is readily identified as the source of perceived injustice.

In June 2003 the government requested the Law Commission to consider the partial defences to murder in circumstances involving provocation, diminished responsibility, and self defence, having particular regard to the impact of these defences in the context of domestic violence. In October 2003 the Commission published a Consultation Paper[20] to which the responses were numerous from among academics, the judiciary, practitioners in the law, professional and nongovernmental organisations. The Criminal Cases Review Commission and the Crown Prosecution Service also responded. The Commission's report was presented to Parliament by the Secretary of State for Constitutional Affairs and Lord Chancellor in August 2004.

Although limited by the scope of its comparatively narrow terms of reference, the Law Commission pointed up the inherent defects in the contemporary law of murder, as a direct response to a substantial body of opinion arguing that

[20] *Consultation Paper No 173.*

there was a pressing need for a review of the whole law of murder[21]. The Commissioners go on to note

> . . . we do regard this strong expression of views by our consultees as salutary and influential upon our work . . .[22]

Acknowledging what they identified as the 'breadth and depth of discontent with the substantive law and sentencing regime', they noted the dissatisfaction that emanated from all shades of opinion, including lawyers and victim groups, and that it was

> particularly articulated in the scathing comments made by Victim Support in their oral and written responses and by SAMM [Support After Murder and Manslaughter] in the course of a very helpful meeting with their officers.[23]

The Law Commission went further than consultation. It conducted independent research on the pleas of provocation and diminished responsibility in operation, and a study of female defendants convicted of murder. It is the survey of public opinion conducted by Professor Barry Mitchell of Coventry University with regard to the partial defences which instantly prompts close scrutiny[24]. Those who will suffer discombobulation by its findings will, doubtless, seek to emphasise the small size of the sample of respondents, but this, far from being an argument for discounting the findings, is a case for replicating the work on a larger scale in order to assess the weight of evidence that the survey discloses. Professor Mitchell should be funded to extend his admirable survey.

The idea that public policy, and in this must be included legal and penal reform, ought to be 'evidenced-based' is one which ought surely to appeal to a New Labour government. This must include evidence that may undermine the basis of the received wisdom of populism that is so often prayed in aid by Ministers intent upon maintaining the *status quo*. 'What works?' is the question that comes immediately and most sensibly to mind. It is a question that we have asked. In our view, Government, in considering the Law Commission's Report, cannot lightly dismiss the strong evidence that indicates:

(a) that the present law relating to homicide generally, never mind that specific to murder, including the penalties available, is certainly *not* working, save in a wholly unsatisfactory way, and that

(b) a great many people across the whole spectrum of society are only too aware of the fact.

---

[21] 'By far the strongest message that emerged from the response concerned matters which we had not addressed in consultation paper No 173 and upon which we had not posed any questions. Many consultees took the opportunity not only to address the questions which we had posed, but to express in the clearest of terms their views on the matters which they felt lay at the centre of the problems with the current partial defences, but which did not fall within our terms of reference'. *Ibid*, 2.12–2.16 p 12.

[22] *Ibid* 2.17–2.21 pp 13–14.

[23] *Ibid* 2.16 p 13.

[24] Published as Appendix C to the Law Commission's Report, pp 180–212.

Those who are so aware, hold views about the nature of homicide and penalties appropriate to it that bear little resemblance to 'public opinion' as it is so frequently represented in the course of Parliamentary debate by Government Ministers. There it is portrayed as something entirely homogeneous in character and mechanistically predictable in its response, the very embodiment of a *soi-disant* trust that cannot be betrayed. Yet there is good reason to doubt that there is, in reality, a public that is unyieldingly and uniformly punitive in its response to homicide. For far from the mandatory sentence of life imprisonment commanding unqualified and universal support, the reverse appears to be the case. To the layman, no less than to the lawyer, it is self-evident that criminally homicidal events are characterised by wide differences which justice demands should be treated on a case-by-case basis and not visited by a single, mandatory penalty. The mandatory life sentence is a 'one size fits all' item of penal footwear, and it avails its enthusiasts nothing to argue that flexibility is provided by a differential tariff. That is no better than saying that the ill-fitting boot may be taken off sooner in some cases than in others, notwithstanding that all are obliged to wear it for a minimum period, whether or not it fits.

Initially, the Government response to the Commission's report was to indicate that, while it would consider the recommendation for a review of the law of murder, it did not intend to abolish the mandatory life sentence. Baroness Scotland of Asthal, the Minister of State at the Home Office, responsible for criminal justice, was reported as indicating[25] that, with regard to the partial defences, doing nothing was not an option but that:

> As their report has demonstrated, this is a highly complex area of law. We would be foolish to rush into quick change.

That the defences to murder, like the entire spectrum of law relating to homicide, constitute a 'complex area' cannot be denied. But it is a complexity that has little claim to a sound and rational base. 'Complex' it most certainly is, but it is the I complexity of the tangled skein that becomes more dysfunctional at each attempt to unravel it. The outcome of centuries of accretion by judicial development, interspersed with legislation with respect to specific aspects of homicide, it is, in short, 'a mess'. The initial response of Government suggests that it is disinclined to do little beyond considering what the Law Commission has had to say about the defences to murder with a view to devising ways in which the law might be amended. But, the reflexive response with respect to the mandatory penalty of life imprisonment, no matter that it is the source of dissatisfaction among judges, practitioners, and not least, the public, is indicative of a stubborn refusal to admit to the defects of its being not merely the imperfect, but also the only possible sentence for what is presently termed 'murder'. It is unclear whether this obduracy to admit to the need for change arises from a fear

---

[25] *The Times*, Friday 6 August 2004.

of public (and likely electoral) displeasure, or whether it is a belief, genuinely held, notwithstanding its patent vulnerability to rational argument.

As the reader will discover, since it is a central feature of our case that all homicides should be consolidated within a single offence of criminal homicide, for which the penalty should be at large, the mandatory life sentence would disappear in the process. We do not argue against severity in its proper context but for proportionality in sentencing based upon an individualised approach to the circumstances of each criminal event. We believe that among the thinking public there is support for an intelligent rather than a mechanistic approach to sentencing. There will always be expressions of a more primitive, authoritarian approach, but that is no reason to regard it as a proper foundation for public policy.

There is no doubt that the outlook for change—certainly if New Labour and Conservative politicians have their way—is bleak. About as bleak, we would think, as it was for the abolition of capital punishment in the early 1950s when the Government sought even to ignore calls for a debate on the report of the Royal Commission. But, for us to be so dispirited as to be deterred would be, to borrow the idea, a betrayal of those who a generation ago laboured and even- tually succeeded in removing one of the last vestiges of the penology of the Middle Ages. Today the goal is a root-and-branch reform of the law of homi- cide itself. It is both necessary and possible, though it might presently appear otherwise.

Barbara Wootton, at the end of her autobiography, *In a World I Never Made*[26] challenged the conventional wisdom that holds politics to be the art of the possible. She wrote:

> In half a century of public and professional life I have not found it so. The limits of the possible constantly shift, and those who ignore them are apt to win in the end. Again and again I have had the satisfaction of seeing the laughable idealism of one genera- tion evolve into the accepted commonplace of the next. But it is from the champions of the impossible rather than the slaves of the possible that the evolution draws its cre- ative force.

Lady Wootton was one of the most doughty and successful champions of the possible. We would like to emulate her, if only in seeing our radical proposals for the reform of the law of murder and its penalty become the received wisdom of tomorrow.

---

[26] (London, George Allen and Unwin, 1967) at 279. A phrase borrowed from AE Houseman; 'I, a stranger and afraid in a world I never made'. *A Shropshire Lad*. xii.

2

The Legacy of
Sr*. Edward Coke, Knight

<hr/>

> Murder is when a man of sound memory, and of the age of discretion, unlawfully killeth within any county of the realm any reasonable creature in rerum natura under the King's peace, with malice aforethought, either expressed by the party or implied by law, so as the party wounded, or hurt, etc. die of the wound or hurt, etc. within a year and a day after the same.[1]

The term 'murder' occupies a place in demotic language, serving as a synonym for those unlawful homicides which are held in the greatest opprobrium. Homicide, by contrast, covers a wider range of actions resulting in death and by no means visited with the same degree of social revulsion. Its meaning is defined in the Oxford Dictionary as:

> One who kills a human being or the killing of a human being.

The term 'homicide' derives from the Latin *homicida*; in turn a conjunction of *homo* (a man or human being) and *caedo* (to cut, cut down, strike or beat.) This etymology is simply descriptive and in no way addresses the subjective issues of circumstance or intention which are essential to the process whereby the law is able to distinguish between different categories of unlawful killing and those accidental killings to which no criminal penalty attaches. Homicide is not, however, a word used with great frequency in common speech.[2] When the body of a person who has clearly suffered a violent death is discovered in circumstances which suggest that the victim has suffered a fatal assault at the hands of some other person, the reports in the public media almost always refer to a 'murder' having taken place. But whereas homicide is an objective description of the criminal event, murder is essentially a term of art. More precisely, it is a legal definition of a criminal event that can only be applied at the conclusion of a trial, initially in the court in which the evidence is put to a jury and finally, should

<hr/>

* A conventional form of address in his day inscribed on his tomb in the church of St Mary at Tittlesham in Norfolk.
[1] Sir Edward Coke, *Institutes of the Laws of England* (1628–34), 3.47.
[2] It is interesting to note that while police forces in the United States have 'Homicide' departments or squads, in England and Wales the term 'murder' is used to describe such specialist units.

there be an appeal, in a superior court. And while a conviction for murder may sometimes be quashed and a verdict of manslaughter substituted, though rare, it has not been unknown for a verdict to go back and forth between the Court of Appeal and the House of Lords.[3] While the term 'murderer' is familiar in the headlines, the word 'manslayer' is unlikely to be seen. The term 'homicide' is inclusive of several legally discrete categories of unlawful killing including not only murder and manslaughter but also infanticide and those parts of road traffic law which relate to causing death by drunken or dangerous driving. Each of these categories of homicide is subject to particular definition but this does not exclude alleged offences from overlapping. Certain defences to murder may reduce the offence to one of manslaughter though, while a death resulting from a road traffic event can result in conviction for manslaughter at common law, the usual choice of the prosecution is to proceed on a charge of causing death by dangerous driving.[4]

The killing of one human being by another, not least when victim and assailant are unevenly matched or when the killing is accompanied by apparently gratuitous cruelty, is regarded by society at large as repellent. While there are individuals at the margins of society whose behaviour indicates otherwise, for the majority, killing other people without lawful excuse is simply wrong. It is important at the outset, however, to consider the sources of the beliefs that inscribe the moral labels that are attached to human conduct. Most of the world's great religions present their followers with a code of conduct in which each prohibition is characterised by a notion of wrong that is generally co-terminous with the idea of sin. It is undoubtedly the case that the common law, like Roman law, has incorporated by a process of social osmosis many of the beliefs and assertions of Western Christianity, itself in debt to the traditions of Judaism; yet it is in no way based upon Christianity (as perhaps some would believe and others might prefer it to be).[5]

The essentially secular qualities of the English law which disengaged itself—though not without difficulty—from the ecclesiastical jurisdiction during the sixteenth century are demonstrated by the fact that its proscriptions are essentially *social* as distinct from 'other worldly' constructs. The matter can be summed up simply; the law is concerned with those things which men[6] living in society have deemed to be of such importance that they should be subject to rules of conduct that are non-negotiable. Equally, they stand to be applied without distinction of wealth, rank or social origin. Moreover, attaching to the rules are sanctions, characterised by varying degrees of coercion, whose object it is to

---

[3] As in *DPP v Smith* [1961] AC 290.

[4] It was the widespread (and not infrequently perverse) refusal of juries to convict drivers at common law, with its attendant maximum of life imprisonment, that Parliament was persuaded in 1956 to identify a separate statutory offence of causing death by dangerous driving for which the maximum penalty was 5 years imprisonment (recently raised to 10 years).

[5] See *Bowman v National Secular Society Ltd* [1917] AC 406.

[6] Throughout this work the terms 'man' or 'men' imply both men and women unless otherwise stated.

deter or to ensure compliance and to visit with penalty should that not be forth-coming. Additionally, the penalties attaching to the infringement of certain rules may be intended or perceived to reflect the social opprobrium with which such rule breaking is thought to be properly regarded. The import of all this is that the categories of behaviour identified by the law as meriting a criminal sanction derive from the way legislators, and those who influence them, think about the world in which they live. Yet the very inclusivity of the criminal law—the fact that it applies without social distinction to those within its jurisdiction and that it is 'non-negotiable'—eclipses, for most of the time, two important considerations. The first is that the laws and the precepts which they embody are derived from the values and beliefs current at the time of their conception[7]; the second is that the provision of new law is not infrequently a response to the demands of particular interest groups—and this was especially true in the past—rather than the expressed priorities of society as a whole. This is a point forcefully made by Dicey[8] and which can readily explain such social inequities as the capital penalties suffered by country labourers convicted of poaching in the eighteenth century, as well as the enclosure Acts which limited the possibilities of subsistence husbandry for the rural poor. It is perhaps the first of these considerations that had the greatest bearing upon the development of the law of homicide; principally, the idea that wrong-doing, whatever the offender might have had in mind, once embarked upon would be sufficient to establish his guilt for the outcome of other consequences, however unintended.

'THINK BEFORE YOU ACT, OR HOW ONE WRONG MAY LEAD TO ANOTHER'

Among those who have stood trial for murder, generally in previous ignorance of the labyrinthine arguments that could accompany its prosecution, was Reginald Woolmington, a 22-year-old Dorset farm labourer of hitherto good character. In 1935, on no less a day for lovers than 14 February, he was convicted at Bristol Assizes of the murder of his 17-year-old wife who having deserted him had returned to her mother. It would seem that he had loved her dearly. The crime itself had the classic ingredients of young love, despair and death; a pastoral tragedy that might have come from the pen of Thomas Hardy. The issue with which the jury had to wrestle concerned Woolmington's claim (subsequently persuasive on appeal to the House of Lords)[9] that his shooting her had been an accident. But it was for the prisoner, the jury were directed, to prove accident. In his summing up, Mr Justice Swift addressed the jury on the law,

---

[7] The ecclesiastical courts of the middle ages provided the death penalty for witches, a task assumed by secular authority by the Witchcraft Acts of 1541 and 1603. A Georgian Witchcraft Act of 1735 remained on the statute book until repealed by the Fraudulent Mediums Act in 1953.

[8] AV Dicey, *Lectures on the Relation between Law and Opinion in the Nineteenth Century*, (London, Macmillan,1905).

[9] *Woolmington v DPP* [1935] AC 462.

employing language having perhaps more in common with the King James Bible than that of the mid-1930s:

> . . . for the law presumeth the fact to have been founded in malice, unless the contrary appeareth. That has been the law of this country for all time since we had law.[10]

Young Violet Woolmington falling fatally wounded by gunshot, the law presumed to be 'a fact founded in malice', no matter what turbulent thoughts might have raged within her young husband's mind. It would be for him to persuade the jury otherwise.

But the final sentence from Foster, quoted by the judge, needs to be considered, since it suggests (and with considerable authority), that in 1935 the law of homicide, and certainly that part which applied to the crime of murder, had stood immutable since time immemorial.[11] This was far from being the case. Moreover, the implication that the young Reginald Woolmington could have been transported back in time to stand his trial before some Saxon or early Anglo-Norman tribunal, without noticing much that was different, must be regarded as something of a fanciful, if elegant, gloss. Not least, the jury would have been a very different assembly indeed. Woolmington was to enter the history books, his name to become as famous as that of the Negro Somersett.[12]

That Mr Justice Swift should have considered a passage from Foster's *Crown Law* of 1762 to be no less relevant some 273 years later, is indicative less of the legal conservatism that characterised the period between the wars than the authority which the great jurists of the seventeenth and eighteenth centuries continued to command long after society had been utterly transformed since their day. And yet the law governing murder and homicides generally had undergone several centuries of evolutionary development before it became the object of attention of the first among them, Sir Edward Coke, in the early decades of the seventeenth century.

IN THE BEGINNING: LAWS FOR LESS ORDERLY TIMES

In the England of the period immediately before the Norman Conquest, the establishment of centralised monarchy was a comparatively recent phenomenon and the institutions of feudalism, with clearly defined rights and obligations based upon land tenure, were the dominant source of effective social and political control. Criminal justice was but one constituent element of the system and

---

[10] Swift was quoting directly from the 'Introduction to the Discourse on Homicide' in Sir John Foster's *Crown Law* (Oxford, Clarendon Press, 1762), p 235.

[11] A term, strictly speaking, denoting a time before the accession of Richard I in 1189 and reliable written accounts of decided cases.

[12] The runaway slave whose case resulted in the declaration by Lord Mansfield that slavery was illegal in 18th century England. Reginald Woolmington survives not merely in legal textbooks, his name for ever associated with a 'golden thread' running through the English law; he has a 21st century website.

was given to being rudimentary in both concept and execution. The coming of the Norman kings and their Angevin successors energised social and political change from which the law was not exempt. While this is not the place in which to rehearse the history of the process whereby the powers of the feudal nobility were finally tamed by the Crown, not least by the establishment of Royal courts of justice and the introduction of itinerant Justiciars offering a superior service to that of the manorial lords, these institutional changes had an important bearing upon conceptions of crime and the penalties applicable to particular offences. The terms *felon* and *felony*, coming from the Old French into the Middle English[13] originally denoted a breach of fidelity in the feudal relationship embodied in homage, but over time came to have a different currency in England from that in mainland Europe, becoming synonymous with the most serious offenders and their crimes. These still contained the same essential ingredient, namely a breach of trust or obligation. Thus the mediaeval law of treason[14] contained what might seem odd nowadays, in that in addition to such things as compassing or imagining the death of the king or his family, violating his womenfolk, levying war against him in his realm, or such assorted mischiefs as slaying the Treasurer, Chancellor or judges sitting in court—the so-called 'High Treasons'—there were also 'petty treasons' which included the slaying of a master by a servant, of a husband by his wife or a prelate by his subject (secular or religious). These 'petty treasons' were not finally subsumed within the common law of murder until 1828. The term 'treason' essentially implies a breach of trust on the part of the offender; the loyalty of the subject to the sovereign, of the servant to his master, of a wife to her husband or of a lesser cleric or layman to a prince of the church. Implicit in this concept of trust is the obligation on the part of the inferior party to the superior.

The term 'murder' has a no less interesting history. In Anglo-Saxon England when a man was killed (whether wilfully or by accident made no matter) the offender was required to bear the feud, or else hand over a sum of money amounting to the worth of the dead man (the *wergild*), normally calculable in terms of the deceased's feudal obligations. This form of compensatory justice has parallels in the social systems of other non-industrial civilisations in which cattle or childbearing women are given by way of compensation to the kin of the dead person.[15] While this suggests a comparatively restrained approach to violent death in the England of long ago, it must be acknowledged that the circumstances of the political economy lent themselves perhaps more readily to what later ages have been able to do by means of civil process, namely; to distinguish tortious liability from criminal guilt and to attempt some degree of restorative

---

[13] In use *circa* 1200–1500.

[14] Statute of Treasons, 1352, 25 Edw III

[15] See Isaac Schapera, *A Handbook of Tswana Law and Custom,* (London & New York, OUP, 1938) 2nd edn, (London, Cassell, 1955). Bohannan notes a similar practice among the Tiv of Central Nigeria, see Paul Bohannan (ed) *African Homicide and Suicide* (Princeton NJ, Princeton University Press, 1960).

justice. But the law could take a firmer line when circumstances demanded. Certainly, in Saxon England, the law had made provision for killings done by way of ambush (*foresteal*)—yet another manifestation of serious breach of obligation or trust—and in the period after the Conquest this notion appears to have become the basis of a more complex jurisprudence with regard to premeditated crimes classified in the Norman French as *assault prepensé* or the Latin *assultus premeditatus*. It is at this period that the term *malitia excogitata*[16] first appears, emerging eventually into the world of Tudor and Jacobean lawyers as 'malice aforethought'.

The term 'murder' derives from the concept of *murdrum*, used in Saxon times to describe what was regarded as an especially heinous crime, that of killing another in secret. After the Conquest, disgruntled Saxons engaged so frequently in deadly ambush attacks on their Norman conquerors that William I enacted that if the perpetrator of such a killing were not found then the Hundred in which the death had occurred should be required to pay a fine known as the *murdrum*, the crime and the punishment described by a single word. This provision for collective punishment in the event of unsolved homicides was abolished in 1340.[17]

It is the presumption of malice in the homicidal event, as distinct from negligence or plain accident, which complicates the law of murder in this early period still further, since it was linked to the offender's entitlement to a pardon, depending upon the circumstances. It has been suggested that pardons were not uncommon.[18] By 1390[19] the statute distinguished pardons sought in respect of such events as self-defence or misadventure from those for 'murders done in await, assault or *malice prepensé*'. It is here that we can observe the origins of the distinctions between various kinds of homicide on the basis of the imputed moral qualities of the act, which were at this time expressed in terms of a hierarchy of sinfulness, an important concern to mediaeval theologians and clerical jurists.

The concept of *sin* was predicated upon the notion of a wrong act having been freely willed by the sinner, the evil intention having been translated into the physical deed. Thus, the knights who had murdered Becket in his cathedral were first and foremost guilty of the sin of sacrilege, never mind what might later have been identified as a murder done in *malice prepensé*, and were required by the Church to do penance. Henry II, thought to have inspired the deed by his incautious expression of exasperation with the Archbishop, was required to undergo a penitential (if somewhat notional) flogging by the monks of Canterbury. Sin and 'wilful murder'[20] could be readily elided in terms of culpability; not so those

---

[16] Coke uses the term *malitia præcogitata*.

[17] 14 Edw III stat Ch 4.

[18] See Theodore Plucknett, *A Concise History of the Common Law*, 4th edn, (London, Butterworth & Co, 1948).

[19] 13 Rich I, stat 2 Ch 1.

[20] A term which first appears in statute in 1532. (23 Hen VIII Ch 1).

homicides in which, although a degree of fault might be identified, it did not amount to an unambiguous intention of bringing about the victim's death. This was at a time when the ability of the agents of the state to protect citizens from robbery, burglary or assault was rudimentary and self-help in such situations was recognised as often the only means whereby the citizen could protect his person or his goods.

What appears to have brought matters to a head in the early Tudor period was the vexed issue of 'benefit of clergy' and for a brief explanation we need to return to the essence of the quarrel between Henry II and Becket.[21] Henry was keen to centralise the power of the Crown by various means, including the extension of royal jurisdiction over all who were deemed to be subjects within the feudal polity. This included clerics, the most powerful of whom (the bishops and abbots) were ranked as peers among the nobility, the 'clerk' being defined as one who was in holy orders, however lowly. Becket, on the contrary, was determined to preserve what he understood to be the liberties of the church for which there was scriptural authority.[22] The Constitutions of Clarendon in 1164 claimed to re-state an earlier arrangement whereby a 'criminous clerk' was to be charged in the King's court, sent to the ecclesiastical court for trial and, if 'unfrocked', then returned to the secular court for sentence. This might, of course, be death. Becket's murder in 1170 set back this movement towards bringing all offenders within the ambit of the royal justice for several centuries. The situation nevertheless moved towards that conclusion; those who sought benefit of clergy claimed it through their ability to recite in Latin the opening verses of Psalm 51.[23] Clerks were, on conviction, supposed to be exempt from the death penalty but subjected to branding[24] (to ensure that they could not claim benefit of clergy twice) but there is reason to think that the system was far from reliable in preventing 'clerks convict' from being hanged as a result of sentence in the royal courts. While Tudor legislation developed to make the most serious crimes 'non-clergyable', the system did not finally disappear until 1827.

From this time on it seems clear that what had been the old felony of murder was now divided into those offences which were 'wilful and of malice afore-thought', not clergyable and consequently capital, and those which, being neither in self-defence nor as a result of misadventure, nevertheless bore culpa-bility.[25] This would seem to have been the result of enthusiasm on the part of the Tudor legislators to limit the unacceptable lenity of the provision whereby those

---

[21] Ironically, it was Henry who had leaned heavily on his old companion Thomas of London, (*aka* Thomas à Becket) to become Archbishop of Canterbury, see David Knowles, *Thomas Becket.* (London, Adam and Charles Black, 1970).

[22] Notably the passage in 1 Chronicles, xvi v 22. '*Touch not mine anointed and do my prophets no harm.*'

[23] '*Miserere mei Deus secundum magnam misericordiam tuam.*' (Have mercy upon me O God according to the greatness of thy mercy.) This became known as the 'neck-verse'.

[24] *Post* 1490. 4 Hen VII Ch 13.

[25] *See* Plucknett, above note 18 .

successfully claiming benefit of clergy were able to escape the death penalty for otherwise heinous instances of homicide. The effect was to drive a great wedge into the law of homicide, splitting off the discrete crime of murder from those other killings which were to become known as manslaughter. The analytical task of distinguishing between murder and manslaughter was increasingly to rest upon the interpretation of the concept of 'malice' and/or the establishment of its presence. The notion of 'malice' if it were not, in its most abstract form, already fraught with problems of definition and identification, was to be subdivided in the ensuing period into categories productive of further complexity.

A FORCEFUL MAN OF LAW; OF MANY PARTS AND GREAT LEARNING

It is at this point that we need to turn in some detail to the contribution of Coke, acknowledged to be one of the great common lawyers whose influence was long to outlive him. For future centuries it was to be immense, in that he provided, for the Common law, a definition of murder which has survived for almost 400 years. But to understand Coke, not least in respect of his promotion of the doctrine of constructive malice, it is important to consider the man himself, his view of the world in which he lived and his highly partisan involvement in its affairs of state.

Born in 1552 he lived, for his time, to the unusually old age of 82. His career in politics and the law, would, by today's standards, be nothing short of extraordinary. At various times he was Speaker of the House of Commons, Solicitor General, Recorder of London, Attorney General Lord Chief Justice. He was no stranger to political controversy and at the age of 70 found himself a prisoner in the Tower for some nine months. At 76 he began on his great four part work, the *Institutes of the Laws of England* completed between 1628 and 1634, the third of which deals with the criminal law. The first attempt to provide a comprehensive view of the law since the treatise of Henry de Bracton in the mid-thirteenth century[26], it had an immense effect, not least on account of Coke's encyclopaedic knowledge of case law and his position was seldom challenged. As Plucknett observes

> Consequently the seventeenth century was apt to see the mediaeval authorities only through Coke's eyes. . . . If every lawyer had gone to the Year books for himself and read them as uncritically as Coke did, it might well be that his idea of the continuity of English law would have broken down. . . . By a careful selection of material Coke

[26] Henricus de Bracton, *De Legibus et Consuetudinibus Angliæ*, vols 1–4, George Woodbine (ed) (New Haven, Conn, Yale Historical Publications, 915–1942). A later edition, setting the original Latin text alongside Woodbine's translation was produced by Samuel E Thorne in association with the Selden Society, (Cambridge, Mass, and London, Harvard at the Belknap Press, 1968–77) (4 vols). De Bracton was working on his *magnum opus* around 1254 and was therefore a contemporary of Aquinas (q.v).

was enabled to conceal the inconsistencies and difficulties which were inherent in his position.[27]

Plucknett observes that there were shortcomings in his writing which had 'few literary graces'. He was also given to employing

passably good Latin maxims which had an air of antiquity about them, in spite of the fact that he himself invented them.[28]

FIG 1: Sr. Edward Coke: inventor of 'passably good Latin maxims'.

As Attorney General he had prosecuted in the treason trial of Essex (under Elizabeth) and Ralegh (under James I). He prosecuted the conspirators of the so-called 'Gunpowder Plot' and later, James' favourite, Robert Carr, Earl of Somerset and his wife, for the murder of Sir Thomas Overbury. His forensic manner was characterised by aggression, insult towards the accused and behaviour generally which, on the part of any advocate, would simply not be tolerated by any modern judge. At the trial of Ralegh at Winchester in November 1603[29] his behaviour was particularly outrageous. Popham, the Chief Justice, and his fellow judges were clearly hostile to the prisoner and

---

[27] Plucknett, above note 18, at 268.
[28] *Ibid* at 267.
[29] Dramatically re-enacted in Middle Temple Hall on its precise 400th anniversary on 17 November, 2003 in the play *Sharp Medicine* by Anthony Arlidge, QC.

failed to provide any summing up for the jury and in this environment Coke's conduct went wholly unreproved. Moreover, the judges had ruled that examination of the prisoner alone could provide sufficient evidence of the alleged treason (for which the death penalty applied) and no witness was required to corroborate the testimony of prosecution witnesses. In the third *Institute* Coke was subsequently to advance quite the contrary opinion notwithstanding that he had earlier been content to take advantage of this ruling in Ralegh's case.[30] Nor was his behaviour as a forensic bully significantly at variance with his actions in private life. His conduct towards his extensive family (his first wife bore him seven children and his second two more) would be readily identified by any contemporary court within the Family Division as unreasonable, even subjecting one of his daughters to abduction and forcible marriage to secure political advantage.

We can but conjecture how far Coke's unattractively egocentric personality,[31] influenced by his attitude towards those who infringed the criminal law, is reflected in his writing on it; perhaps more important, and bearing upon his extreme interpretation of the concept of constructive malice, is his social position in Jacobean England. He belonged to a class of gentry with close connections with the nobility, and which enjoyed substantial privilege in what was an extremely unequal society. Earlier generations of it had grown rich upon the loot of monastic property but the security of this new class, unlike that of the various 'estates' of feudal times, was far more vulnerable.[32] Above them stood the Crown, in this instance in the person of the petulant and unpredictable James I, while beneath them were the rural poor, and a politically volatile element in the towns[33] besides large numbers of those made landless and destitute by a combination of enclosures and economic circumstance. The 'sturdy beggars' identified by the vagrancy laws of Elizabeth had by no means disappeared. The privilege of the class to which Coke belonged was thus secured on the one hand by royal benevolence but, more importantly on the other, by a system of social control of which a repressive criminal law was a dominant constituent. Moreover, such capital crimes as treason as were prosecuted in the great state trials of which we have good historical accounts, were infrequent compared

---

[30] In this trial Coke was quite openly serving the King's interest, whose approbation he was overtly seeking to gain. Master Bruce Williamson, *Lector Autumnalis* in the Middle Temple in 1935, expressed a trenchant view on the honesty of Coke's position:

> What would be thought today of a Counsel who took advantage of a ruling he believed to be erroneous to secure a conviction on a capital charge? I do not think he would long wear his Barrister's gown or be suffered to remain in any Inn of Court which had the misfortune to number him among its members.

Sir Walter Ralegh and his Trial, (London, Sir Isaac Pitman and Sons, 1936) at 29.

[31] In the language of a contemporary pre-sentence report he might well be considered, notwithstanding his undoubted intellectual qualities, possibly to have had some personality disorder.

[32] As Ralegh and others among Elizabeth's favourites had learned to their cost.

[33] London was unsafe for Charles I at the outbreak of the Civil War in 1642.

with those of petty malefactors who went quickly and largely unrecorded to their deaths on public gallows.[34]

Constructive malice, in that it patently disadvantages the defendant on a charge of murder, not merely offends against widely held notions of natural justice but represents a kind of premium or excess penal liability upon what has been the primary criminal act. It is Coke's interpretation of the concept which is significant in its socio-political context; intellectually, its roots were in the theology of the Middle Ages which was deeply influenced by Aristotelian philosophy, whose great exponent was Thomas Aquinas (1225–1274), a contemporary of de Bracton. In his *Summa Theologiæ*[35] he identifies what he terms voluntary homicide (*homicidium voluntarium*). This, he says, can come about in two ways, the first when a man engages in activities in which he should not have done (*rebus illicitis*) or when he does not take due care (*solicitudinem*). Where the activity is legitimate and due care has been exercised there is no guilt of homicide, but where the activity is illicit, or even when it is but due care is not taken, then there is guilt for any resultant homicide. Considering those unlawful homicides arising from *rebus illicitis* there is clearly discernible the kernel of the notion of a 'premium' or culpable excess. It would have been logically consistent for the Tudor lawyers to extend it and for Coke to complete the task by formalising it in the *Institutes*. By Coke's time we have a clear distinction between those homicides predicated upon deliberate intention (malice) and those, although there is fault sufficient to generate culpability, which are exclusive of malice prepensed or constructed. However, it is important to recognise that Aquinas (like de Bracton) was writing in Latin and there is a certain capacity for elasticity in translation. The three words, *culpa, delictum* and *peccatum*, may all be translated as 'fault'. Aquinas, however, employs the word *culpa* to mean 'fault' and *peccatum*[36] to mean 'sin'. Aquinas is, of course, concerned here in Volume 38 of the *Summa,* with injustice in the context of moral theology and not with the dimensions of criminal guilt which by the end of the sixteenth century had acquired a definitely secular meaning.

In the *Institutes*[37] Coke distinguishes between malice aforethought that is *express* as distinct from that which is *implied*. It is express:

> . . . when one compasseth to kill, wound or beat another, and doth it *sedato animo*. This is said in law to be malice aforethought, prepensed, *malitia praecognitata.*

---

[34] The rapidity of the criminal trial of common people charged with capital offences persisted well into succeeding centuries and as Alexander Pope was to observe in *The Rape of the Lock*:

> The hungry judges soon the sentence sign
> and wretches hang, that jurymen may dine.

Less of a *memento mori* in the philosophical sense, the corpse of a highway robber that swung from a crossroads gibbet was more akin to a specimen displayed in a gamekeeper's larder.

[35] Vol 38 (trans Marcus Lefébure, OP, London, Blackfriars in conjunction with Eyre and Spottiswoode, 1975).

[36] Though the word can also be translated as 'mistake' he does not use it in this sense.

[37] 3. 51–52.

He then identifies three categories of malice implied:

(1), '*in respect of the 'manner of the deed'*. Thus in the case of unprovoked killing malice is implied;

(2), '*in respect of the person killed'*. 'As if a magistrate or known officer, or any other that hath lawful warrant, and doing or offering to do his office, or to execute his warrant, is slain, this is murder, by malice implied by law.';

(3), '*In respect of the person killing'*. 'If A assault B to rob him, and in resisting A killeth B, this is murder by malice implied, albeit he (A) never saw or knew him (B) before.'

Malice, notwithstanding that it is express in the sense that the offender forms a clear intention of killing his victim, cannot, as a matter of course, presume the rationality of the act, but Coke was not concerned with defences based upon the accused's mental state; the same applies to his first category of implied malice where there is killing without provocation. It is in the second and third of his categories of implied malice that the social dimension of the 'constructive' element—the 'penal premium'—comes into focus.

Notably, it is magistrates and others concerned with the enforcement of the law who are the first to be identified, not on account of their especial vulnerability as victims *per se*, but on account of their office. Given that the law was often disadvantageous to the relatively powerless, their resort to physical violence would not be beyond the bounds of possibility—for example in the context of the enforcement of the vagrancy laws, or evictions from enclosed common lands. Nor is it without significance when Coke goes on to amplify the doctrine of constructive malice in instances of poaching. If the offender

shooting at a cock or a hen, or any tame fowl of another man and the arrow, by mischance kills a man

then this is murder because the intention had been to do an unlawful act and is held sufficient to warrant the penalty for murder. The penal premium, with its consequential penalty of death is thus applied to those who challenge the social order, whether by offering violence to its agents of control or by violating the proprietorial rights of others when these actions result in the unintended consequence of death.

Having effectively invested the penal premium with the authority of a statement of the substantive law, succeeding generations of commentators went little further than to modify some of the detail, the *corpus* of the doctrine of constructive malice remaining unaffected. Stephen[38] was of the view that it was not accepted by Hale[39] and Chief Justice Holt expressly limited it to cases of

---

[38] Sir James Fitzjames Stephen, *History of the Criminal Law* ((London, Macmillan, 1883).

[39] Sir Matthew Hale, (1609–1676), *Historia Placitorum Coronae: The History of the Pleas of the Crown* (Edited posthumously by Sollom Emlyn. 2 vols, London, 1736).

felony,[40] a view shared by Foster[41] in the mid-eighteenth century. Even limited this far, Stephen considered it to be 'cruel and monstrous'[42] perhaps because of the very large number of offences defined as felonies. It would appear that by the end of the eighteenth and in the early nineteenth century, courts were nevertheless becoming less confident about the automatic application of the principle in felony cases.[43] Both *Lad* and *Greenwood* had concerned instances of children who had died as a consequence of rape, anticipating some of the issues to be raised many years later in the case of *Beard*.[44] A case in 1862[45] (which bears some comparison with the modern case of *Hyam*) involved the demise of an unknown tramp who had been burned to death following the arson of a straw stack. In summing up to the jury, the trial judge, Baron Bramwell, had indicated:

> . . . though it may appear unreasonable, yet as it (the doctrine of constructive malice) is laid down as law it is our duty to act upon it. The law, however, is, that a man is not answerable except for the natural and probable result of his own act; and therefore, if you should not be satisfied that the deceased was in the barn or enclosure at the time the prisoner set fire to the stack, but came in afterwards, then, as his own act intervened between the death and the act of the prisoner, his death could not be the natural result of the prisoner's act, and in that view he ought to be acquitted on the present charge.[46]

There are few homicides in which the person responsible for the death does not have some 'intention', whether formed on the spur of the moment in reaction to some stimulus, or long before what emerges as a criminal event. Since the law presumes a substantial degree of rationality, foresight and demonstrable intention on the part of the offender, the establishment of both *actus reus* and *mens rea* present, in theory, few intellectual problems. The questions are very straightforward; 'Was it the defendant who did it?' 'Is what is alleged that which was actually done?' 'Did the defendant intend to do what he did?' The forensic reality, however, is often a very long way from that atmosphere of seminar-room simplicity. The history of homicide is replete with instances in which the offender, by his initial act, precipitates an avalanche of happenings over which he has decreasing, if indeed any credible control, and in which he, along with his victim, is swept to a conclusion as unintended and ùnwanted as it is invariably tragic. These are the crimes, which, catastrophically, 'go wrong'; in which 'intention' becomes hard to identify and 'motive' something long lost in the often swift passage of events.

---

[40] *R v Keate* (1697) Comb 406; also (1697) 1 Comyns 13; 92 ER 934; also *R v Plummer* (1700) Kel. 109; also (1700) 12 Mod 627; 88 ER 1565.

[41] Sir John Foster, above note 31.

[42] Royal Commission on Capital Punishment, 1949–53, *Report*, Cmnd 8932 (1953), Appendix 7.5 at 384.

[43] See *R v Lad* (1773) 1 Leach 96; also (1773) 168 ER 150, and *R v Greenwood* (1857) 7 Cox CC 404, a case in which it was held that words alone did not amount to provocation.

[44] *Beard v DPP* [1920] AC 479.

[45] *R v Horsey* (1862) 3 F& F 287; also 176 ER 129.

[46] See, Royal Commission on Capital Punishment, above n 63, Appendix 7.8, at 385.

The normal place for the exchange of such insistent contradiction is the pantomime theatre, certainly not the courts. Yet the case of 'Gypsy' Jim Smith in 1961 involved contradictory judgments that, as perceived in the public mind, inspired confusion and some sense of absurdity. A verdict of murder was replaced by one of manslaughter, in turn replaced by another which restored a conviction for murder. It seemed to mirror an Alice in Wonderland World in which those who were in charge at a particular moment said that the facts meant what they decided they should mean, with one court saying 'Yes', another 'No' and yet a third 'Yes', once more.

In the *Smith* case, which was to have an important effect upon the law of murder, we can observe how the presumed objectivity which the law seeks to impose on the criminal event has a capacity to invest the situation with a quality of unreality, divorced from the way things generally happen in the real world. Smith was driving his car (which had a quantity of metal scaffolding clips—of dubious provenance—in the boot) when approached by one PC. Meehan by whom he was apparently known. Rather than stop, Smith accelerated away but Meehan hung on the car until, after having been struck by several oncoming vehicles, he was thrown into the roadway where he was run over by a bubble car and killed. The charge was one of capital murder,[47] since the victim was a police officer acting in the execution of his duty. Smith argued that he had never intended killing or indeed doing grievous bodily harm to Meehan; the trial judge, Mr Justice Donovan, spread before the jury the test of how the 'reasonable man' (he who travelled daily upon the Clapham omnibus) would have behaved. Smith was convicted and sentenced to death on 7 April, 1960. The argument in the Court of Criminal Appeal was that the jury should, in contrast, have been invited to consider his actual intention at the time of the death. The appeal was successful, perhaps surprisingly, and the conviction for capital murder was quashed and one for manslaughter substituted. If these had stood, then this might well have been the point at which the bell finally began to toll for the demise of that punitive criminal jurisprudence regarding the law of murder of which Coke was the undoubted progenitor; but it was not to be. The Director of Public Prosecutions, having obtained leave to appeal to the House of Lords on this point of law, successfully persuaded their Lordships to overturn the judgment of the CCA and on 28 July the following year the court restored both the capital conviction and the sentence of death.[48]

---

[47] Pursuant to the Homicide Act, 1957.

[48] [1961] AC 290. Smith was fortunate in that the Home Secretary, RA Butler, was a man of great humanity. Butler announced, in advance of the Lords judgment that should the death sentence be re-imposed it would be commuted to life imprisonment. There is a parallel between *Smith's* case and that of *Hedley and Jenkins* in 1945. Escaping from the scene of a shop-breaking in the City of London in December, 1944, they had been seen in their stolen car by a Captain Binney who, in an effort to stop them, jumped in front of it. Hedley continued to drive and Binney was caught beneath

The judgment, given by the Lord Chancellor, Lord Kilmuir (but widely believed to have been drafted by the Lord Chief Justice, Lord Parker) met with little approval and much dismay; the reform of the doctrine of constructive malice, or preferably its effective consignment to the dustbin of legal history, seemed as far away as ever. Criticism was both wide and immense.[49] Professor Glanville Williams remarked that if the Lords were correct in *Smith*, then it was now possible to commit murder by accident. The Homicide Act 1957 had, by abolishing 'constructive malice', removed the automatic attachment of the penal premium in cases of death in the context of the commission of felony or specifically in resisting an officer of justice; most reformers, however, had regarded the Act as little more than an unsteady stepping stone on the path to the abolition of capital punishment and, if statutorily banished from the substantive law, the ghost of constructive malice seemed to lurk in the shadows of its forensic interpretation. There were those who suspected that the new statute had 'not killed the snake but scotched it'. No attempt had been made to attempt a similar despatch for 'express' or 'implied' malice.

The matter was referred to the Law Commission whose recommendations[50] became the basis for section 8 of the Criminal Justice Act, 1967[51] By now, even if Coke's grand construction embodying the penal premium was not yet entirely demolished, it had become an intellectually uninhabitable ruin.

'WHATEVER HAPPENED TO JUSTICE?'

In the post-war period during which capital punishment was either mandatory, or, after 1957, the penalty for specific categories of murder, there remained other unresolved issues whose consequences remained morally troubling. It was not

---

the vehicle and dragged the length of London Bridge, sustaining injuries from which he later died. Hedley, convicted of murder, was sentenced to death but surprisingly for the times was reprieved and sentenced to penal servitude for life. Jenkins was sentenced to 8 years penal servitude for manslaughter. Two years later, Jenkins' younger brother was hanged for the murder of Alec de Antiquis, yet another spirited member of the public, who had attempted to apprehend him and his accomplices after a robbery in the West End. The second, Geraghty, was also hanged, but the third, Rolt, being a juvenile, was sentenced to be detained at His Majesty's Pleasure.

[49] See, Glanville Williams, 'Constructive Malice Revived', (1962) *Modern Law Review*, 605. J Salmon 'The Criminal Law relating to Intent,' (1961) 14 *Current Legal Problems*, 1. Rupert Cross 'The Need for a Redefinition of Murder' (1960) *Criminal Law Review*, 728.

[50] *Imputed Criminal Intent: Director of Public Prosecutions v Smith.*

[51] Section 8 of the Act provides:

'A court or jury in determining whether a person has committed an offence,

(a) shall not be bound in law to infer that he intended or foresaw a result of his actions by reason only of its being a natural and probable consequence of those actions; but
(b) shall decide whether he did intend or foresee that result by reference to all the evidence drawing such inferences from the evidence as appear proper in the circumstances.'

Section 8 only went half way towards the implementation of the proposals, being concerned only with *how* intention or foresight must be proved, not *when*.

until the end of the twentieth century that it became possible, through the agency of the Criminal Cases Review Commission to go some way to rectifying the errors and injustices of earlier cases. One such concerned the conviction and hanging of Derek Bentley.

One Sunday evening in the early winter of 1952, two youths, Christopher Craig (16) and Derek Bentley (19) burgled a confectionery warehouse in Croydon. They were surprised by police and Bentley, the older youth, was quickly taken into custody. Craig, not yet taken up, discharged a gun at one of the arresting officers who died as a result. It had begun as a joint enterprise in theft; it concluded, as the law was to demonstrate, as a joint enterprise in homicide to which the death penalty applied. The prosecution alleged that though in custody, Bentley had called to Craig *"Let him have it, Chris!"* meaning 'fire at him!' Both were convicted of the murder of PC Miles; Craig, being below the age of 18 was, as a juvenile, sentenced to be detained at Her Majesty's Pleasure. Bentley, being of 'gallows years', was put to death at Wandsworth prison in January, 1953.[52] The case was a strange echo of events that followed another warehouse-breaking some 12 years before. Two men engaged in the enterprise had been surprised by police and attempted to escape. On the brink of capture, one fired a shot which killed one of the policemen. At the trial the prosecution alleged that the other, according to the policeman in a dying deposition, had been heard to say, *"Let him have it, he's all alone!"* Both were convicted of murder on the basis that they were united in their common resolution to resist by violence any constable who opposed them in their escape.[53] The case for the exercise of the prerogative in Bentley's case was immensely powerful if not wholly compelling; he was not the principal in the crime of murder notwithstanding he had been engaged in the joint enterprise of breaking into the warehouse. That he was barely old enough for the gallows argued for some mercy, but not so much as the fact that the principal in the crime was too young to hang. The Home Secretary, Sir David Maxwell Fyfe who, as Lord Kilmuir was later to become Lord Chancellor, decided otherwise. Yet only seven years before, in the case of Hedley and Jenkins, who had been convicted of killing Captain Binney whilst fleeing from a scene of crime, Hedley, the driver, had been reprieved from the gallows and his companion Jenkins sentenced to eight years for manslaughter. It has been often argued that the explanation for Maxwell Fyfe's decision was that in the early 1950s the country was in the grip of a moral panic about the growth of crime, especially amongst the young. The killing of a policeman was held to be especially heinous, not least since the figure of the friendly 'bobby', immortalised in the character of Dixon of Dock Green greeting the world under the blue lamp, was one of reverential affection. While

---

[52] Bentley's conviction has, a generation later, been quashed, his remains removed from Wandsworth and decently interred. The patent injustice of the comparative fate of the two youths involving death for the one who had not even handled the gun, but a prison sentence and subsequent release for the one who had, did much to increase support for the abolition of the death penalty.

[53] *R v Appleby* (1940) 28 Cr App Rep, 1 (CCA).

the country mourned the death of PC Miles it was, at the same time, unable to accept as just a situation in which Craig, his actual killer should escape the death penalty while Bentley would die. As the law then was, if Bentley had been safely and soundly convicted, the mandatory death sentence could be moderated only by the exercise of the prerogative. Though the decision 'to let the law take its course' which was the responsibility of the executive, seeking no doubt to balance an individual mercy with the demands of what was perceived to be the public interest, the Bentley case brought certain features of the law into sharp focus. The law relating to joint enterprise embodied aspects of the penal premium that had its origins in Coke. In essence, it was predicated upon the same argument as that in any other instance of constructive malice. The wrongness of their joint malfeasance would ensure that each would bear responsibility for the actions of the other. Five years after Bentley was put to death, the Homicide Act of 1957 was to remedy the situation, limiting the death penalty to the offender who was actually responsible for the killing.[54]

Although it was not the subject of specific comment at the time, the case also demonstrated the shortcoming of the principle of the mandatory sentence. Having defined a particular set of circumstances as 'murder' in distinction from other homicides, the retention of the mandatory penalty of death was testimony to the principle of 'one size fits all'. This is, of course, logically consistent with a jurisprudence that is focused upon the abstract definition of a crime, rather than the constituent elements of a criminal event, or indeed, any event. But as such, it saps at the very roots of the concept of judgment since, by the denial of any latitude, it offers no possibility of its exercise.

THE LEGACY: A WORTHY INHERITANCE OR A CURSE TO THOSE WHO CAME AFTER?

The common law has among its champions those who take the view that among its central propositions are some, hitherto immutable, which ought to remain exempt from any attempt at change. The identification of murder as a crime apart from all other homicides on account of its special heinousness is the instant case. Like all institutions of long standing, such as Parliament or monarchy, the Common law (and not least that part concerned with criminal homicide) can be vested with an aura verging upon the sacred, seen to encapsulate all that is best in a past which mirrors standards of morality whose loss deserves to be mourned. But, like the jury system, it is enveloped in myth and misunderstanding.

All law is the product of particular philosophical, religious and political views that have at some time been in the ascendant; it has no apocalyptic pedigree. For the most part, and certainly in centuries previous to the last, these were

[54] s 5 (2).

expressed not by any popular or democratic will, but rather, by those whose power—almost always (but not invariably) derivative of their wealth—could never be effectively challenged. Yet, since the very idea of crime is a social construct, certainly that which is statutory, it cannot pretend to a quality of immutability, either in its substance or the arrangements for its prosecution. Law is created by men for their own purposes; as a convenient statement of contemporary morality, inevitably subject to a time lag. As Devlin argued[55], it is often a filter for social change and there is much to support that view; reforms of the law relating to such diverse topics as suicide and obscenity, prostitution and homosexuality are merely examples. Increasingly, if public confidence in criminal justice is to be maintained, its intellectual content must become more accessible. The citizen should be able to make sense of the law by perceiving it to relate to a world inhabited by real people.

But there is a dimension of that world which cannot be neglected. There are numerous opportunities for the expression of populist views about the nature of crime and its punishment, which, though sincerely held, can be based on misunderstanding or even misinformation. In a mature democracy it is possible to tell the difference between public clamour and the persuasiveness of argument based upon careful assessment of all aspects of the situation. The arcane distinctions that are sometimes made between murder and other forms of homicide, can often be perceived as resulting in manifest injustice. The remedy is not difficult to identify, yet, four centuries after Coke, we still lack a statutory definition of murder, never mind a coherent law of homicide that is appropriate to our times.

---

[55] Sir Patrick Devlin, *The Enforcement of Morals* (London, OUP, 1965).

3

Murder will out: the substantive law today

Mordre wol out, that we see day by day.

Geoffrey Chaucer, 'The Nun's Priest's Tale' *Canterbury Tales* (Circa 1386)

Between 1867 and 1908 no fewer than six Bills came before Parliament that sought to amend either the law of murder or the law of homicide generally, none of which was to be enacted.[1] Another 40 years were to elapse before the matter again came before the legislature. It cannot be other than a cause for reproach that since the Second World War, Parliament, while willing to debate (frequently in the 1980s) and to legislate (generally in 1957 and 1965/1969, and extensively in 2003[2]) for the *penalty* for murder, has (with one minor exception[3]) stubbornly declined to define the *offence*. In 1957 Parliament did, however, marginally amend the law, in respect of the partial defence of provocation and by introducing the concept of diminished responsibility. Murder is the only offence in the criminal calendar which has been left to be defined by the common law and then only through the extensive body of case law.

Parliament's omission to settle the arguments about the law of homicide might not be a matter of great moment, were it not for the fact that the law of homicide has consistently occupied the persistent attention of the appellate courts in a seemingly endless search for clarification and certainty. Judicial efforts, in a myriad of cases, to rationalise the law of murder and manslaughter have cried out for Parliamentary intervention, unavailingly.

---

[1] In contrast to the situation regarding other violent crimes hitherto prosecuted at common law which were to come within the provisions of the Offences Against the Person Act, 1861.

[2] We discuss the provisions in the Criminal Justice Act, 2003 (the 'Blunkett proposals') later.

[3] s 8 of the Criminal Justice Act 1967 abolished the doctrine of constructive malice, revising the much-criticised decision of the House of Lords in *Smith v DPP* [1961] AC 290. The government proposal in May 2003 to bring in legislation to define corporate manslaughter will provide another instance.

Thirty years ago in *Hyam*[4], Lord Kilbrandon said:

> It is not so easy to feel satisfaction at the doubts and difficulties which seem to sur-
> round the crime of murder and the distinguishing from it the crime of manslaughter.
> There is something wrong when crimes of such gravity . . . call for the display of so
> formidable a degree of forensic and judicial learning as the present case has given rise
> to. I believe this to show that a more radical look at the problem is called for . . . since
> no homicides are now punishable with death, these many hours and days have been
> occupied in trying to adjust a definition of that which has no content. There does not
> appear to be any good reason why the crimes of murder and manslaughter should not
> be both abolished, and the single crime of unlawful homicide substituted; one case will
> differ from another in gravity, and that can be taken care of by variation of sentences
> downwards from life imprisonment.

Parliament ignored that powerful judicial entreaty, as it did a similar plea
twenty years later when Lord Mustill said,

> Murder is widely thought to be the gravest of crimes. One could expect a developed
> system to embody a law of murder clear enough to yield an unequivocal result on a
> given set of facts, a result which conforms with apparent justice and has a sound intel-
> lectual base. This is not so in England, where the law of homicide is permeated by
> anomaly, fiction, misnomer and obsolete reasoning. One conspicuous anomaly is the
> rule which identifies the "malice aforethought" (a doubly misleading expression)
> required for the crime of murder not only with a conscious intention to kill but also
> with an intention to cause grievous bodily harm.[5]

In the last 30 years no fewer than 12 appeals—an astonishing number—have had
to be decided by the House of Lords which is authorised to entertain criminal
appeals only if the Court of Appeal (Criminal Division) certifies that the case
raises an issue of general public importance and leave is granted either by that
court or the Law Lords themselves. The case of *Hyam* was upset in 1985, since
when all shades of culpability and fine distinctions have peppered the judgments
by our senior judiciary, to the point where the law of homicide is in desperate
need of parliamentary attention. It is only the popular—widely misunderstood—
view of murder as more serious than manslaughter that might be thought to
stand in the way of its replacement by a simple offence of criminal homicide.

The mindless and mechanistically repetitive statement that murder is the
most wicked of all crimes, and that it must be sharply distinguished from all
other forms of unlawful homicide, is thoroughly discredited. Given the variables in homicidal events and the moral opprobrium attaching to any one individual killer, there is no need in contemporary society to label unlawful killings
other than by the rubric of a single crime. This chapter seeks to demonstrate
both the variable nature of homicides and the moral responsibility for each case.

The traditional (or old) definition of the offence of murder was unlawful
killing, with malice aforethought, resulting in death of the victim within a year

---

[4] *Hyam v DPP* [1975] AC 55 at 98.
[5] *Attorney-General's Reference No 3 of 1994* [1998] 1 Cr App Rep 91 at 93.

and a day. In modern times, the emphasis has invariably focused on the state of mind of the accused (the malice aforethought). It is a common misapprehension among non-lawyers that a person can be convicted of murder only if it is proved that the accused intended to kill; in fact only a minority of people convicted of murder possess that intent. It is sufficient for the prosecution to prove an intention to cause really serious injury. If death ensues, however unexpected, unpremeditated, lacking in intention to kill, the offence of murder is made out, and the mandatory sentence of life imprisonment must follow. It is possible to commit a murder not only without wishing the death of the victim but without the least thought that this might be the result of the assault. Few would think that this represents a system of justice.

By contrast, where the accused is charged only with an attempt to murder, it is necessary for the prosecution to prove a specific intent to kill; an intention to cause serious injury would not suffice. The case of Dr Nigel Cox points up the absurd illogicality of the law. Dr Cox was tried and found guilty of the attempted murder of a terminally ill patient by giving her a lethal injection. He received a 12-month suspended sentence. If, on the facts (as might well have been the case) it was proved that the injection had been the cause of the patient's death, the charge would have been murder, and the penalty would have had to be life imprisonment.

The laudable aim of contemporary lawmakers in the Anglo-Saxon legal system, be they legislators or judges, has been to establish a consistent moral basis to the law of homicide, and that is attainable only by an accurate assessment of the degree of culpability of the individual killer. If the general justification for the prosecution, conviction and punishment of offenders were to be the utilitarian aim of preventing harm, the law might be content to apply objective standards of human conduct towards those that kill. Oliver Wendell Holmes Jr (Mr Justice Holmes of the US Supreme Court) in his classic work, *The Common Law*[6] took pains to emphasise that:

> the tests of liability are external, and independent of the degree of evil in the particular person's motives or intentions.

Holmes' purpose in championing an external standard of liability was to strip the criminal law, like other legal subjects, of the 'baggage of morals'; in particular Holmes was fond of converting terms, such as 'malice'[7] or 'intent' from subjective to objective concepts.

> 'Acts', he wrote, 'should be judged by their tendency under the known circumstances, not by the actual intent which accompanies them.'[8]

---

[6] Oliver Wendell Holmes, Jr. *The Common Law* 1st edn (Boston, Little Brown & Co, 1881) at 50. Holmes is quoted in the judgment in *Smith* (see below n 10). See also Holmes' judgment in *Commonwealth of Massachusetts v Pierce*, 1895, 138 Mass, 165, 168–9 (1884).

[7] Although principally remembered for the 'golden thread' running through the English law, that places the burden of proof upon the prosecution, the judgment in *Woolmington* (delivered by the Lord Chancellor, Lord Sankey) importantly addresses in some detail the history of the term. *Woolmington v DPP* [1935] AC 462.

[8] Holmes, *The Common Law*, above n 6, at 66.

A Holmesian view finds modern expression in an essay by Lord Irvine of Lairg:

> . . . it is surely not for the accused himself to decide what level of risk he is permitted to take. That must be for the law to decide. And we have to decide these perplexing questions, with a level head and an open mind, perhaps best under the shade of a coolibah tree.[9]

Apart from an occasional dalliance with such notions,[10] English law has adhered rigidly to the principle that for all serious crimes, principles of justice and fairness to accused persons must prevail over the public interest in preventing harm, thus desisting from the punishment of those who lack the capacity or fair opportunity to obey the standards of society. Moral culpability for the criminal event alone can justify the imposition of any penal sanction.

Had the Holmes' doctrine of foreseeability, tested by objective standards, become the established rule of the English Common Law, there would be no room for the concept of oblique intention, that is to say an intention inferred indirectly from the individual's actual foresight of his actions and their perceived consequences. But lawmakers—and in the case of murder and manslaughter they have been almost exclusively the judges, sections 2 and 3 of the Homicide Act being the sole statutory exceptions—have had to grapple with the complexities of the mental processes of human beings behaving in a disorderly fashion. Once the objective judgment of conduct is abandoned, what suffices to constitute the requisite intention, in contradistinction to unintentional conduct, which is treated from a moral and legal point of view as nonculpable in terms of criminal responsibility? Inevitably, the courts need to resort to indirect ('oblique') aspects of desire or foresight on the part of the accused. Any analysis of the extensive case-law will demonstrate the fluid, not to say confusing state of the law.

If jurisprudence has directed (or misdirected) the shape and form of the law relating to the question of intent to kill or cause really serious harm, the resultant case-law has to be viewed in the context of the criminal justice in which the verdict of the court of trial is distributed as between the judge and jury, the distinction being that the judge rules on the law (but, *quaere*, whether that is decisive of the case at the hands of an uncontrolled jury) and the jury which must decide whether its findings of fact constitute a proper inference of the criteria for concluding the requisite intention.

That important qualification to a logical analysis of the case-law is manifest in the speech of Lord Scarman in *Hancock and Shankland*.[11] A year earlier, in

---

[9] 'The English and Australian Law of Criminal Culpability' ch 20 in *Human Rights: Constitutional Law and the Development of the English Legal System,* (Oxford, Hart Publishing, 2003) at 346.

[10] *DPP v Smith* [1961] AC 290, 327–28. Citing Holmes, Lord Kilmuir, LC, said; 'The test of foresight is not what this very criminal foresaw, but what a man of reasonable prudence would have foreseen.'

[11] *R v Hancock and Shankland* [1986] 1 AC 455.

Moloney,[12] the House of Lords held that judges should generally avoid using the term 'intention' beyond explaining that it does not encompass motive. Lord Bridge of Harwich, interpreting what their Lordships had variably (and unhelpfully) said in *Hyam* about the requisite intention of an arsonist of a residence in which known individuals were the accused's former lover and her children who were killed, said:

> the probability of the consequence taken to have been foreseen must be little short of overwhelming before it will suffice to establish the necessary intent.

Lord Bridge's observation about the 'natural consequence' flowing from an act would seem to cover the actor who has knowledge of a high degree of certainty that his or her behaviour is likely to result in death. In *Nedrick*[13] Lord Lane, CJ, used the language of 'virtual certainty' of death or serious harm to reflect the result of the actions of the accused and that there was appreciation that such was the case. The language of certainty is dangerous, if only because it is an absolute. In so far as in common parlance we all talk of degrees of certainty, such imprecision merely gives rise to differing views about how near to certainty one must get.

The vagueness of the phrase 'natural consequence' was considered in *Hancock and Shankland* to be too misleading for the jury. Lord Scarman expressed himself as being concerned less with intent and more with the way in which a jury might go about determining intent. A jury should be aware:

> the greater the probability of a consequence the more likely the consequence was foreseen and if that consequence was foreseen the greater the probability is that the consequence was intended.

This ruling on intent shifts the question towards the evidentiary (a jury issue) rather than function as a substantive mechanism with which to direct (or even guide) a jury to find intent or not. That, however, did not bring the judicial debate to an end. Another trip to the House of Lords was necessary. In *Woollin,*[14] it was held that the jury should be told that it could 'find' the requisite intention rather than 'infer' it from the circumstances of foresight, but—a big 'but'?—that it would be a misdirection to tell the jury that intention could be inferred from foresight that there was a 'substantial risk of death or serious harm'. This blurs the dividing line between intention and recklessness, and demonstrates that the law has given more than simple accommodation to oblique intention. Recklessness may, it seems, spill over into the realm of intent.

A presently unanswered question is what a jury should understand, in terms of foresight, about an intention on the part of an accused to endanger life. Should the law require not merely an intention to cause really serious harm but incorporate an intention to endanger life? A decision of the Court of Appeal in

---

[12]   *R v Moloney* [1985] 1AC 905.
[13]   *R v Nedrick* [1986] 1 WLR 1025.
[14]   *R v Woollin* [1991] 1 AC 82.

Northern Ireland in April 2003[15] would seem to suggest an affirmative answer. Whether this extension to the established rule about what constitutes 'really serious harm' is affected by Articles 3, 6 and 7 of the European Convention on Human Rights raises the spectre of yet further uncertainty in the law. The obliqueness of intent comes in a European garb. Can the English Common Law resist the incoming tide of precepts in international human rights'? Judicial criticisms concerning the concept of really serious harm abound. In *(Attorney-General's Reference No 3 of 1994)*,[16] a re-run of the doctrine of transferred malice, Lord Mustill stated[17] that

> the grievous harm rule is an outcropping of old law from which the surrounding strata of ratiocinations have withered away.

Again, in *Powell (Anthony)*,[18] Lord Steyn said that the rule turned

> murder into a constructive crime resulting in defendants being classified as murderers who are not in truth murderers

The remedy—another form of obliquity—lies in the recommendation of the Select Committee on the House of Lords on Murder and Life Imprisonment[19] that a person commits murder if he causes death of another

> intending to cause serious personal harm and being aware that he may cause death.

If there is any room in the English Common Law for a concept of oblique intent, it does no more than import a theoretical underpinning of the law of homicide. It must be concluded that, willy-nilly, the law in action has accommodated obliquity in its endless search for a consistent moral basis by way of establishing the *mens rea* for murder. In its pragmatism, the judiciary has effectively consigned the statement to the archives of the criminal justice system.

The task of the criminal court today is to determine whether the ultimate aim of the accused, as distinct from the preceding stages of the accused's activities, is intended or unintended. The substantial and shifting body of case-law reveals an unwillingness, or perhaps even an inability, to define intent and to leave to the jury the task of deciding whether the circumstances disclose intention or inattention. The result is a confused and confusing mosaic, a piecing together of judicial directions and jury verdicts. 'What a muddle!' exclaimed the leading academic criminal lawyer of his day, the late Professor Sir John Smith, QC. He was right.

The distinction between murder and manslaughter is not derived from the physical harm contemplated, since in both cases the proscribed harm is the same unlawful killing of a human being. What sets them apart is the moral principle that intentional wrongs are generally more heinous than unintentional ones.

---

[15] *R v Anderson (Samuel)* [2003] NICA 12. Leave to appeal to the House of Lords was refused.
[16] Above n 5.
[17] [1998] AC 245 at 258.
[18] [1999] AC 1.
[19] HL Paper 78–1, Session 1988–1989, para 71.

There's the rub. The task of identifying the killer's intention in relation to the specific victim is difficult enough for both judge and jury, the less so for the former whenever he sits alone (as in the Diplock courts in Northern Ireland since 1974) and is required to give a reasoned decision which is susceptible to an unqualified appeal. The comparative study of one killer's intention with that of another for the purpose of assessing appropriate penal sanction is infinitely more complicated. Since in the case of murder that exercise is not performed by the trial court, it can only be gauged by the appellate court which supervises the sentencing policy and practice, or by the post-conviction process of tariff-fixing by the judiciary and in the process of determining the killer's ultimate discharge from prison. If the trial verdict be manslaughter, the penalty available to the court is at large.

In mediaeval times, European legal systems gave effect to the distinction between intentional and unintentional killing at the stage of sentencing by varying the punishment in the light of the presence or absence of intention; this being done *after* liability had been determined according to the doctrine of causation—not invariably an easy task in cases of homicide, as we have witnessed in contemporary cases of mothers killing their babies supposedly by suffocation or violent shaking. The ascertainment of causation has often been limited by the extent of medical knowledge, notably regarding those particular instances commonly referred to as 'cot-deaths'.[20]

In principle, there is no reason why that same approach, considering the issue of intent at the sentencing stage, could not be adopted today. But since the Middle Ages the authors of the common law, in unintentional collusion with legislators, have long since decreed otherwise. For the last four centuries they chose instead to tie intention to liability. They attached greater moral turpitude to intentional killing; thus murderers and manslayers were convicted of different criminal offences according to the perceived public heinousness of the criminal event, the infliction of harm, and the death of the victim, being precisely the same. Everything in a murder trial focuses on the alleged intention of the accused in order that the correct legal label may be affixed to the event, so vital for the imposition of the penalty; in the instance of murder, fixed and immutable, in that of manslaughter, at large. Since the nature and circumstances of the criminal event of an unlawful killing are infinitely variable, it hardly seems sensible to pigeon-hole its unlawfulness into different legal compartments. One label should readily suffice.

The weight of contemporary academic opinion[21] is that the language of risk-taking belongs to the realm of recklessness rather than to intention. This smacks

---

[20] While in a pre-scientific era the techniques of forensic pathology were rudimentary, the sophistication of modern science is no warranty that in some instances it will not prove extremely difficult to establish the facts. Expert witnesses are not infrequently at variance in their opinions as to how the evidence should be interpreted to establish the facts. See below chapter 5 *Expert Evidence on Trial*.

[21] See F McAuley and G McCutcheon, *Criminal Liability* (Dublin, Round Hall Sweet & Maxwell, 2000) at 300.

of semantics rather than a reasoned method of stating the substantive law. If the dichotomy of murder/manslaughter were swept away and replaced by a single offence of criminal homicide, any distinctions in moral culpability between a reckless disregard of a risk to human life and well-being, and an intention to cause death or serious injury, could be reflected in the degree of punishment imposed. Nor would that sentencing exercise be encumbered by legal tests—subtle or unsubtle—of criminal responsibility, but would provide all the necessary flexibility of graduated punishment.

Stripped of the elusive element of intention, other forms of unlawful killing are subsumed by the law under the rubric of involuntary manslaughter as risk-taking activity, such as causing death by dangerous driving, which fall short of being murder. There are, however, three ways in which death resulting from risk-taking can constitute manslaughter.[22]

First, where the defendant subjectively foresees a risk of death or serious injury (but the degree of foresight fails to come within the narrow confines of the test in *Woollin* such as to constitute murder) there is liability for manslaughter. In practice, this category covers instances in which the jury rejects the verdict of murder and finds the defendant guilty of manslaughter. It is a common experience that the Crown Prosecution Service indict for murder on the basis that the jury is the proper forum for the decision as to which side of the dividing line the case falls. Not infrequently, of course, the defendant will plead to the lesser offence of manslaughter. This practice on the part of the prosecution was neatly illustrated in the case of *Moloney*. The defendant was a young soldier at home on leave, engaged in a celebration which went on late into the night. The young man killed his stepfather (with whom he was on affectionate terms) with a shotgun. He would not in any way have desired the victim's death which occurred in the course of a contest between them to see who could be quicker on the draw. When the defendant drew first, the victim dared him to shoot. He did just that, with the fatal result. The trial judge, Mr Justice Stephen Brown (later to become President of the Family Division of the High Court) told the jurors that they were entitled to convict the defendant of murder if they were satisfied that the defendant foresaw that his actions were likely to cause serious bodily harm. The jury convicted. Ultimately the House of Lords put matters right, but it is worth tracing the course of the criminal proceedings to demonstrate the judicial conflict about the law and the public's understanding of the law of homicide.

The killing, on any view, was a human and family tragedy. The defendant had instantly given himself up and was charged with murder. When the case came before the local magistrates, they declined to commit the defendant to the Crown Court for murder, and substituted a charge of manslaughter—no doubt a sensible layman's view, and right, as it turned out to be! The prosecution (as

---

[22] Strictly speaking, there is no separate offence of 'involuntary' manslaughter, but for convenience the three ways are so described.

it was entitled to do, though if somewhat lacking in good judgment, and no doubt relying on *Hyam*) restored the charge of murder on the indictment. The defendant appealed to the Court of Appeal (Criminal Division). The appeal failed, miserably. The Court, with a display of judicial reluctance, certified that the case raised a point of law of general public importance, but emphatically refused to give leave to take the case to the House of Lords.

Leave was in fact readily granted by the Law Lords, and the appeal succeeded, resoundingly.[23] That there should have been such a divergence of view among the senior judiciary in 1985—nothing in this regard would seem to have changed[24]—on the question of intention as the mental element in the crime of murder is itself a sad commentary on the law's failure to declare with certainty the ingredients of a serious criminal offence. What then happened to the law?

Secondly, where the defendant commits a *dangerous* and *unlawful* act which results in death, manslaughter is the appropriate crime.

Thirdly, where the defendant owes a duty of care to the victim of homicide and breaches that duty in a negligent manner causing death—the negligence is usually stated to be 'gross', but it is not clear what that adds to the negligent act—there can be liability for manslaughter. In short, the requirement of the law is that the risk of physical harm be foreseeable. This category would, in theory, catch those cases once popularly known as 'motor manslaughter' before the legislation making statutory provision for the offences of causing death by dangerous driving or causing death while driving under the influence of drink or drugs. Prosecutions are invariably brought under the road traffic legislation.[25] Corporate manslaughter for train disasters and the like is a rarity, but the campaign to broaden the responsibility appears to have persuaded the Government to legislate in the near future.

The unsatisfactory state of the law has been comprehensively and critically reviewed by the Law Commission,[26] but its recommendations remain unenacted. There is no need for us to rehearse the difficulties in the law on involuntary manslaughter or the possible solution. The Law Commission's review of 1996, together with the cascade of contemporary case-law from the House of Lords, has, one must concede, at least made the darkness of the law less completely impenetrable, but the greyness of the jurisprudence remains without clear landmarks in what is, nevertheless a mist of uncertainty. Moreover, the

---

[23] [1985] AC 905. The issue was considered the following year by Lord Lane, CJ, in the Court of Appeal in *Nedrick* (1986) Cr App Rep 267.

[24] See *R v Smith (Morgan)* [2001] 1 AC 146; also *Partial Defences to Murder,* Law Commission Consultation Paper 173 (2003) at 4.69–4.161.

[25] Road traffic offences are, for the most part, subject to substantially less social opprobrium than other crimes. This is a matter of immense significance to the relatives of the victims of such crimes who are frequently at a loss to perceive either logic or justice when what they hold to be homicides are nevertheless often visited for the most part with comparatively lenient sentences within a specified maximum which falls well short of that of the discretionary life sentence available to the courts in cases of 'ordinary' manslaughter.

[26] *Legislating the Criminal Code: Involuntary manslaughter,* Law Commission, Paper No 237, (1996).

legitimate (or what are, arguably, less intellectually legitimate) defences—partial or otherwise—to a charge of murder make no contribution to answering the primary question of how, through its criminal law, a civilised society should respond to unlawful killings.

NECESSITY, DURESS AND SELF-DEFENCE

Necessity

A hundred and twenty years ago the Lord Chief Justice of the day, Lord Coleridge, in a case involving cannibalism at sea, explained why the law provided no defence of necessity to a charge of murder. The yacht *Mignonette*, outward bound from Southampton for Australia, foundered off the African coast and her crew took to her small dinghy. Adrift, and without food or water, the master and mate killed the cabin boy (the physically weakest, and therefore the most likely to die first if they were not rescued) and had begun to eat the body when help arrived. In his celebrated judgment, Lord Coleridge observed:

> It must not be supposed that in refusing to admit temptation to be an excuse for crime it is forgotten how terrible the temptation was; how awful the suffering; how in such trials to keep the judgment straight and the conduct pure. We are often compelled to set up standards we cannot reach ourselves and to lay down rules which we could not ourselves satisfy. But a man has no right to declare temptation to be an excuse though he might himself have yielded to it, allow compassion for the criminal to change or weaken in any manner the legal definition of the crime.[27]

Lord Coleridge dismissed the claim that self-preservation was a lawful defence[28] and held it to be 'unworkable and dangerous in practice'.

---

[27] *R v Dudley and Stephens* (1884) 14 QBD 273 at 288. The two, who were rescued, were subsequently found guilty of murder and sentenced to death. Sir Henry James (Attorney-General) and Sir Farrer Herschell (Solicitor-General), implored Harcourt to exercise mercy, stating that public opinion was in sympathy with the defendants. On 5 December 1884 James wrote to Harcourt:

> 'If you announce a commutation to penal servitude for life or even to any shorter term you will never be able to maintain such a decision and you will have to give way';

to which Harcourt replied:

> 'It is exactly to withstand an erroneous and perverted sentiment on such matters that we are placed in situations of very painful responsibility'.

Harcourt relented to the extent that the death sentence was commuted to one of imprisonment for six months.

[28] It may be argued that the necessity of preserving life, not least one's own, constitutes perhaps the most extreme form of duress. The House of Lords was, many years later, to confirm that duress did not constitute a defence to murder; even if the defendant's own life is threatened it cannot be justifiable to take another innocent life. *R v Howe* [1987] AC 417. This issue is discussed *ex hypothesi* by Professor Andrew Ashworth in the context of a more recent maritime disaster, the sinking of the *Herald of Free Enterprise*: Ashworth, *Principles of Criminal Law*, 3rd edn (Oxford, OUP, 1999).

'Certainly I would', he said 'rather be in an open boat with companions who accepted [this] principle than in company with lawyers who accepted necessity as a defence to murder'.

Two distinguished academic lawyers have written that it would be premature to conclude that necessity can never be a defence to murder.[29] The suggestion is that where the person sacrificed has innocently imperilled the lives of others— for example, by falling over a precipice while roped to another climber, who then cuts him loose to save his own life—the defence might be available. An incident which emerged from the inquest into the deaths caused by the sinking of the *Herald of Free Enterprise*—the Zeebrugge disaster—impliedly supports such a suggestion.[30]

Justice Benjamin Cardozo, in a remarkable instance of eloquent extra-judicial writing, has probably best expressed the approach of the English Common Law:

> Where two or more are overtaken by common disaster, there is no right on the part of one to save the lives of some by the killing of another. There is no rule of human jet-tison. Men there will often be who, when told that their going will be the salvation of the remnant, will choose the nobler part and will make the plunge into the waters. In that supreme moment the darkness for them will be illuminated by the thought that those left behind will ride to safety. If none of such mould are [*sic*] found aboard the boat, or too few to save the others, the human freight must be left to meet the claims of the waters. Who shall choose in such an hour between the victims and the saved? Who shall know when the masts and sails of rescue may emerge out of the fog?[31]

The extreme caution of Justice Cardozo in entertaining a defence of the choice of the lesser evil in homicide is not the prevailing one, as the treatment of the problem by the US Model Penal Code shows. In its commentary on the passage from Cardozo's statement, the Code states:

> It would be particularly unfortunate to exclude homicidal conduct from the scope of the defence (of choice of evils) . . . Conduct that results in taking life may promote the very value sought to be protected by the law of homicide. The life of every individual must be taken . . . to be of equal value and the numerical preponderance in the lives saved compared to those sacrificed surely shall establish legal justification for the act . . . Although the view is not universally held that it is ethically preferable to take one innocent life than to have many lives lost, most persons probably think a net saving of

[29] Sir John (JC) Smith and Brian Hogan, *Criminal Law*, 8th edn, (London, Butterworths, 1996) at 258. See also JC Smith, *Justification and Excuse in Criminal Law* (London, Sweet and Maxwell, 1989) at 73–79.

[30] The incident involved a passenger who, it seems likely in a panic born of terror, blocked an escape route to others by continuing to cling to a rope ladder. The unfortunate individual was said to have been eventually pushed off. No prosecution resulted. See also JC Smith, *Justification and Excuse in Criminal Law*, previous note, at 73–79.

[31] Benjamin Cardozo, *Law and Literature and Other Addresses* (New York, Harcourt Brace, 1931) at 113 (Originally published in (1925) 14 *Yale Law Review*, 699). The passage quoted is repro-duced in Adam Bedau, *Making Moral Choices: Three Exercises in Moral Casuistry* (Oxford, OUP, 1997) at pp 30–31 and cited in McAuley and McCutcheon, *Criminal Liability*, above n 21, at 800.

lives is ethically warranted if the choice among lives to be saved is not unfair. Certainly the law should permit such a choice.[32]

Assuming that the principle of choosing the lesser evil were to become available as a defence to a charge of homicide, Dudley and Stephens, the two crew members of the *Mignonette*, might succeed to-day. Lord Coleridge's statement,

> it is admitted that the deliberate killing of this unoffending boy was clearly murder, unless the killing can be justified by some well recognised excuse admitted by the law

confuses justification with excuse. The distinction clearly exists. One *justifies* causing harm to another by showing that one did it deliberately and after due reflection nevertheless concluding that in the circumstances it was the right—or the best—thing to do. One *excuses* someone from blame for the harm done to another by conceding that it was wrong to cause the harm, but that nevertheless, in the circumstances, it could not be helped and therefore one cannot really be blamed for it. The latter might be a partial, or a complete excuse. We think the law should now establish the distinction. There are signs of such a development from a case four years ago in the civil jurisdiction, where the Court of Appeal was asked to decide whether, in the exceptional circumstances of a planned surgical operation to separate conjoined babies, the doctors, knowing that death would ensue for one of the twins, could lawfully proceed with the surgical operation without fear of committing murder. Without disturbing the decision in *Dudley and Stephens*, the Court in *Re A (children)*[33] distinguished the different human predicaments faced in the facts of the decision. Lord Justice Brooke stated that the defence of necessity could be available to an accused. He said:[34]

> According to Sir James Stephen, there are three requirements for the application of the doctrine of necessity: (i) the act is needed to void inevitable and irreparable evil; (ii) no more should be other than is reasonably necessary for the purpose to be achieved; and (iii) the evil inflicted must not be disproportionate to the evil avoided.

The Court found all of these requirements had been met in *The Conjoined Twins* case, thus giving the surgeons the green light to go ahead without the fear of facing a criminal prosecution. On the Court's findings, the twins had to be separated if the death of both twins was to be avoided, but in the process of avoidance one of the twins was bound to die. Translated to a case of necessity pleaded in defence to a charge of murder (or criminal homicide) the test laid down by Lord Justice Brooke might avail an accused in a *Dudley and Stephens* situation: the choice of the lesser evil would be a sustainable defence to criminal liability.

---

[32] The Code was drafted in the late 1950s and was prepared and published by the American Law Institute, the Official Draft appearing in 1962. The Code has served as a guide for measuring possible and proposed reforms in procedural and substantive criminal law in the various jurisdictions of the United States.

[33] [2000] 4 All ER 961.

[34] *Ibid.*, p 1052.

Duress

Duress as a defence to murder has had a more chequered career than its counterpart, necessity, in coping with the expedient taking of human life. While duress may be raised as a defence to most non-homicidal offences, the common law has not accorded such status generally to the crime of murder. Almost 30 years ago[35] the House of Lords, by a majority of 3 to 2, did find that the defence was available in a case of attempted murder, but that was to be rejected by a unanimous House in 1987 in *Howe* and again in 1992 in *Gotts*.[36] Duress can now be regarded as a plea of general application available to all crimes except murder, attempted murder and some forms of treason. In any event, the courts have been able to negative a plea of duress to a charge of murder whenever the killer was a voluntary member of an organisation, thereby committing himself to an unlawful campaign; the killer was not permitted to take advantage of the pressure exercised on him by his fellow criminals. In Northern Ireland, in a case involving a member of the Official IRA, Lord Lowry observed, it was not possible to do so,

> in order to put on, when it suits him, the breastplate of righteousness.[37]

Speaking of the defence of duress in the *Fitzpatrick* case, Lord Lowry said that if the conscious intent to commit a crime, including logically to kill or cause really serious injury, was formed under a compulsion so strong that it could be said that the perpetrator ought not reasonably be expected to resist it, the moral excitability erases the criminality of the guilty act. He added:

> Putting the matter thus, one can appreciate an argument for saying that duress, if proved, should merely be reflected in the severity of the punishment and not in exculpation of the crime, but it is now too late to pretend that this approach would reflect the common law.

Yet it is never too late for Parliament to decide that this mitigation, too, can be appropriately assigned to the sentencing stage. Lord Mackay of Clashfern in *Howe* said,

> I have not found any satisfactory formulation of a distinction which will be sufficiently precise to be given practical effect in law and at the same time differentiate between levels of culpability, so as to produce a satisfactory demarcation between those accused of murder who should be entitled to resort to the defence of duress and those who are not.[38]

Touché. Once it is acknowledged that the killing was unlawful, claims that the killer was under duress can safely be left to the stage of sentencing.

[35] *DPP for Northern Ireland v Lynch* [1977] AC 653.
[36] *R v Gotts* [1992] 2 AC 412.
[37] Lowry, LCJ in *R v Fitzpatrick* [1977] NI 120.
[38] [1987] AC 417, 453.

Self-defence

Where a person kills in self-defence, the law adopts an 'all-or-nothing' approach. If the killer, in order to protect himself, or even his home, uses more force than is reasonable, he is liable for murder; there is no half-way house in a partial defence of excessive force. This is a time hallowed view enunciated by Aquinas 800 years ago, who maintained that

> . . . it is legitimate to answer force with force provided it goes no further than due defence requires.[39]

Yet, here again, in modern times, the law has tended to waver. An Australian initiative contemplated a lesser homicidal offence than murder where the killing narrowly crossed the threshold between a reasonable and an unreasonable amount of force.[40] The Privy Council in 1971[41] rejected that idea, on the ground that the full application of self-defence could adequately favour those who used such force as they instinctively thought necessary in the circumstances.

In its 4th report in 1980 the Criminal Law Revision Committee disagreed, recommending that a verdict of manslaughter should be possible where the use of some force which the killer used was reasonable in the circumstances. The High Court of Australia set the clock back in 1987 by denouncing the doctrine of excessive force as too complicated for juries.

But the issue has not gone away. Private Clegg, a soldier in Northern Ireland, had been convicted of murder as a result of shooting at a car which drove through an army checkpoint. The House of Lords upheld the conviction although Lord Lloyd of Berwick, while expressing some sympathy for the soldier's dilemma, thought the question of reform was a matter only for the legislature.[42] The Government's response was to contend that whatever the force of the argument for a compromise verdict of manslaughter, it was outweighed by the complexity that would ensue by a change in the law.[43]

The recent case of the Norfolk farmer, Tony Martin, brought the issue of self-defence into a sharp, contemporary focus and is a subject which has excited a great deal of public interest. Martin was originally convicted of the murder of a teenage burglar, and sentenced accordingly to life imprisonment. Martin's subsequent appeal against conviction for murder was allowed on the grounds of evidence of diminished responsibility and sentenced to five years' imprisonment for manslaughter. In December 2003 the BBC Radio 4 Today programme

---

[39] 'Vim vi repellere licet cum moderamine inculpatæ tutelæ', *Summa Theologiæ*, 38 (trans M Lefébure, OP, London, Blackfriars in conjunction with Eyre and Spottiswoode, 1975) at 43.

[40] *R v McKay* [1957] ALR 648 and *R v Howe* (1958) 100 CLR 448; *R v Zecevic* (1987) 71 ALR 641.

[41] *Palmer v R* [1971] AC 814 and *R v McInnes* (1971) 55 Cr App Rep 551.

[42] *R v Clegg* [1995] 1 AC.482, 499–500. Subsequently at a re-trial, on fresh evidence, Clegg was convicted of a lesser (non-homicidal) offence.

[43] *Report of the Interdepartmental Review of the Law on Use of Lethal Force in Self-defence or the Prevention of Crime* (London, Home Office, 1996).

invited listeners to put forward suggestions for law reform; the proposal that proved most popular was for a law to permit householders to use any means to defend themselves or their property against criminal threat.[44] Public opinion appeared to be divided about the correctness of the jury verdict of murder. What is clear from the various responses to the outcome of the Martin case, is the degree of public dissatisfaction—and misunderstanding—of the law. That Martin should be imprisoned for life having killed the youth who was engaged in committing a serious crime against *him* represented for some a kind of dissonance between the law and a commonsense notion of what was equitable. Clearly, manslaughter was, for many, a preferable outcome, but one must retain an element of scepticism about how far that arose from an intellectual concern about the distinction between murder and manslaughter rather than the more practical consideration that manslaughter carries an essentially discretionary sentence, likely to result in a shorter term of incarceration. Indeed, on his successful appeal the Court of Appeal subsumed a sentence of five years imprisonment. The issue which the Martin case raises, yet which has passed with little public comment is the successful promotion of the defence of diminished responsibility, the defence of self-defence having initially failed. In recent years this statutory defence[45] has been advanced in some instances in which its legislative progenitors might well have considered it inappropriate, though it is not unknown for a law, to be enacted for one purpose, but used by succeeding generations for another. Diminished responsibility has been used in attempts to enlarge the scope of provocation and in this instance appears almost to have pushed the issue of determining the nature of reasonable force in self-defence into a secondary place. Our view is that the defence of diminished responsibility, if it is to be retained, ought to be confined to demonstrating that there is, where the defendant is suffering from some form of mental impairment or disorder, insufficient evidence of the *mens rea* required for the crime of murder. The long view must surely be that diminished responsibility, like any other currently available defence having the effect of reducing the crime from murder to manslaughter, raises issues that can only properly be addressed at the sentencing stage, being essentially mitigatory in character. In any event, the abolition of the distinction between murder and manslaughter, which we would strongly argue can be the only logical direction for the long overdue reform of the law of homicide, would render this axiomatic.

---

[44] Although scarcely likely to be a representative sample of pubic opinion, the poll revealed the intensity of feeling the issue has aroused through appearing to suggest that having once embarked upon a criminal enterprise, the offender should be seen as having effectively forfeited anything beyond the most vestigial consideration of his welfare. In this we might hear an echo from Coke, perhaps the most articulate advocate of the 'penal premium'. At the time of writing (January 2004) a Private Members bill has been introduced to embody this expression of public sentiment but disavowed by the Leader of the Conservative Party, Michael Howard.

[45] Deriving from the Homicide Act, 1957.

DEFENCES RELATING TO ISSUES IN MENTAL HEALTH

Insanity

The relationship between the mental competence of a person charged with a criminal offence and the establishment of the responsibility sufficient for the proper imposition of a penal sanction is a problem that is far from new. In the thirteenth century the jurist Henry de Bracton devised his so-called 'wild beast' test[46] while in the nineteenth century, the problem still unresolved, the judges were exercised to produce the M'Naghten Rules. Although applicable to all crimes, the issue of the insanity defence became entangled with the mitigation of the capital penalty at an early stage. This was due, no doubt, to the fact that the offences committed by those suffering from various forms of mental illness tend to attract attention when they are of a very serious nature, such as homicides, arson and, in particular, the assassination of public figures, crimes which in the past carried the death penalty. Add to this the aggravating feature that they are often accompanied by bizarre circumstances and anxieties concerning risk to the community at large are readily amplified. A deep-seated fear, not so much of mental illness *per se* but of mentally ill people, has been a feature of many societies throughout history, our own contemporary world included. Indeed, Bracton's 'wild beast' has by no means become extinct in the popular vocabulary within which some sexual and other violent offenders are categorised. If what might be considered a populist approach to sentencing philosophy has moved forward it has been from a demand that such 'beasts' be put down to an insistence that they be caged securely for natural life.

The special verdict of 'not guilty by reason of insanity' is found, on average, in only three cases a year. Since the only outcome of this verdict is that the defendant is detained in a Special Hospital (or other hospital specified by the Home Secretary) with the same status as restricted patient under the Mental Health Act 1983, the defence of insanity is worth raising only when the prospect of indefinite hospital detention is thought preferable to the likely period of imprisonment for the offence, i.e. life imprisonment for murder. By comparison, the verdict of guilty to manslaughter by reason of diminished responsibility provides a wider and more flexible alternative although it provides no guarantee that a defendant suffering from mental illness who advances this defence will necessarily receive treatment as part of the sentence of the court. Research conducted by the present authors into the operation of the Homicide

---

[46] Applied in 1724 by Mr Justice Tracey in *Arnold's Case* (6 State Trials, 764, 765). This is unsurprising in view of the fact that in the *Institutes* Coke, in his account of *Beverley* (1603), notes that a beast, being incapable of reason was similarly incapable of felonious intent. For a fuller discussion see: Terence Morris. 'Mad, Bad or Simply Dangerous? Homicide and Mental Disorder' in Gavin Drewry and Charles Blake (eds) *Law and the Spirit of Inquiry: Essays in Honour of Sir Louis Blom-Cooper* (London, Kluwer Law International, 1999).

Act 1957[47] indicated considerable variation in the nature of disposal by the courts, including determinate sentences of imprisonment, Hospital Orders and periods of supervision on Probation. The 'insanity' defence for murder seems then to be obsolescent, if not in practice obsolete, although it is still raised occasionally for cases other than murder. It is occasionally invoked to establish unfitness to plead[48] which essentially comprises an inability, deriving from some condition of the mind, to understand the evidence before the court, to give evidence as a witness, or to give instructions to counsel.

The so-called 'McNaghten Rules' were once famously described by the American criminologist Sheldon Glueck as having both the flexibility of the bed of Procrustes and the rigidity of an army mattress.[49] Certainly, since their original formulation in 1842 judges were to provide juries with a range of interpretations, though the process was influenced by the theoretical constructs that were promoted by medical authorities in the field until comparatively recent times. It was widely held that there was a distinction to be drawn between the 'sane' and the insane' and the latter were considered to be identifiable by errors of cognition. Half a century ago it was still possible for textbooks on criminal law to contain examples of hypothetical defendants unable to distinguish between cutting a woman's throat and slicing a loaf of bread, or killing the victim under the delusion that D was breaking a jar.[50] The Victorian psychiatrist Henry Maudsley had paraphrased the two principal elements of the rules as consisting in either the defendant not knowing the nature and quality of his actions or, if he did know them, did not know them to be wrong. The first criterion, like that of the 'wild beast' test, led to the 'all or nothing' dichotomy between sanity and insanity. The second rendered impossible the serious defence of those whose evident paranoia was nevertheless expressed in the most lucid fashion. If the first criterion applied a test of cognition, extreme to the point of such absurdity as to be useless as a test of the defendant's understanding of his actions, the second applied a test of knowledge and conformity to the law which automatically excluded the defences of those who, however articulate, were deluded by the mental disorder from which they suffered.

These shortcomings relating to the 'insanity' defence have been long regarded by psychiatrists as inappropriate in that the most disturbed person labouring under the severest delusions usually understands the nature of the act he has committed and knows that the act is regarded as morally wrong by society at large, even though he may have been driven by fear, anger or 'the voices' to

---

[47] Terence Morris and Louis Blom-Cooper, *A Calendar of Murder*, (London, Michael Joseph, 1964).

[48] See *R v Johnson*, 27 June 2002 [2002] EWCA Crim 1900.

[49] Sheldon Glueck, *Law and Psychiatry: Cold War or Entente Cordiale?* (London, Tavistock, 1962).

[50] Gordon Hewart who was Lord Chief Justice from 1922 to 1940 reflected in an extra-judicial observation that, 'The mere fact that a man thinks he is John the Baptist does not entitle him to shoot his mother' in Gordon Hewart, *Not Without Prejudice*, (London, Hutchinson, 1937).

override his own moral concerns. The key point is that the majority of mentally disordered offenders are still possessed of both reason and memory together with a capacity for cognition; only those with what are severe mental health problems (sometimes amplified by learning disabilities) are likely to be entirely without competence.

Every now and again the insanity defence is complicated by the arguments over whether or not someone is suffering from an 'insane automatism' or should be totally acquitted on the grounds that the offence was committed as a result of 'non-insane automatism', a transient state produced, for example (in theory) by drugs, the post-ictal phase of focal epilepsy, hypoglycaemia,[51] sleepwalking or any organic cause of reduced consciousness.

Psychiatrists believe that the courts will always enjoy arguments about automatism, a 'condition' which has no medical meaning other than to refer to the behaviour observed in the aftermath of the fit in Jacksonian (focal) epilepsy. Memory loss has also been raised as an issue, perhaps most notably in the case of Günter Podola charged in 1960 with the murder by shooting of a police officer.

In summary, the M'Naghten Rules are widely regarded as 'past their sell-by date' while the insanity defence may be said to be in a terminal state of decline. Medical knowledge has effectively consigned the plea into oblivion and as a forensic device its eclipse by diminished responsibility is almost complete, a situation unlamented by lawyers. Reform is unnecessary; it exists only now to establish fitness to plead. Nor is there any enthusiasm for the recommendations made in 1975 by the Butler Committee on Mentally Abnormal Offenders[52] that there should remain a special verdict renamed 'not guilty on evidence of mental disorder' which would include transitory abnormal mental states and apply both to mental illness and learning disability.

There seems recently to have been a shift in medical thinking, at least among those leading forensic psychiatrists, who now feel that if people are fit to plead, they should have the right to be tried on the evidence of the facts, and that the main role of psychiatrists should be confined to the sentencing and disposal phase. Theirs may not be the opinion of the membership of the Royal College of Psychiatry as a whole, which by its nature tends to a more conservative view of any proposed change and may be less willing to relinquish the verdict which is meant to absolve the 'patient defendant' from all blame or punishment. In practice, patients are not keen on being labelled as 'insane', whether or not it attaches to a 'not guilty' verdict, particularly as incarceration in a hospital on a restriction order is often regarded by those with either previous experience or good inside knowledge as substantially less preferable to a prison sentence.

---

[51] It was used successfully in the Northern Ireland case of Ian Hay Gordon in 1953. See: *R v Gordon*, 20 December 2000 (Unreported) when, in a reference by the Criminal Cases Review Commission the NI Court of Appeal quashed the verdict of 'guilty but insane'.

[52] Cmnd 6214.

Diminished Responsibility

The partial defence of diminished responsibility was introduced for the first time in England by section 2 of the Homicide Act, 1957, with the express purpose of mitigating the effects of the death penalty for the mentally disordered. It is now the preferred and commonest route for those (numbering about 130 cases a year) whose mental state is considered to be relevant to the homicide with which they are charged. It is a defence which, almost half a century after its introduction, receives virtually universal condemnation from those psychiatrists who are called upon to give evidence. Effectively, it exists only to provide the courts with the flexibility provided by the wide range of sentencing options available following a conviction for manslaughter, in contrast to the inflexible rigidity of the mandatory penalty for murder. The criteria for the defence, the accused being of

> such abnormality of mind as substantially impaired his mental responsibility for his acts or omissions in doing or being a party to the killing

is arguably wide enough to cover socially unacceptable behaviour during bouts of irritability brought on by a head cold, but the evidential proof necessary to establish the defence causes profound difficulties for those forensic psychiatrists who do not feel qualified to make judgments on the moral dimension of 'responsibility'. Nevertheless, they are often invited by judges to express an opinion. There is, moreover, a temptation to which some psychiatrists succumb, to pontificate on degrees of responsibility as if there exists a sliding scale of this essentially abstract moral phenomenon. It often comes down to 'well, how *bad* is this person, and how morally wrong in this instance?'; terms of art having little meaning in the realms of forensic science. Thus the scene is set for a psychiatric protagonist to argue in court about a topic for which none of his or her colleagues would claim any expertise outside of court!

Forensic psychiatrists agree that this is unseemly, bringing psychiatry into disrepute, if not ridicule. They are agreed that, if the mandatory life sentence were abolished and range of penalties for murder as flexible as that for ordinary manslaughter, these farces would be avoided. The types of cases in which psychiatrists experience most unease are those where ascertainment of mental abnormality, either transient or chronic, is feasible, but in which lawyers, quite frequently, hope for a helpful quota of 'emotional instability' to be dug out of the psyche.

How far a psychiatrist is willing to go in support of a claim of diminished responsibility owes more to his or her own moral judgment on the imputed wickedness of the defendant, than to psychiatric training or medical knowledge.

It would be hard to over-emphasise the dislike expressed by forensic psychiatrists of the defence of diminished responsibility which is regarded as a blot on psychiatric practice and a poor mechanism for dealing with the wide range of individuals whose circumstances demand widely differing judicial responses.

The case-law on section 2 of the Homicide Act, 1957 is, moreover, jurispru-dentially unedifying. After abolition of the death penalty in 1965/1969, the *raison d'être* of this defence to murder ceased to exist, save for the desire by some to avoid the stigma of a conviction for murder and the consequent sentence of life imprisonment. Juries might also be reluctant to convict those offenders they consider are not morally reprehensible, if they did not have the option of the less stigmatising verdict of manslaughter to fall back on. The abused spouse, the 'mercy killer' as well as the deluded individual—are they all to be labelled mur-derers? Of course, if the distinction between murder and manslaughter were to be abandoned and all unlawful killings subsumed within a general category of homicide, the problem of differential stigma would be resolved.[53] In general, psychiatrists feel that the stigma attached to the verdict of murder would not be greatly lessened by any change in the court's discretion to sentence, and there-fore they acknowledge the force of the argument for maintaining a lesser verdict for some cases. Their concern is to see psychiatrists removed from the forum of arguments for it.

Infanticide

Infanticide is now used to cover cases of women who kill their babies as a result of circumstances which can include personality problems, difficulties in making a relationship with the baby, failure to cope, social deprivation and poverty. It clearly covers a lot more than the effects of birth and lactation. Brenda Hoggett (now Lady Hale of Richmond) poses an incisive question:

> Should these amount to an excuse at all? If they should, why should they not apply to fathers? Or to other people who are driven to killing by the intolerable pressures of their surroundings, although unprovoked by the victims?[54]

An offence of criminal homicide would adequately cover the killing of children by their parents in situations of great stress, and those living under the strain of mental illness induced by the situation within the family, including mothers suf-fering from post-puerperal depression. The courts are able, within the existing law relating to offenders suffering from mental illness or disorder, to deal appropriately with those convicted of such culpable homicides in ways that meet both the needs of the offender for treatment by which the interests of the community are best protected.

---

[53] As it is, offenders who kill children or elderly pedestrians whilst committing other road traffic offences such as dangerous or drunken driving or driving without licence or insurance are regarded for the most part with greater opprobrium than those responsible for so-called 'mercy' killings.

[54] Brenda Hoggett, *Mental Health Law*, 3rd edn (London, Sweet & Maxwell, 1990).

Provocation

Killing when the offender is provoked reduces the crime of homicide from murder to manslaughter. However, the law lays down strict pre-conditions before a jury can convict of the lesser offence of manslaughter. Section 3 of the Homicide Act, a restatement of the Common law, but with the addition of 'words spoken' to 'acts done' reads:

> Where on a charge of murder there is evidence on which a jury can find that the person charged was provoked (whether by things done or by things said or by both together) to lose his self-control, the question whether the provocation was enough to make a reasonable man do as he did shall be left to be determined by the jury; and in determining that question the jury shall take into account everything both done and said according to the effect which, in their opinion, it would have on a reasonable man.

It is unclear whether the defence of provocation is classified as a partial justification or a partial excuse. If the former, it accepts that the intentional killing (or causing of serious injury) was partially warranted. If the latter, a defence which operates as a partial excuse is based on the understanding that the killing was wrongful but that the accused was only partially to blame. The defence varies according to whether the criminal event is perceived as a partial justification, which concentrates on the deceased's wrongful conduct in provoking the homicide, whereas a partial excuse rests on the accused's loss of self-control. In the Northern Ireland case of *Winchester*, the observation of Lowry, LCJ that

> one has to consider in provocation cases the enormity of the crime, the gravity of the provocation (and here it was grave indeed) and the excusability of loss of control on the part of the accused[55]

would seem to endorse the defence as being a partial excuse.

What has long been regarded as the classic test of provocation was set out more than half a century ago by Devlin, J in *Duffy*:

> Provocation is some act, or series of acts, done by the dead man to the accused which would cause in the accused, *a sudden and temporary loss of self-control*, rendering the accused so subject to passion as to make him or her for the moment not master of his mind.[56] [Italics supplied].

Devlin's test enunciated in the context of the common law was modified by the Homicide Act, 1957 section 3, providing:

> Where on a charge of murder there is evidence on which the jury can find that the person charged was provoked (whether by things done or things said or by both together)

---

[55] *R v Winchester* [1978] 3 NIJB p 1.
[56] *R v Duffy* [1949] 1 All ER 932.

to lose his self control, the question whether the provocation was enough to make a reasonable man do as he did shall be left to be determined by the jury; and in determining that question the jury shall take into account everything both done and said according to the effect which, in their opinion, it would have on a reasonable man.

There have been critics of both the test set out in *Duffy* and of the statutory modification, particularly in those cases in which the provocation did not prompt immediate reaction, i.e. a sudden and temporary loss of control. In other words, if there is sufficient lapse in time between the provocative conduct and the passion to cool, such that the passion abates and the accused's self-control is restored, the defence is unavailable. This test barely accommodates the lapse of time between provocative behaviour and the reaction experienced by battered wives or partners. Modern authority still stresses the importance of the element of immediacy,[57] while treating the persistently violent behaviour by the male, husband or father, as a factor to be taken into account by the jury, rather than in immediacy being itself a legal requirement. The Court of Appeal has adapted the immediacy test to accommodate the 'battered woman syndrome' alone or in conjunction with a personality disorder, on the ground that the reasonable person with those characteristics might have reacted suddenly to provocative conduct although the provocation had built up over a period of time.

The test of the reasonable man has itself given rise to discussion and legal debate. The courts generally, have emphasised that the objective approach is to evaluate the act of the accused by reference to a standard form of conduct. Thus in the Privy Council case of *Philips*,[58] it was held that the reaction of the accused must not exceed the reaction of a reasonable man. In earlier cases such as *Mancini*[59] the law required an element of proportionality between the provocative act and the reaction of the accused: like should be met with like. Thus, it was stated that a provocative blow could not be met by the use of a deadly weapon. Resort to a firearm was disproportionate to a blow by the fist. Subsequently this has been modified, post-1957, by holding that a reasonable retaliation is not required as a matter of law, but as with the immediacy factor it is to be taken into account by the jury. But the legal test, that the reaction of the defendant to the provocation must not exceed what would have been the reaction of the reasonable man, remains intact.

Proportionality is, therefore, the guide to the question of what is 'reasonable' retaliation. In *Philips* counsel for the appellant[60] contended that once a reasonable man loses self-control as a result of the provocative conduct of the deceased, he ceases to be a reasonable man and cannot be accountable on those

---

[57] *R v Thornton (No 1)* [1992] 1 All ER 306; *R v Thornton (No 2)* [1996] 1 WLR 1174; *R v Ahluwalia* [1992] 4 All ER 889; *R v Savage* [1991] 3 NZLR 155.

[58] *Philips v The Queen* [1969] 2 AC 130.

[59] *Mancini v DPP* [1942] AC 1.

[60] Sir Louis Blom-Cooper, QC.

terms. Lord Diplock, giving the judgment of the Privy Council, firmly rejected that argument, stating the submission was

> based on a premise that loss of self-control is not a matter of degree but is absolute; there is no alternative between the detachment and going berserk. This is false. The average man reacts to provocation according to its degree.

The judicial view reflects the supposed common experience. Loss of temper is typically moderated by the degree of provocation experienced. But is it the common experience that there is invariably proportionality? The reaction to provocative behaviour may depend on the accused having, as in cases involving the 'battered woman' syndrome, a personality disorder which prompts a disproportionate response. The excessive retaliation thereby generated should not automatically disqualify the accused from claiming an excuse. A psychological approach can have special application with regard to the reliability of eyewitness testimony and the mental state of the defendant. Medical evidence may be used to show that a witness, including of course, the defendant, suffers from such disease or defect or abnormality of mind that it affects the reliability of the evidence. Such evidence is not confined to a general opinion of the unreliability of the witness but may display all the characteristics of mental ill-health, not only the foundation and reasons for the diagnosis, but also the extent to which the credibility of the witness is affected.[61]

If the defence on provocation is to be retained—and not all commentators agree that it should[62]—both the statute and the case-law are ripe for review. If the penalty for murder were to cease to be the mandatory sentence of life imprisonment, all cases of provocation would readily be accommodated at the sentencing stage, where partial justification and/or partial excuse for criminal homicide could be invoked. Moral innocence is as much a concern of the law as is moral culpability. Lord Hoffmann, in *Smith (Morgan)* thought that the abolition of the mandatory sentence would not necessarily render the defence of provocation superfluous, He said:

> It might be thought desirable to allow the jury to decide whether provocation was a reason why the killer did not deserve the degree of moral condemnation and severity of sentence associated with the crime of murder.

We profoundly disagree. A jury verdict of criminal homicide would suffice to condemn the killer morally, and the 'severity of sentence' is emphatically not a task for the jury.

At the time of writing (January 2004) the Law Commission has issued a consultation paper on *Partial Defences to Murder*[63] in response to a reference from the Home Secretary in June 2003, to consider and report on provocation and

---

[61] *Toohey v Metropolitan Police Commissioner* [1965] AC 595.

[62] Jeremy Horder, *Provocation and Responsibility*, (Oxford, OUP, 1992) chapter 9. See also McAuley and McCutcheon, *Criminal Liability*, above n 21, at 885.

[63] Consultation Paper No 173, 31 October 2003, at 249.

diminished responsibility (Sections 3 and 2 of the Homicide Act, 1957 respectively) and on whether there should be a partial defence to murder in circumstances in which the defendant, though entitled to self-defence, killed because the force used in self-defence was excessive. The Law Commission's work is a hugely impressive piece of scholarship and will indubitably inform and excite a public and political response. We do no more than highlight the main thrust of the Law Commission's exhaustive review of the three partial defences. The review does not cover necessity and duress; otherwise we commend every attention to its detailed report.

On provocation the Law Commission believes that the law cannot remain in its present state[64] on the ground that it has serious logical and moral flaws, and that its defects are incurable by judicial development of the law. If abolition is the favoured option, a possible corollary would be the abolition of the mandatory penalty of life imprisonment.[65]

On the subject of diminished responsibility, the Law Commission is less inclined to propose the alternative of abolition. Were the concept of diminished responsibility in its statutory form to disappear, the spectre of M'Naghten would instantly arise and with it all the forensic difficulties with which the law of homicide was afflicted for more than a century. In our view, a worse state of affairs would be difficult to envisage.

It is unsurprising that the topic of the defences to murder should have been on the agenda of public discussion, given the number of cases involving battered women, to householders defending their premises against intruders, and to the use of guns. But there is generally a difference in approach, sometimes reflected in a tension, between governments and politicians on the one hand and practitioners and expert observers on the other on the issues of reform. In this instance Ministers are sensitive to what they perceive to be the preferences of the electorate—the consumers, as it were, who have a choice between political leaders no less than between different supermarkets and the goods on their shelves. The practitioners of the law, who have an interest both in its utility and in its fitness for purpose, share meanwhile, some common ground with those who note its operation from a distance and may reflect upon its wider social and moral perspectives.

We would argue that the task of considering the defences to murder in isolation from the substantive law, while of great importance, is to be given the wrong brief. That is a proposition which can be demonstrated by reflecting that the distinction between murder and other unlawful homicides is essentially artificial. 'Murder' is a term used in common parlance,[66] often without much discrimination, to describe incidents of violent and unnatural death to which social opprobrium is attached, notwithstanding that a court may conclude at

---

[64] Para 12.2.

[65] See para 12.26.

[66] Newspapers almost invariably report homicides as if they were already defined as murders.

trial (if any) that the proper verdict under the law is one of manslaughter. Murder is essentially a term of art; a construct having its origins in the intellectual patchwork of the common law that, responsive to the currents of opinion but without any over-arching logic—still less philosophy—that has evolved over the centuries. In no way can it be regarded as a phenomenon *sui generis*, since the boundary between murder and manslaughter shifts as readily as the precise limits of a sand bar under the influence of wind and tide.

The defences which may be employed to identify the crime as manslaughter, rather than murder, are as chimerical in character as the attempts to create categories of murder to which may be attached a range of differential penalties. The question must, therefore, be posed whether it is profitable to expend further intellectual energy and resources in pursuit of the *ignis fatuus* of their perfection.

Were the mandatory penalty of life imprisonment for murder to be abolished, the incentive for defendants to persuade the courts that, if they plead guilty it is to manslaughter and not to murder, would cease to exist, and with it the problems of interpretation of motives and states of mind that presently demand so much legal attention. That incentive removed, the existence of a common sentencing tariff to reflect the proportionality of penalty to the specific nature of the criminal event, would make plain the underlying intellectual imperative; the establishment of a single offence of criminal homicide.

4

Hunting the Chimæra[1]

The jurists of the Middle Ages and their successors in the seventeenth century were concerned with the law of murder largely in terms of the issues of malice and its constructive extensions. Apart from the sanctions applicable in the 'clergyable'[2] exceptions, homicide, like many other offences, was punishable by death. In the nineteenth and twentieth centuries the focus had shifted away from definitions of the law of homicide and towards its limitation in the context of capital punishment. By the second half of the nineteenth century, limitation of the death penalty had become so extensive that it effectively applied only to what the law now defines as murder[3]. The pressure for the total abolition of capital punishment, however, continued to grow, predicated for the most part upon the argument that it was a barbarous relic of past times which ought have no place in a modern society which saw itself located at the pinnacle of contemporary civilisation. In the event, progress towards abolition was to prove very protracted.

Perhaps as with no other criminal offence, discussion about its definition became increasingly inextricable from consideration of its penalties. Indeed, this has been the besetting problem for reforming the law of homicide, as distinct from the penalties attaching to it. By presuming the jurisprudential legitimacy of fragmenting homicide into distinct offences, each with its specific penal consequences, murder became, quite literally, 'a crime apart'. The wider issues

---

[1] The phrase 'hunting the chimæra'—a figure for the pursuit of the non-existent—was used by Sir Ernest Gowers, Chairman of the Royal Commission on Capital Punishment 1949–53 in conversation with the present authors in 1963 after the law of murder had been modified by the distinction between capital and non-capital murder provided by the Homicide Act. The Commission's Report in 1953 noted (p 189 at Para 534) that:

'We began our inquiry with the determination to make every effort to see whether we could succeed where so many have failed, and discover some effective method of classifying murders . . . .. We conclude with regret that the object of our quest is chimerical and that it must be abandoned.'

He repeated to us his view in the light of what Parliament had done in the face of his counsel. The Chimæra, a fabulous monster of Greek mythology, described by Homer as having a goat's body, a lion's head and a dragon's tail, was born in Lycia, and slain by Bellerophon. Such an ungainly hybrid might well serve as a figure for the Homicide Act 1957 itself.

[2] See chapter 2.

[3] Exceptions remained, largely those related to national security in times of war.

of legal liability and moral culpability were eclipsed by attempts to identify malicious intent, express, implied or constructive. In May 1864 after a debate in the House of Commons on capital punishment a Royal Commission was appointed:

> To inquire into the provision and operation of the laws under which the punishment of death is now inflicted in the United Kingdom, and the manner in which it is inflicted, and to report whether it is desirable to make any alteration therein.

The Commission reported in January 1866[4] in a mere six pages.[5] The Commissioners could not agree on the subject of abolition, but they were of one accord in finding the current law of murder unsatisfactory. While accepting the agreed definition of the crime as killing unlawfully with malice aforethought, they were exercised by the way in which the courts had variously interpreted these terms. Interpretations of malice aside, the defence of provocation was by no means uniform in character. Provocation, by means of words, looks, gestures, or trespass to land or goods, were held to be insufficient to reduce the crime to manslaughter. The Commission did, however, make an attempt at distinguishing between two degrees of murder, only the first being capital. The first degree was to consist of those murders deliberately committed with express malice aforethought, such malice to be found as a fact by the jury. Additionally punishable by death were to be those committed in the context of other acts such as escape after or in the perpetration, of the felonies of murder, arson, rape, burglary, robbery or piracy. For the rest, the penalty was to be penal servitude for life, or for any period of not less than seven years, at the discretion of the court. Prior to the Consolidation Acts of 1861, the judges had enjoyed the power to record the death sentence but not pronounce it; if this were to have been restored, it would have had the effect of giving the judges the discretion to decide whether a defendant convicted of first degree murder would suffer the death penalty rather than this remaining within the Royal Prerogative of Mercy.[6] Fitzjames Stephen, Recorder of Newark at the time, was strongly in favour of retaining the death penalty and he believed public hangings were a powerful deterrent.[7] While he would have reduced the scope of the crime of murder he considered that the proposed bifurcation of murder into two degrees

---

[4] *Report of the Capital Punishment Committee*, Cmnd, 3590, 1866.

[5] In contrast to the 700 pages or so of Minutes of Evidence and other material.

[6] No longer exercised by the sovereign after the accession of the 17 year old Victoria in 1837, but by the Home Secretary.

[7] James Fitzjames Stephen, *A History of the Criminal Law of England* (London, Macmillan, 1883), vol 2 at 89. He argued that such a shameful death was 'much harder to go through in public than in private.' Stephen had a tendency towards the hyperbolic in expressing some of his most punitive views. He favoured making more felonies capital on grounds of deterrence and thought that such an extension would result in short time, in 'really bad offenders' becoming 'as rare as wolves'.

would be productive of nothing but further complication in the definition of murder, bringing numerous injustices in its train[8]

Four months after the publication of the Royal Commission's report, the Lord Chancellor, Lord Cranworth, introduced a Bill in the Lords with this precise intention, based upon the recommendations of the Commission. The voting for and against was equal and Cranworth substituted a new clause limiting the definition of murder to instances in which the accused intended to kill or do grievous bodily harm to the person killed or any other person. Although this managed to survive a Third Reading, a change of government frustrated its successful passage through the Commons. But for this quirk of political events reform of the law of murder, as distinct from the penalty, might have made a quantum leap in the direction of constructive reform. Throughout the next two decades there were a number of attempts to tackle the issue, none successful. The Bill introduced in 1867 is of particular interest in that it anticipates the approach embodied in the Homicide Act 1957, by identifying five conditions having the effect of defining the crime as capital, namely:

(i)   a deliberate intention to kill or do grievous bodily harm to the deceased or another;

(ii)   that the crime was committed with a view to, and in or immediately before or immediately after the commission of the felonies of rape, burglary, robbery, piracy, or arson to a dwelling house any person being therein;

(iii)   that the crime was committed for the purpose of thereby enabling himself or any other person to commit murder or any of the above mentioned felonies;

(iv)   that the crime was committed in the act of escaping from, or for the purpose of enabling himself or any other person to escape from or avoid lawful arrest or detainer, immediately after he or such other person had committed or attempted to commit murder or any of the above mentioned felonies;

(v)   that the accused murdered a constable or other peace officer, acting in the discharge of his duty.

Neither this Bill, nor any of its successors[9] was to reach the Statute Book.[10] Stephen's draft Bill of 1874 was referred to a Select committee of the House of Commons; it is notable in respect of a clause (Clause 24) which, had it become law, might have avoided what was to prove to be almost a century of ensuing debate about the so called 'insanity defence'.

---

[8] Stephen, writing in *Frasers's Magazine* of February 1866. In 1872 Stephen, who enjoyed a substantial reputation as a jurist, was invited to draft a Bill that would define and amend the law relating to homicide. It was presented in 1874.

[9] Murder Law Amendment and Appeal Bill (1871), Homicide Law Amendment Bill (1874), *ditto* (1876), Homicide Law Amendment Bills (1877 and 1878), Law of Murder Amendment Bill (1908), Criminal Justice Bill (1948) (Clause 1 and Schedule of Government Amendments to Lords Amendments, also clauses proposed by Mr Basil Neild, KC, MP and Mr Hector Hughes, KC, MP).

[10] The passage of these various Bills in the later Victorian period is considered in detail by Leon Radzinowicz and Roger Hood in volume 5 of their seminal *History of English Criminal Law*, (London, Stevens & Sons, 1986) 661–76.

Some seven decades were to elapse before major reform of the law of murder once more became the concern of government as distinct from individual Members of Parliament seeking to promote the abolition of capital punishment. The Criminal Justice Bill of 1948, promoted by the Labour government elected in 1945, was, not unlike British motor cars in the immediate post-war period, a pre-war design in almost every respect. In this instance it was based very broadly upon the Bill of the same name proposed in 1938 by a Conservative administration but overtaken by events that were to bring about World War II. The abolition of capital punishment was, however, a 'bolt on' modification that has to be understood in the context of the enormous pressure for abolition that had been building on the Government back benches, led by the indefatigable Sydney Silverman, MP. In the event, a combination of hostility in the Lords and the doubts entertained by the Prime Minister, Clement Attlee, that abolition consequent on a constitutional battle with the Upper House would be a politically hazardous enterprise[11] proved fatal. It was not for a further decade that Parliament was again to be exercised on the issue, once more in the context, not of reform of the law of homicide *per se*, but its modification in order to reduce the scope of capital punishment. Although abolition was clearly not going to be recorded in history along with the foundation of the NHS as one of its great achievements, the Attlee administration was responsible for the establishment of the Royal Commission on Capital Punishment in 1949 under the chairmanship of Sir Ernest Gowers.[12] It combined a powerful and intellectually incisive chairman with some notable specialists among the Commissioners. It had the advantage of having as its Secretary Francis Graham Harrison, who was to emerge as one of the ablest figures in the post-war Home Office. The Report, which appeared in September 1953, was, however, made to a Conservative Government headed by the elderly Churchill.[13] Its essential findings were that, short of abolition, there was no way in which it was practically possible to reform the law, and that the idea of 'degrees' of murder was a non-starter. Attempts to get a Commons debate on the Report in February 1954 were stonewalled by the Home Secretary, Sir David Maxwell-Fyfe.[14] The Lords had debated the Report in the preceding November. Further attempts were made, but to no avail, to persuade the Government to change its mind; nor would it even indicate what steps, if any, it proposed to take with respect the Commission's recommendations. Not until a further year had elapsed, did the opportunity for debate finally arise on 10 February 1955. Silverman, his

[11] There is reason to believe that Herbert Morrison, Attlee's deputy, and effectively his political manager, urged this counsel. Morrison, (a policeman's son) was opposed to abolition.

[12] The membership of the Gowers Commission is listed in Annex 1. Hitherto, Gowers, himself a distinguished civil servant, had been better known for his work in attempting to persuade others in the Civil Service to employ plain English.

[13] How far he was, in his eightieth year, concerned with such issues is a matter for speculative doubt. The onset of old age was beginning to take its toll of this gargantuan figure.

[14] Maxwell-Fyfe is elsewhere remembered as the Home Secretary whom Goddard, LCJ, had *expected* to reprieve Derek Bentley, but chose to let the law take its lethal course.

Parliamentary energy seemingly inexhaustible, attempted to amend the government motion to 'take note' of the Gowers Report by moving that the death penalty be suspended for five years. Maxwell-Fyfe had meanwhile been succeeded as Home Secretary by Major Gwillym Lloyd George, and Sir Reginald Manningham-Buller[15] was now Attorney General. The combination of an Attorney General and a Home Secretary, neither of whom favoured change, together with a divided House ensured not merely the defeat of Silverman's amendment but sterilised the debate about capital punishment in the immediate future—or so it seemed in the early months of 1955.

But once more, it was to be public disquiet with individual cases involving the death penalty that guaranteed that the issue simply would not go away. The hanging of Timothy Evans in 1950 (subsequently pardoned) and the subsequent conviction of his landlord John Christie (for serial murders in the same house) in 1953 had projected into popular consciousness the spectre of an innocent man going to the gallows; the hanging of Derek Bentley, aged 19, while his accomplice, Christopher Craig, (accused of firing the fatal shot) had been too young to do so, aroused a sense that the law was capable of monstrous unfairness which offended the common man's sense of justice. The execution of the death sentence on Ruth Ellis in the summer of 1955,[16] served to re-ignite the debate which the government thought had been quenched some five months earlier. These three can be identified as being the cases which changed the law. But the politics of abolition at this period were complex[17] and the outcome scarcely surprising in view of the resistance to abolition which was still marked, certainly in Parliament. What was to emerge could most charitably be described as little more than a legislative botch. It failed to placate the diehards among the retentionists, but succeeded, simultaneously, in providing ammunition to be used in the cause of abolition.

The Homicide Act 1957[18] must rank as one of the most unsatisfactory examples of legislation affecting criminal justice in the twentieth century. Instrumentally reactive rather than constructively pro-active, it began its working life with few friends and the number of its critics grew with the passage of time.

To be fair, it began bravely. It served to abolish the doctrine of constructive malice. That, at least, was the intention, though how far 'constructive malice'

---

[15] In his forensic style, Manningham–Buller had not a little in common with Sir Edward Coke.

[16] Although much 'played down' by both the Metropolitan Police and the Home Office, accounts of the scenes outside Holloway on the morning of 13 July suggested outrage, with the crowd chanting 'Evans!, Bentley!, Ellis!' Official 'denials' of the circumstances surrounding the execution of the death penalty remained until almost the very end of capital punishment. As it happened, Ruth Ellis was to be the last woman to be hanged in the United Kingdom.

[17] See Brian P Block and John Hostettler, *Hanging in the Balance* (Winchester, Waterside Press, 1997) and Terence Morris, *Crime and Criminal Justice in England since 1945* (Oxford, Basil Blackwell, 1989) 77–85.

[18] Elizabeth II Ch 11. It was not long before it became known among lawyers as the 'Reggie-cide' Act since the Attorney-General Sir Reginald Manningham-Buller (later to become Lord Chancellor as Lord Dilhorne) was one of its principal architects. Its detailed provisions are set out in Appendix 2.

lingered on in other guises suggesting that the snake had been scotched rather than killed, is a matter for some debate. It plunged, with not a little courage into the deep and dimly illuminated waters of what had become known since the days of M'Naghten[19] as the 'insanity defence' by introducing the concept of diminished responsibility (the burden of proof to be on the defence) and upon a jury thus finding, providing for a substitute conviction for manslaughter. The grounds for provocation were extended to cover 'things said' as well as 'things done' or a combination of the two, and, to deal with the tragic predicament of the surviving party to a suicide pact (the burden of proof of fact again being upon the defence) a further provision for a manslaughter verdict. Thus far, the new Act was to liberalise the law of homicide by making concessions to a long line of critics that stretched back for years, if not centuries.

However worthy these intentions, they were largely set at nought by the fact that, contrary to the advice of the Gowers Commission—and indeed, to many of the critics who had taken part in the Parliamentary debates in later Victorian times—the Act forged ahead with categorising murders into capital and non-capital. We cannot be certain what was the source of this initiative; certainly, there was at the time a current view that public opinion, by no means enthusiastically abolitionist, would only tolerate so much by way of change and would look ill upon the hangman becoming redundant.[20] It is not impossible that the political managers considered the Act as a way of getting the issue of total abolition put to sleep for many years to come. On the other hand, there were among the younger generation of Conservative politicians, especially those who were lawyers, a recognition that, complete removal of the death penalty apart, changes were needed. Each of these is likely to have weighed advantageously in the balance against taking the advice of the Royal Commission and, as for the lessons of history; they could be readily set aside as having little relevance to the mid twentieth century,[21] yet it requires little imagination to imagine the reaction of Stephen to the proposal.

The five categories of capital murder were those done:

(a) in the course or furtherance of theft
(b) by shooting or causing an explosion
(c) in the course or for the purpose of resisting or avoiding or preventing a lawful arrest, or of effecting or assisting an escape or rescue from legal custody
or (d) any murder of a police officer acting in the execution of his duty or of a person assisting a police officer so acting

---

[19] See chapter 3 at 49.

[20] Part of the problem was that public sentiment was volatile; those convicted of horrific murders would enjoy little sympathy and many would wish them speeded on their way to the gallows, while others would engender a sense that to inflict the death penalty was unjust or unfair. *Vox populi* might chant the names of Evans, Bentley and Ellis, but not those of Heath, Haigh or Christie.

[21] There is a view, attributed to George Santayana, that those who know no history are destined to re-live it.

or (e) in the case of a person who was a prisoner at the time when he did or was a party to the murder, any murder of a prison officer acting in the execution of his duty or of a person assisting a prison officer so acting.

Provision was also made for the death penalty for those convicted of murder who had been so convicted in Great Britain of another murder done on a different occasion.

In these categories echoes of the past resonate with a familiar clarity. We see homicides done in the course of other crimes singled out for the capital penalty. Theft, which included robbery, being one of the old felonies remains capital. Similarly, homicides done whilst resisting arrest or escaping from custody. Officers of the Peace are, however, limited to police officers, and prison officers emerge as a new category of those specially to be protected by the sanction of the death penalty.

In the case of those murders for which a court was to be precluded from passing sentence of death, the Act provided that the sentence should be one of life imprisonment. The comparatively brief life span of the Act was one factor that ensured that the meaning of life imprisonment was unlikely to become a contentious matter, but, in any event, the assumption appeared to be that such life sentences would be no different from those life sentences served by those who had been reprieved from the gallows. Reprieve was traditionally granted in compassionate cases and non-capital murders were now statutorily differentiated as less heinous than those for which the penalty of death was reserved. Only since total abolition has the meaning of the life sentence become a matter for what is almost exclusively, political debate. As we shall consider later,[22] the concept of imprisonment for life currently arouses feelings in politics and the media that equal, if not surpass, those generated by the debates about capital punishment. Indeed, the situation is multi-dimensional, since it involves the legal definition of 'life' as well as the implications of the cumulative increase in the 'lifer' population for the administration of prisons.

While it can be argued that imperfections could be discerned everywhere in the 1957 Act, it was in the distinctions between capital and non-capital offences that its flaws were most transparent. Every attempt to categorise the various manifestations of homicide is predicated upon the presumed existence of a hierarchy of heinousness. In plain language, the law is employed to say that *this* kind of killing is worse than *that* and therefore deserves a greater penalty to be inflicted on the offender. The assumption is that there is a readily discernible consensus on the matter. But neither in 1957, nor, for that matter, today, is such uniformity of view other than an illusion.

The inclusion of police officers was no surprise, not least since the time of Coke various agents of justice had been identified as requiring special protection[23] and

---

[22] In chapter 7.
[23] Whether this was significantly afforded by the law relating to constructive malice is a matter for argument.

it was widely believed that the deterrent quality of the death penalty provided this. The inclusion of prison officers occasioned some surprise, not least since the phenomenon of prison staff being killed by their captives was, (and indeed, remains) exceptionally rare. The inclusion of killings in the course or furtherance of theft was again, historically consistent with the view that it was deemed appropriate for certain felonies to be marked by some penal premium.

Since the death penalty was to remain the centrepiece of the legislation, the Home Secretary, Major Gwilym Lloyd George (later Lord Tenby), elaborated on the reasoning behind the new role of capital punishment. The government had a prime duty to maintain order in society and it recognised a real fear in the public mind that to remove the ultimate penal sanction would lead to increased violence. Those murders involving such violence as to be inimical to public order and those most likely to arouse fear in the minds of members of the public at risk were deemed to be prime instances of capital crimes. The progenitors of the Act failed to consider either the incidence of such crimes or the way in which the circumstances of particular offences or the characteristics of many of the offenders involved might result in anomalies, let alone apparent injustices.

The present authors examined each of the 764 cases of persons indicted for murder in England and Wales between the coming into force of the Act on 24 March 1957 until 31 December 1962.[24] In practice, not all popular conceptions of heinousness were recognised in the Act by the identification of certain offences as capital. Killings that involved poisoning—for long regarded as one of the most despicable homicides—those occurring in the course of sexual offences and the killing of children after abduction, were excluded from the capital category.[25] The use of firearms, thought to be the preserve of professional criminals, was by no means absent from what are more accurately termed domestic homicides. *Walden* (1959) shot and killed the young woman with whom he was infatuated and her boy-friend[26] while *Neimasz* (1961) shot his male victim but killed his female companion with the butt of the shotgun immediately afterwards.[27] *King* (1959) was acquitted of capital murder but convicted of s 2 manslaughter and sentenced to life imprisonment. In the course of a domestic dispute during which King appears to have been under the influence of alcohol, he terrorised his estranged wife and her parents. When a constable attempted to get the gun away, King shot him in the groin; he then shot his wife in the back. A police inspector who tried to pacify him was then shot in the chest and died later. The trial of Günter Podola (1959) who shot and killed Det. Sgt.

---

[24] Terence Morris and Louis Blom-Cooper, *A Calendar of Murder* (London, Michael Joseph, 1964).

[25] In 1961 *Jones* was convicted of non-capital murder of a 12 year old girl whom forensic evidence indicated had been raped. The defendant had previously been convicted of raping an 11 year old. Consequent upon the failure of his appeal to the Lords his sentence of life imprisonment, consecutive upon the existing sentence of 14 years imprisonment for rape was upheld: *R v Jones* [1962] AC 635.

[26] Walden was hanged at Leeds on 14 August 1959.

[27] Neimasz was hanged at Wandsworth on 8 September 1961.

Purdy was beset with the issue of fitness to plead, since it was claimed he was suffering from hysterical amnesia following events at the time of his arrest. The truth of the matter will never be known, since he was hanged[28] having been refused the Attorney's *fiat* for an appeal to the Lords. At most it can be said that Podola seemed far removed from the average passenger on the Clapham omnibus.

But perhaps an instance of how the law remained in an unsatisfactory state during the currency of the 1957 Act was the case of *Vickers*. The Act had been in force barely a month when Vickers (22) killed a woman of 72 who had attacked him as he attempted to burgle her shop. Knocking her down with a blow from his fist he searched for money and finding none fled the scene. His only one previous conviction was for theft at the age of 11. The killing was done in the course of theft, but was it murder when a pathologist report suggested that the blows inflicted on the victim were moderately severe to slight? Far from being a straightforward instance of the kind of violence which would normally result in serious harm to the victim, the blows were such as to put the implication of malice in some considerable doubt. In the Court of Criminal Appeal[29] it became clear that while the Act had, as it were, struck a mortal blow against the doctrine of 'constructive' malice, the notion of implied malice was alive and flourishing; a full court of five judges dismissed his appeal. The Attorney General subsequently refused his *fiat* for an appeal to the Lords, provoking a motion of censure upon on the part of some 68 Labour MPs who argued that the case raised a point of law of exceptional public importance.

Four months from the date of his original conviction Vickers became the first person to suffer death under the new Act and was hanged at Durham.[30] It is not without irony that the first trial for capital murder under its provisions should have demonstrated, and so clearly, that the notion of 'malice', the relic of three centuries of criminal justice, should continue to present problems of interpretation. The issue of what constitutes 'serious harm', though the case of *Vickers* is now almost half a century distant, remained unresolved. The House of Lords recently refused to entertain two questions arising from a case recently in the Court of Appeal in Northern Ireland.[31]

1. Whether implied malice (an intention to commit grievous bodily harm) constitutes sufficient *mens rea* for the crime of murder, or whether the prosecution must prove express malice (an intention to kill.)

2. If implied malice constitutes sufficient *mens rea*, whether it must be proved that the defendant knew or foresaw that his act might endanger the victim's life.

During its brief lifetime, the Homicide Act 1957 could be accounted a success in at least one regard; it succeeded in pleasing no one. If concern about the conviction and hanging of Vickers was limited to articulate abolitionists, a reverse

---

[28] At Wandsworth 5 November, 1959.
[29] [1957] 2 QB 664.
[30] On 23 July 1957.
[31] *The Queen v Anderson (Samuel)* [2003] NICA 12.

concern undoubtedly existed in the public mind about the fact that the majority of the most serious instances of homicide in the context of some form of sexual activity were not only excluded by statute from the capital category but also appeared to provide some form of penal discount through the medium of the verdict of manslaughter by reason of diminished responsibility.

In 1958 *Matheson* (52), a casual labourer had met his victim, a 15 year old boy, and had gone with him to premises in Newcastle for the purpose of homosexual relations. He killed the boy with blows from a bottle and a hammer and then took £35 in cash from his person. Hiding the body until the following day, he crudely dismembered it and put the body parts into a drainage sump in the building. He finally surrendered to police in Glasgow. Two issues, central to the new Act, emerged at his trial at Durham Assizes; the first relating to the definition of murder 'in the course or furtherance of theft' and the second with regard to his plea of diminished responsibility. The trial judge,[32] observing that the term was entirely new, raised the question of its interpretation; was theft the motive or intention that led to the murder, or was the intention of the accused to murder, perhaps during the course of the sexual offence, and the theft just followed?

On the question of diminished responsibility, three doctors, including the Medical Officer of the prison in which he had been remanded to await trial, gave evidence of his mental history. Most of his life had been spent in various penal institutions and he had been a voluntary patient in a mental hospital. He had sought treatment for his sexual condition but suffered from the handicap of an IQ of only 73, having a developmental age of 10. He was also described as having a psychopathic personality. His appeal to the Court of Criminal Appeal was heard before a full court of five judges, with Goddard, LCJ presiding.

The appeal was grounded primarily in the argument that the jury had come to an unreasonable verdict, against the weight of the evidence of diminished responsibility. Three doctors had testified on the matter and there was no evidence the other way. On this argument the appeal was allowed, and a verdict of manslaughter (under s 2 of the Act) and a sentence of 20 years imprisonment substituted.[33] In giving judgment the court affirmed that it was for the jury to decide the question of diminished responsibility; it must be founded on the evidence offered.[34]

---

[32]   Mr Justice Finnemore.

[33]   [1958] 1 WLR 74. Matheson's eventual discharge from prison was not back into the community but into a secure mental hospital.

[34]   A similar issue had arisen in *Spriggs*, convicted of capital murder a month or so before *Matheson* (by shooting a barman who had earlier ejected him from licensed premises on a relatively trivial issue). Mr Justice Austin Jones, having meticulously rehearsed the medical evidence to assist the jury, then confined himself to handing them a copy of the terms of s 2. Dismissing the appeal in the CCA, Goddard, LCJ had observed

> It was not for a judge, where Parliament had defined a particular state of things, as they had here, to redefine or attempt to define the definition. ([1958] 1 QB 270).

The Attorney-General refused his *fiat* for appeal to the Lords but Spriggs was reprieved by the Home Secretary (R A Butler) three days before execution of the death warrant and the sentence commuted to one of life imprisonment.

In 1960 there were two instances of murders with powerful sexual overtones that arrested public consciousness by their horrific details but which were, again, defined as non-capital under the Act.

Patrick *Byrne*, a 27 year old labourer was a voyeur who prowled about a women's hostel. Entering the room of a resident he strangled her and having done so embarked upon the savage mutilation of her body. Byrne entered a plea of diminished responsibility and medical witnesses gave evidence of his being an aggressive psychopath with a long history of sexual pathology. Despite the fact that this evidence was not rebutted, the jury convicted him of non-capital murder. It was argued on appeal that the trial judge[35] had misdirected the jury by so interpreting s 2 that the jury were effectively precluded from finding a verdict under the section. The CCA allowed the appeal arguing that, properly directed, the jury could not have come to any other conclusion than that the defence of diminished responsibility was made out. A verdict of manslaughter pursuant to s 2 was substituted and a sentence of life imprisonment affirmed.[36]

A third homicide involving substantial mutilation in an overtly sexual context was prosecuted in the case of Michael *Dowdall* some three months before. A 19-year-old Guardsman, he went with a prostitute to her home where, after intercourse, a quarrel degenerated into physical violence between them. The defendant took a large ornament and battered her to death, subsequently subjecting the body to mutilation and other indignities. The defendant was not in fact arrested until eleven months later, following a similar attack on another woman who fortunately survived and was able to give a description. Forensic evidence was sufficient to link him positively with both crimes. In support of a plea of DR, substantial evidence was offered, the Senior Medical Officer at the remand prison describing him as a psychopathic personality liable to act aggressively and to become physically violent without evident provocation. He had apparently attempted to hang himself at the age of 17. He was not the material of a good soldier, thought to be difficult, and given to the heavy consumption of spirituous liquor. A senior officer thought he exhibited delusions of grandeur, occasioned by the fact that he was in fact 'weak and insignificant'. So compelling did this evidence appear that the Crown offered nothing by way of rebuttal and following a conviction for section 2 manslaughter a sentence of imprisonment for life was imposed.

It so happened that on the day that Dowdall was sentenced at the Old Bailey[37] James *Barclay* was on trial at Newcastle Assizes. The defendant had gone with a prostitute to an hotel where her naked body was later discovered, indicating signs of battering and other assault. A plea of DR having been entered,

[35] Mr Justice Stable.
[36] The court's interpretations of 'abnormality of mind' and 'mental responsibility' in s 2 were subsequently approved by the Judicial Committee of the Privy Council in *Rose v The Queen* [1961] AC 496.
[37] 21 January 1960.

substantial evidence of the defendant's long history of mental disorder combined with a propensity to violence towards women was given. The verdict was s 2 manslaughter and a life sentence was imposed.

While it can be argued that the Act at least ensured that, when presented with compelling evidence of mental illness or abnormality in the context of a s 2 plea, juries had an opportunity to make a finding for other than murder. In the years of mandatory capital punishment juries had not infrequently felt constrained to make recommendations for the exercise of the prerogative of mercy in distressing and compassionate cases—which included instances of apparent mental disorder of various kinds as well as provocation, so-called 'mercy' killings and unwanted survival in suicide pacts. In practice this had meant that while substantially mitigating factors were identified by juries—of whom it could be said that they were as close to the evidence as anyone—there was no guarantee that the Home Secretary would necessarily act upon their recommendations, however forcefully urged at the conclusion of their verdict. The existence of the provisions whereby verdicts of manslaughter could be returned in cases involving mental disorder, a wider definition of provocation and suicide pact survival, meant that their conclusions could be both intellectually assured and legally secured. That there were categories of murder, specifically identified as capital could, however, frequently vitiate this process. In capital cases, these considerations, though they might go to the heart of the matter, whether the circumstances of the offence or the character of the offender, were largely subordinated to determining the issues which identified the killing as capital murder.

While there were capital cases which undoubtedly involved the kinds of professional criminal activity that did not eschew the commission of homicide, by no means all those charged with the commonest form of capital murder—a killing committed in course or furtherance of theft—were aware of the kinds of killings that were capital and those that were not. The desire to be hanged was expressed in a disturbing minority of instances of non-capital murder, suggesting that the Act, when poorly understood, by no means offered the universally appreciated deterrents that its authors had believed would be clear to all intending killers.[38]

Experience of the 1957 Act strongly indicated that the deterrent effect of the death penalty remained as variable as it had always been, and the situation was complicated in some instances by offenders being unaware of the differences between capital and non-capital crimes. But this could be numbered among the least of the weaknesses of the Act. The attempt to distinguish certain offences as particularly heinous failed, and miserably, to persuade the public that it had been done with any sense of logic, still less with any reference to how the public at large viewed the nature of particular crimes. That the killers of children, espe-

---

[38] In our original research based on those indicted for murder under the 1957 Act we were able to identify at least eight such instances.

cially those who had sexually assaulted them beforehand, should merely go to prison for life,[39] while the killers of policemen went to the gallows, was perceived as inequitable in terms of desert. Quite apart from the uncertainties of interpretation that were never entirely absent from the minds of either judges or juries, the public increasingly perceived its workings as frequently capricious. In the so-called 'towpath' murder there was but a single criminal event; the brutal killing in the course of an attempted robbery of a young man by a group of four youths aged between 23 and 17. One, aged 20 was convicted of non-capital murder and sentenced to life imprisonment. The 17 year old, who had injured the victim, was sentenced to be detained at Her Majesty's pleasure; the remaining two were sentenced to death and hanged though only one had caused injury, the other having merely gone through the victim's pockets. The prosecution established a common purpose or design involving all four in the crime; yet, though on this point the conclusion of the criminal law mirrored that of common sense, the imposition of three kinds of sentence on four defendants, including the death penalty on two who were clearly not equally responsible (in the physical sense) for the death of the victim, appeared to many people if not as capricious then powerfully indicative of the law's capacity for absurdity.

The Homicide Act 1957, by any test, was a legislative failure. But it was more than that. It was a demonstration of a belief that an argument that had been around for almost a century—that it was impossible to identify distinctive categories of homicide based upon their heinousness and embody them with clarity and no ambiguity with the substantive law—could somehow be overcome. The pressure for reform in the face of the public disquiet generated by particularly troubling cases provided the stimulus for what rapidly proved to be an unsatisfactory law enveloped in a political fix. In the event, the fix turned out to be a botch, creating new problems rather than radical solutions to old ones. If it did anything, it was to serve the interests of those who were pressing for total abolition of the death penalty.

The Act, in so far as it sought to establish a hierarchy of heinousness that mirrored the gradient of public opprobrium, is now long gone, though its provision of the defences relating to diminished responsibility and certain forms of provocation, in their essence, remain. Politically, however, it would seem to have come back to haunt us, albeit in a somewhat disembodied guise, its *geist* an echo in the penal philosophy of New Labour. In place of the arguments that once raged over the provision of the death penalty there is now a new division of opinion over the interpretation of the meaning of 'life' imprisonment. And, as alarming as it is inexplicable, save in the context of appeasing a perceived populist desire simply to punish (to the exclusion of all other objectives within the framework of criminal justice) the Criminal Justice Act 2003 enshrines, yet again, a hierarchy of heinousness in criminal homicide. No matter that to do

---

[39] 'Whole life' sentences at this time were not only extremely rare, but in effect only resulted from the continuing perceived dangerousness of the offender.

so has been proclaimed impossible, not least by Parliamentarians for almost a century and a half; no matter that the 1957 Act lies in the sands of the political desert, like the fallen image of Ozymandias for all to see and reflect upon; the government is determined once more, to hunt down that elusive and mythical creature, the Chimæra.

5

Expert Evidence on Trial

This Court understands how the jury came to the verdicts which they did which, on the evidence presented to the jury, in our view, were perfectly reasonable once it could not be effectively disputed by defence counsel that [the victim] had been unlawfully killed. We accept [Prosecution counsel's] submission that the jurors who reached these verdicts should not feel that they were to blame for [the appellant] having spent some 23 years in custody.

We allow this appeal because the pathological evidence that this was an unlawful killing and natural causes could be excluded has now been shown to be unreliable.

In allowing this appeal we wish to express this Court's great regret that as a result of what has now been shown to be flawed pathological evidence the appellant was wrongly convicted and has spent a very long time in jail.

Lord Justice Roch's peroration to a judgment in R. v Nicholls in the Court of Appeal (Criminal Division) 12 June 1998.

Fictional representations of the criminal trial may nourish in the popular mind the idea that, among those who stand in the dock, the innocent may be as numerous as the guilty; the experience of practitioners is that the guilty will probably be in the majority. When scientific evidence enters upon the forensic scene, it can often be compellingly persuasive to a jury of the defendant's guilt. But in trials for murder, things do not always go as smoothly, not least in cases of infant deaths that are in some way 'unexplained' and which are enveloped in a suspicion that stems from such uncertainty. Violent and brutal parents are generally not difficult to identify, but what of evidently loving and caring parents whose infants—sometimes more than one—suffer deaths that remain unexplained, or in which the cause appears 'unascertainable'? Among those parents standing trial in recent cases for the murder of their children in such circumstances have been Sally Clark, Angela Cannings and Trupti Patel. Sally Clark and Angela Cannings were both convicted of murder and sentenced to the mandatory penalty of life imprisonment; Trupti Patel was acquitted by the jury. This trilogy of cases in the first decade of the twenty-first century will undoubtedly be noted by future historians of the criminal law as cases which were to change it, not least in consequence of the judgments given in the appeals of Sally

Clark and Angela Cannings quashing their convictions. In each of these cases the jury was confronted with a mass of highly complex expert medical evidence. If there is a lesson to be learned here, it is that there is an urgent need for the court itself to take early possession of expert evidence, not least within the context of court management, if juries are not to become confused and, more importantly, if those parents to whom no blame should be attached are to be spared the humiliation and public obloquy that follow a conviction for murder, not to mention the loss of their liberty.

Every trial of a defendant charged with an offence of homicide will involve the calling of expert medical (and sometimes other scientific) evidence, if only to ascertain the cause of the victim's death. Usually, the evidence of the forensic pathologist who conducted the post-mortem will suffice. The pathologist conducting the autopsy is both a witness of fact—of what he finds respecting the condition of the corpse—and an expert witness as to the import of those facts. It will normally be uncontroversial and uncontradicted, simply because the cause of death will be manifest. It will establish readily whether the death was from natural or unnatural causes, but even if a violent or unnatural death, the precise instrument that killed may be in doubt.

The problems associated with the reception and assessment of forensic evidence in a system of trial by judge and jury are anything but new; they have become accentuated over the passage of time and advances in medical knowledge. Writing in 1859 James Fitzjames Stephen (later to become Mr Justice Stephen) said:

> Few spectacles, it may be said, can be more absurd and incongruous than that of a jury composed of twelve persons who, without any previous scientific knowledge or training, are suddenly called upon to adjudicate in controversies in which the most eminent scientific men flatly contradict each other's assertions. How, it might be asked, can ordinary tradesmen and farmers, who have never been accustomed to give sustained attention to any subject whatever for an hour together, be expected to weigh evidence, the delivery of which occupies many days and which bears upon subjects which can only be described in language altogether new and foreign to their understanding?[1]

and he concluded:

> . . . we ought to take seriously that when scientific questions are involved in a criminal trial, the verdicts upon which courts of justice pronounce judgment should represent the settled opinions of men who have made a special study, and not the loose impressions of unscientific jurors.[2]

How to handle scientific or technical knowledge in the context of a criminal trial before a jury as the exclusive fact-finder is an issue of increasing complexity and importance. Is the jury the right instrument to adjudicate upon conflicting

---

[1] James Fitzjames Stephen, *Trial by Jury and the Evidence of Experts* (London, Papers of the Juridical Society, 1858–1863) volume 1, Paper XIV, at 236.
[2] *Ibid.*

medical evidence? If so, how can it be assisted by the manner in which that evidence is elicited, set out and placed before the court, either before or at the trial? Failure to heed the words of Fitzjames Stephen and to accommodate opinion evidence on scientific or technical matters constitutes a reproach to successive administrators of criminal justice over nearly a century and a half.

No criminal trial, heavily dependent upon expert (medical) evidence has exposed so demonstrably the deficiencies in our system of criminal justice than the recent case of Sally Clark. The quashing of Sally Clark's conviction (at the second attempt in January 2003) was fully justified, but it was achieved in circumstances that give cause for disquiet about the procedure for adducing expert evidence in criminal justice. Nor does it not stand alone. Similar concern was expressed at the trial of Trupti Patel (acquitted by the jury at Reading Crown Court later in that year) and most recently, in the appeal by Angela Cannings in January 2004 where there was no extraneous non-medical evidence. The earlier case of Damilola Taylor[3] threw up the problem of a delayed medical report challenging the Crown's version of the cause of the victim's death. Sally Clark's case, however, is an exemplar.

At Chester Crown Court, before Mr Justice Harrison and a jury on 9 November 1999, Mrs Clark, a solicitor, was convicted of the murder of her sons, Christopher and Harry, when they were aged eleven weeks and eight weeks respectively. At her trial no fewer than 14 experts were called—belatedly—nine by the prosecution and five by the defence. There was some other non-forensic evidence, which may have tilted the scales against the accused, but clearly the prosecution relied primarily and heavily on the medical evidence supporting the opinion that each child had either been suffocated or had been subject to severe shaking at the hands of their mother. They were not, the Crown argued, deaths from natural causes.

Sally Clark's appeal to the Court of Appeal (Criminal Division) on 2 October 2000 was unsuccessful. The Court, composed of Lord Justice Henry, Mrs Justice Bracewell and Mr Justice Richards, delivered a judgment of 274 paragraphs (approximately 40,000 words). Under the heading, *The strength of the case at trial*, it concluded:

> We have considered with care the extensive evidence placed before the jury at trial, and we have concluded that there was overwhelming evidence of the guilt of the appellant on each count. (There were two separate counts, one for each of murder.)

At paragraph 272/3 the Court had stated:

> . . . we consider that there was an overwhelming case against the appellant at trial. If there had been no error in relation to the statistics at the trial—a reference to a piece of evidence from [Professor] Sir Roy Meadow, a consultant paediatrician and an

---

[3] The trial of those thought responsible for the death of the young schoolboy Damilola Taylor ended in acquittal, the evidence of one juvenile witness having seriously affected the strength of the Crown's case.

expert on cot deaths[4]—we are satisfied that the jury would still have convicted on each count. In the context of the trial as a whole, the point on statistics was of minimal significance and there is no possibility of the jury having been misled so as to reach verdicts they might not otherwise have reached. Had the trial been free from legal error, the only reasonable and proper verdict would have been one of guilty . . . The error of approach towards the statistical evidence at trial . . . did not render the convictions unsafe.

On July 2002 the Criminal Cases Review Commission referred the case back to the Court of Appeal, on the basis that there was a real possibility that the Court would find that

> . . . the new evidence renders Mrs Clark's convictions for the murders of Christopher and Harry unsafe.

The 'new evidence', which the second Court of Appeal admitted as 'fresh evidence', related to hospital records of the result of microbiological tests performed on samples of Harry's blood, body tissue and cerebrospinal fluid gathered at the post-mortem on the child. The resulting microbiological tests were not disclosed at trial, but when submitted to medical experts it was suggested that Harry might not, after all, have been killed, but may have died from natural causes.

At the Court of Appeal hearing on 28/29 January 2003 Mrs Clark's counsel made what were identified as 'two essential points'. First, and principally, the failure of the Crown to disclose the information contained in the microbiological reports meant that important reports relating to the cause of death were never considered at trial. Secondly, it was contended that statistical information given to the jury about the likelihood of two sudden and unexpected deaths of infants from natural causes misled the jury and painted a picture which was now considered as overstating, very considerably, the rarity of two such events happening within the same family.

Counsel for the appellant did not seek to argue any other point—in particular, she did not review the effect of the expert evidence given at trial, which the first Court of Appeal comprehensively covered in concluding that it presented an overwhelming case of unnatural death at the hands of the children's mother.

The Court of Appeal, comprised of Lord Justice Kay, Mr Justice Holland and Mrs Justice Hallett,[5] delivered its judgment on 11 April 2003. The judgment ran to 182 paragraphs (approximately 20,000 words). Nearly two-thirds of the judgment was devoted to a rehearsal of the expert evidence at trial, and concluded as follows:

> The medical evidence at trial, which we have set out in detail, made clear that on any view this was a difficult case. There was a wide difference of views in respect of each

---

[4] The term 'cot death' is a popular term employed to describe otherwise inexplicable deaths in infants. The term 'Sudden infant death syndrome' or 'SIDS' has greater scientific currency.

[5] Mrs Justice Hallett had been the trial judge in the case of Angela Cannings.

death as to the conclusions that could properly be drawn from the available evidence. However, a number of factors seem to us to emerge, which are of relevance to this appeal:

1. In each case, before a conclusion adverse to the appellant could be drawn, the jury would have had to be sure that they could rely upon the evidence of Dr Williams [the forensic pathologist who conducted both post-mortems]. There were important features said to have been found at each post-mortem examination which depended both upon the competence of Dr Williams in carrying out the post-mortems and upon the extent to which he could be considered as a reliable and objective witness as to his findings. There were features at that time that must have caused the jury to hesitate. His change from a conclusion that Christopher died of a lower respiratory tract infection, to an opinion that there was no evidence that he had such an infection that could have led to death, and the acceptance by the Crown that Professor Luthert [a consultant ophthalmologist] was right about the intra-retinal haemorrhaging of the eyes being the result of an error in slide preparation were the most obvious examples of the need for caution. Anything further that cast doubt upon the approach of Dr Williams must, therefore, have been of potential significance to the jury's conclusions.

2. It was of potentially crucial importance that there was no evidence of any illness or infection suffered by Harry that might have explained his death. If this was not a true SIDS case, as the doctors were largely agreed, and since there was no apparent natural explanation for the death, the evidence pointed towards unnatural, death. The only disagreement between the doctors was whether it did so to sufficient degree to permit a firm conclusion that the cause of death was unnatural, or whether the case had still to be classified as an unascertainable cause of death. Thus any evidence which positively suggested that Harry died from natural causes was of potentially crucial relevance to the jury's considerations and might very well have resulted in different verdicts.

3. The evidence in respect of Christopher's death, if it had stood in isolation would not have justified a finding of murder and if, therefore, there had been evidence that suggested that Harry died from natural causes so that the jury accepted this was a possibility, it seems inevitably to follow that they could not have been sure that Christopher was murdered.

The Court of Appeal dealt peremptorily with the statistical evidence:

Finally, we should say a little about the statistical evidence led before the jury. The matter was the subject of only brief argument before us and we certainly heard none of the evidence.[6]

and observed:

The Court of Appeal on the last occasion would, it seems clear to us, have felt obliged to allow the appeal but for their assessment of the rest of the evidence as overwhelming. In reaching that conclusion, the Court was as misled by the absence of the evidence of the microbiological results, as were the jury before it. We are quite satisfied that if the evidence in its entirety, as it is now known, had been known to the Court it would never have concluded that the evidence pointed overwhelmingly to guilt.[7]

---

[6] At para 172.
[7] At para 179.

Thus, in effect, the sole argument before the second Court of Appeal was the non-disclosure to the Court of the hospital records of the microbiological tests on Harry. That non-disclosure in itself either constituted an unfair trial, or was insufficiently serious to justify the sobriquet of unfairness.

Since the sole issue was the failure of the prosecution to disclose the microbiological tests (which had a significant impact on the question whether the deaths of the two infants were the result of natural or unnatural causes), it mattered not one wit, for the purpose of concluding the verdict to be unsafe, how and why the reports were undisclosed, or indeed who was to blame for the failure to disclose.

For the purpose of determining the appeal, on the legal consequences of non-disclosure of important evidence, the court had no need to review the case, since it had been contested without the undisclosed material. The statistical evidence provided a basis for adjudication distinct from the undisclosed evidence, and did not affect the ultimate result. Why then did the Court engage in a lengthy, even prolix, rehearsal of the medical evidence given at trial and fully reviewed by the Court of Appeal in October 2000, minus the fresh evidence of the microbiological tests? Unfortunately, one can only speculate.

Reviewing (and re-reading) paragraph 93 of the judgment, we conclude one of two possibilities.

> 1. By implication, the second Court of Appeal had come to the conclusion that their judicial brethren in October 2000 had wrongly concluded that the case was overwhelmingly proved against Mrs Clark. A review of the experts' evidence disclosed that there was no consensus about the cause of death, but a clear conflict between those whose were in favour of death from natural causes and those who were doubtful whether the cause was simply 'accidental', 'unascertained' or even 'unascertainable'. On that analysis, the jury should have entertained a reasonable doubt. Surprisingly, it did not. It may be that the jury, utterly confused by the welter of conflicting medical evidence, plumped for the non-forensic evidence of the accused and her husband, to guide them to their verdict. If that was so, what an appalling way in which to treat forensic evidence in a criminal trial!
> 2. If that is the true interpretation, either the second Court of Appeal should have declined to say anything about its predecessor's decision (and dealt only with the question of non-disclosure), or it ought to have stated that it positively disagreed with the earlier decision: it should have said that the jury's verdict was unsafe, whether or not the microbiological tests had been disclosed.

If neither of the two possibilities is correct, the only other explanation is that the second Court of Appeal, for the purposes of public relations, was desirous of quelling public disquiet about other cases in the pipeline for review on appeal. One gleans that much from a somewhat unusual final paragraph in the judgment, in which the Court wrote:

> We are aware that there is public speculation as to whether other convictions of mothers for killing their babies where the babies have died sudden deaths, are similarly unsafe. The matters to which we have referred are directly referable only to this case. If any other case is brought before this Court, it will receive the same anxious scrutiny by the court that we would like to think we have given to this case.

That 'other case' must surely be a reference to that of Angela Cannings, hearing of whose appeal came before the Court in December 2003 with the judgment at the end of January 2004. If, in Sally Clark's case, the Court had felt obliged to engage in the exercise of publicly demonstrating its familiarity and full understanding of the medical evidence, it might, more profitably, have turned its attention to the practice in our criminal courts of adducing evidence which produced such a flawed procedure. But it singularly failed to address the problem of how courts in a modern world should handle scientific evidence.

In its judgment of 2 October 2000 the first Court of Appeal in the Sally Clark case had observed that it was not until the medical witnesses for the defence were called to give oral evidence on the ninth day of a thirteen day trial, that it became clear that those medical experts called by the defence accepted that neither the death of Christopher Clark nor the death of Harry Clark 'was a true SIDS death'. It is a grave reflection on the English criminal process that an issue so crucial to the outcome of the trial could be exposed only at such a late stage in the proceedings. It stems from the fact that expert evidence (as with the testimony of eye-witnesses) is fitted procedurally into an adversarial system that requires the Crown to prove its case. Only if there is a *prima facie* case, will the defence then call its evidence which, at best, will reveal fully the nature of its case against conviction.

In the case of expert testimony, the totality of such evidence (whether emanating from Crown or defence) might sensibly be heard in a discrete fashion as a preliminary body of evidence, to be evaluated by the trial judge alone, or by the judge leaving the jury to assess its weight in the light of other, non-expert, evidence adduced by the parties. This evaluation after judicial examination could be incorporated within the process of court management.

Our recommendations hereafter are designed to promote a procedure which gives effect to that overriding need for a separate function for expert evidence in the criminal jurisdiction, especially in homicide cases. The recommendations are made in the light of the provisions of section 30 of the Criminal Justice Act 2003, which inserts into the existing procedure in section 6 of the Criminal Procedure and Investigations Act 1996, a requirement on the defence to notify the Crown of experts instructed by the accused. Section 6D(1) follows the wording of Part 35 of the Civil Procedure Rules in that

> . . . if the accused instructs a person with a view to his providing any expert opinion for possible use as evidence at the trial of the accused . . .

the expert's name and address must be supplied to the court and the Crown. Thus, experts' reports, which are sought for the purpose of advice and not for potential use at trial, are not subject to notification and possible disclosure. It is not clear whether the Crown can seek disclosure of any notified expert's report. We suggest that, in accordance with the recommendations of Sir Robin Auld in his *Review of the Criminal Courts of England and Wales*,[8] such reports should

---

[8] Published 8 October 2001.

be disclosed, but not any other reports outwith the provisions of s 30 of the Criminal Justice Act 2003. We think that expert evidence, which is opinion evidence based on given data—such as a post-mortem report in a homicide case—ought to be treated as available to the court, whether its provenance is the Crown or the defence. While we would not support any replica derived from Part 35 of the Civil Procedure Rules of 'a single joint expert', we do think that there should not be any proprietorial interest in any experts' reports. They belong to the criminal court of trial, irrespective of their origins.

Additional to the provision of the expert evidence emanating from the parties, we suggest that, exceptionally, the trial court might call for expert evidence in a particular area of expertise relevant to the issues at trial, the Sally Clark case providing just such an example. The Court might in the instant case have required the Macclesfield Hospital to send the results of the microbiological tests performed on the one child. These were tests which the jury had requested to see, but were told were not available. Under our proposals, the Court could have required them to be produced at an early stage. At the pre-trial stage, a report might also have been sought from an obstetrician and gynaecologist to explain whether the fracture to Harry's rib could have been caused by a breach birth[9] even if, as appears, the birth was a normal vaginal delivery.

An initiative from the Court to call additional expert evidence might conventionally be subject to the concurrence of the parties. But should the parties not agree, the court should be empowered to order such evidence. Likewise, the court should have the power to limit the number of experts from a particular speciality. Mr Justice Harrison at trial observed that the jury

> might be forgiven perhaps for thinking that you had heard almost too much medical evidence.

The judge's explanation,

> ... that a murder trial involves very serious issues and therefore these matters must be investigated thoroughly ...

we think, is misguided. On the contrary, the sheer volume of evidence from the pathologists (five from the prosecution and three from the defence) and from neurological pathologists, paediatricians and ophthalmologists may well have served only to confuse, rather than to elucidate the cause of death of two babies. Indeed, the parties seem to have indulged in a protracted expedition to find medical experts to support their respective cases. The Crown Prosecution Service has explained its actions publicly:

> The experts were instructed and as the case unfolded it became clear that the prosecution required specific expert evidence. For example, the pathologist Dr Alan

---

[9] See para 271(c) of the judgment of the Court of Appeal.

Williams suggested that the Crown contact Professor Green. In a similar way, the other prosecution experts were selected. Naturally, every report and statement from prosecution experts has been served on the defence and made available to the Court.

We have been asked to explain why a microbiologist was not instructed at the outset. The answer is that there was nothing to indicate that the microbiology was of any significance, and expert evidence in this regard was therefore not required.

The judgment in *Cannings* delivered by Judge LJ, offers an important point of reference when considering the problems arising from a plethora of expert witness evidence:

> We have some sympathy for the jury. We have to reflect an anxiety which has struck us throughout our own deliberations, whether notwithstanding these clear directions, [by Hallett J, which were found to be faultless] the whole course of the trial, the sheer numbers of experts called by the defence, and the complex specialist fields in which these distinguished men and women worked, the jury may not, inadvertently, unconsciously, have thought to itself that if between them all, none could offer a definitive or specific explanation for these deaths, the Crown's case must be right.

We shall need to return to the judgment in *Cannings* later, since it must now be regarded as a landmark, not merely for the present but for the future conduct of trials of parents arising from infant deaths in suspicious circumstances where direct evidence of violence, deliberate neglect, or the involvement of third parties such as carers is absent.

But why should decisions about the calling of expert evidence be so perilously left to the parties, effectively unregulated in the way they conduct their case and delayed in their presentation until trial, often many months after the event? This is a very particular species of evidence. Frequently its significance may be demonstrated only after the specialist language of experts has been translated into a vernacular that can be readily understood by a jury. Moreover, lawyers, however keenly their professional skills in the techniques of presentation and cross-examination may have been honed by years of experience, are rarely independently possessed of qualifications in medicine and forensic science. In criminal trials in which the issue of proof can be so finely balanced upon the evidence of expert witnesses, not least those in which the charge is murder, the volume and availability of expert evidence cannot be subject to *laissez-faire* arrangements. Even if there are to be a great number of witnesses giving a prodigious volume of evidence, it must be a predictably ordered process.

Our considered view, based on examination of cases in which reliance has been placed upon such evidence, and especially those which have been the subject of successful appeal, is that the court, at a pre-hearing stage, should have the power to restrict the number and nature of expert witnesses to be called to give oral evidence. Experts' reports should, wherever possible, be advanced by way of opinions written for the purpose of the court, and not for the parties.[10] In the Sally Clark case the parties appear to have sought sequentially to identify medical experts who would put a favourable gloss on what was up till then very ambiguous opinion evidence.

We think, nevertheless, that such a power should be conditional on some distillation of the evidence contained in the written reports. The condition would be that the parties should identify those areas in which there is agreement and those in which there is disagreement. The matters thus identified would need then to be further explored by formal discussion among the experts.

In the civil courts, and particularly in the Family Division, there is a long tradition of a not dissimilar practice whereby experts enter into discussions before trial, often held face-to-face. With the introduction of the Civil Procedure Rules 1998, such discussions have become widely used in civil litigation of all kinds. The discussions assist the court in defining the matters of agreement and disagreement between opposing experts. Sometimes, the discussion obviates the calling of expert evidence at trial, for there is no substantive point of difference; an agreed statement is submitted. More commonly, where agreement is not complete, the experts are able to tell the court which points of difference remain.

Applying this principle to the criminal jurisdiction would have considerable advantage in the case of complex medical evidence. It would, in the trial of Sally Clark, have revealed at a stage long before trial the extent of agreement between the pathologists that the cause of death of both Christopher and Harry was unascertainable, but that they were certainly not cot deaths (SIDS), something that was to emerge only nine days into the trial.

But there are also important questions of interpretation of expert evidence in which it is important that juries are properly directed. Angela Cannings, had originally been charged with the murder of her daughter Gemma—a charge not proceeded with—as well as those of her sons Jason and Matthew of whose murder she was convicted. The jury was to hear evidence, not only about the deaths of Jason and Matthew but also about a number of so-called 'ALTE's' (Acute or Apparent Life-Threatening Events) relating to Jason, Matthew and a surviving daughter, Jade. In her directions to the jury Hallett J reminded them that both sides were inviting them to look at all the evidence:

> ... be careful how you approach Gemma's death. It was a long time ago. ... It is part of the background and it is relevant. It may, for example, be relevant as to whether or not there is a genetic defect. But be very wary how you approach Gemma's death. You know the pathologists carried out a very careful post-mortem and decided that the death effectively was SIDS, or cot death, and no suggestion of maltreatment. You have not heard about Gemma's death to justify the kind of approach referred to by Mr Mansfield;[11] the Lady Bracknell approach. This is not a case whereby you could say

---

[10] There is a well established model for this in the pre-sentence reports prepared *for the court* but made available to the defendant.

[11] Michael Mansfield QC, counsel for Angela Cannings.

"to lose one baby is misfortune, two carelessness, three murder." As you will appreciate members of the jury, that is just inappropriate—totally.[12]

The jury at Winchester went on to convict Angela Cannings, though their reasons for doing so are likely to remain as inscrutable as the present law requires. The jury at Reading Crown Court hearing the case against Trupti Patel was directed in not dissimilar terms by Jack J:

> You have heard from some of the Prosecution witnesses the idea that the fact of three deaths makes it more likely that the cause was unnatural. Certainly with three deaths one must be suspicious and look the more carefully, for potentially it is a very serious situation. But I am going to ask you to put out of your minds the idea that because there are three that makes it more unlikely that the causes are unnatural: . . . I think that would be a dangerous approach in this case. . . .[13]

We interject only to say that we think the Bracknell test might well be reversed; to lose one baby who appeared healthy enough is suspicious, two arouses concern as to the possibility of a killing, and three points in the direction of a plausible genetic explanation.

The jury in the Patel case, eschewing that 'dangerous approach' took the different view and acquitted the defendant. It would, of course, be quite wrong simply to contrast the finding of one jury with that of another, notwithstanding that in both instances the directions of the trial judge were clear and unambiguous. Indeed, one might be forgiven for thinking that there are times when, whatever social and mental processes there may be at work, ratiocination may be for some jurors the very last tool they employ to assist them in their task. What is almost certainly more relevant to the task of understanding the verdict in *Patel* is the chronology of final outcomes in each of the three cases to which we have referred. In the case of Sally Clark it required more than one attempt in the Court of Appeal before the jury's verdict was quashed following a reference back by the Criminal Cases Review Commission, on the basis of new evidence supplied by those advising Sally Clark. The outcome was known by the time of the Patel trial.

Clark can be portrayed as the initial movement of a critical stone in the existing forensic structure which did not, however, dislodge it, *Patel* was responsible for knocking it away; while the successful appeal in *Cannings* can be thought of as the forensic JCB which cleared away the debris, leaving the intellectual ground ready for a new and more efficient construction.

In January 2004, shortly after the Court had delivered its reasons for quashing the convictions of Angela Cannings, the Attorney General, Lord Goldsmith QC ordered a review of the 258 cases in which a parent or carer has been convicted of killing a child under two years old, since 1994. The Director of Public Prosecutions, Mr Ken MacDonald, QC undertook at the same time to review

---

[12] *R v Cannings* [2004] transcript, paras 167, 168.
[13] Quoted in *R v Cannings*, at para 165.

personally the 15 prosecutions pending in order to determine whether they should proceed. The announcement occasioned criticism that in Family Court proceedings children had been removed from the care of their parents on the basis of not dissimilar expert evidence; this prompted a further announcement that a similar review of old cases would take place, but with the *caveat* that the process in these civil cases might well take substantially longer.[14] The reported comments of the DPP on the broader issues are not without interest. Commenting that

> One can hardly imagine a worse miscarriage of justice than a woman who has lost her baby is then convicted of murder, and then sentenced to life imprisonment.

he also observed that there was an 'attraction' in the procedures employed in some other European countries:

> . . . in other jurisdictions, these cases don't come into the criminal justice system. They go before a family law panel.[15]

The application of the practices employed in the civil jurisdiction with respect to expert evidence can scarcely present any significant difficulty. Guidelines on the conduct of such discussions have been published in the Code of Guidance on Expert Evidence, produced by the working party established by the Head of Civil Justice in December 2001 and published in the Spring 2002 edition of the White Book. Central to their success is the production of closed questions, on a tight agenda, usually to be agreed by the parties but the court retaining the ultimate power to set the agenda. A similar procedure should apply to the criminal jurisdiction. Nowhere would it be better to make a start than in all homicide cases.

It is worth questioning, however, whether the current procedure for handling expert evidence in the criminal jurisdiction complies with Article 6 of the ECHR; and whether the reforms we suggest would be compliant. Our view is that the present English law, which procedurally favours the accused in relation to pre-trial disclosure of expert evidence, is entirely compatible with Article 6(1). Nor however, would any change in English law which might hereafter equiparate, as between prosecution and defence, the treatment of expert reports, violate Article 6(1), in that, by itself, such treatment would fail to maintain the principle of the equality of arms. Only if the trial were subsequently, on consideration of the entirety of the proceedings, held to be unfair, would the court, so finding, be bound to take account of the manner in which the expert evidence functioned.

---

[14] Whereas in criminal cases involving the death of a child or children the quashing of convictions and the release of prisoners goes some way towards righting an injustice, the situation in civil proceedings is altogether more complicated. In may not be in the best interests of a child for it to be restored to it parents if it is now well settled in foster care; in instances where adoption has taken place the presenting problems appear intractable.

[15] Reported in *The Guardian* of 11 February 2004.

The European Court of Human Rights would not regard the multiplicity of experts, even if numerically favouring the prosecution, as unfair. Nor would the Court also regard any restrictions on the number of experts, given parity in quantity and quality, as a violation of Article 6(1). Likewise, a court-appointed expert, where the existing experts disagreed, would not be an unfair practice. A procedure whereby experts meet to decide the areas of agreement and disagreement would also not constitute any violation of a fair trial.

That the situation needs urgently to be addressed is underlined by the fact that some medical experts have expressed a growing sense of unease about becoming involved as expert witnesses. In March 2004 the Royal College of Paediatrics and Child Health published the results of a survey questionnaire sent to all paediatricians in the United Kingdom of whom a very substantial proportion (78%) responded. The survey results indicated that the number of complaints against paediatricians involved in child protection work had increased from fewer than 20 in 1995 to over 100 in 2003. Of these, some 11% were sufficiently serious to be referred to the General Medical Council. Of the cases so referred, 41% were dropped and 59% were found not proven.[16] At the same time, the BBC *Today* programme reported that just under a third of members of the Royal College had expressed fears of being made scapegoats or the subject of malicious complaint if they became involved in child protection work; some have been the recipients of 'hate' mail and one the subject of a death threat.[17]

There can be little doubt that the high profile of a number of recent cases has attracted a great deal of attention in the media, which in turn has had a bearing upon public perception of the phenomenon commonly known as Munchausen's Syndrome by Proxy (MsbP), in which the children of those affected with the condition will either have a fabricated illness or an induced illness. Both the Royal College and the Department of Health now use the term Fabricated Illness (FiI) rather than MsbP. What has happened in these cases, in which expert evidence has effectively come to grief in the appellate process, is that the prominent conjunction of what is an unsafe conviction (with its attendant consequences for the parent concerned) and the importance of such evidence in securing the original conviction has placed some expert witnesses in a highly unfavourable light. It is a short step to generalised criticism on a 'profession wide' basis.

Expert witnesses are there to give an expert opinion upon the evidence which is before the court, based upon their knowledge and experience; witnesses of fact are there to be just that. But whereas a witness of fact, assuming he or she is not lying in the witness box, can be *mistaken*, the situation with an expert witness is quite different. Opinion evidence given by one expert is no more than that, and may well be at variance with the import given to the same facts by another expert; the dichotomy of truth and falsehood has no relevance as is

---

[16] Royal College of Paediatrics and Child Health *Press Release* of 8 March 2004.
[17] Press Association News, 8 March 2004.

frequently the case with those who are no more than witnesses of fact. But for the jury comprised of ordinary men and women, frequently quite unfamiliar with the sophisticated nuances of the forensic process, the task can often be far from easy. Experts, of necessity, need to employ technical language, but even if this can be translated into the demotic, an array of expert evidence (the meaning of which may be the subject of the differing expert opinion) can be bewildering, not least when it is presented for many hours, day after day.

In our view, however, the substantially greater source of difficulty resides in the unsatisfactory way in which the management of the court process in the criminal trial presently permits the presentation of expert evidence in a manner which precisely reflects the adversarial character of the trial process itself. The feature with which the public is probably most familiar from fiction and television drama is the cross-examination of a witness. It is the entirely proper task of the cross-examiner to test the witness's evidence in such a way as to cast doubt upon its reliability, whether by challenging the witness about its factual basis, or—and by no means uncommonly—by challenging the probity of the witness. This, of course, must apply to witnesses of fact; with the expert witness, who offers an opinion, the challenge must of necessity be on a different basis. The view of one distinguished lawyer[18] was that the forensic offensive should be mounted against the expert's methodology rather than be directed at his probity.

But because in the popular mind the distinction between the two types of witness is imperfectly understood or not even appreciated to exist, when expert evidence is successfully challenged it is perceived as having been *untrue* rather than unreliable as a consequence of some flaw in analysis or methodology. It follows that when a conviction in a high profile case which is quashed, in which expert evidence has played a substantial part, it can be readily (if quite wrongly) assumed that the expert evidence was in some way incompetently mistaken or inaccurate or, at worst, derived from some malice or hostility towards the defendant.

The remedy, in our view, is for the courts to take ownership and responsibility for expert evidence, particularly at the pre-trial stage. In homicide trials the Crown will always need the evidence of a forensic pathologist, stating the facts found on a *post mortem* examination; the witness who conducts the *post mortem* will bestride the roles of witness of fact and expert witness. If specialists who are willing to serve the administration of justice are deterred from participating in criminal trials, an imbalance between prosecution and defence may well develop, to the detriment of the quality of opinion evidence before the court upon which homicide trials are so frequently dependent.

---

[18] The late Sir Frederick Lawton (a retired Lord Justice of Appeal) who had long experience at the Criminal bar.

CONCLUSIONS

Our practical proposals for change can be summed up as follows:

1. In any prosecution, where the case involves difficult, controversial expert evidence, a judge in a pre-trial direction should decide whether trial of such issue should be by jury, or by judge alone. In the event that the matter goes before a jury, opinion evidence from expert witnesses should be treated as forensically residing within the province of the judge.

2. In any event, where the trial by jury primarily involves complicated expert evidence, arrangements should be made for all the expert witnesses to be called in succession in a trial-within-a-trial. There should not be a division between experts called by Crown and defence. While experts are called by the parties, they are all the court's witnesses.

3. Whenever possible, experts should be advised pre-trial to attend a meeting among themselves, with a view to defining the areas of agreement and disagreement, thereby reducing the areas of conflicting evidence.

4. The trial judge should draw a distinction between those experts giving eyewitness testimony (eg, a pathologist conducting a post-mortem) and those giving opinion evidence only, on established data.

The matters which we have examined in this chapter, at times technically complicated in both the scientific and legal sense, and baffling as they might appear to a jury, go to the very heart of that justice which is itself at the epicentre of the criminal prosecution. For Sally Clark, Angela Cannings and Trupti Patel, the possibility of a mandatory sentence of life imprisonment, imposed for crimes of which they protested their innocence, could have been nothing if not awesome, even mind-numbing. Perhaps the best we can say is that those who sit captive in the dock, charged with the murder of their own children, yet fervently clinging to the hope, if not expectation, that their innocence will appear transparent, no longer risk perceiving the outline of the hangman's noose in some chance shadow upon the courtroom wall. But there remains for such defendants the prospect of a sentence which some would wish to be transformed from being a constructive punishment for those convicted of homicide, with the prospect of rehabilitation and eventual release, into a symbolic entombment characterised by punitive retribution alone. If guilt in cases so reliant upon expert evidence cannot be ascertained with certitude, then that 'dreadful possibility' to which Lord Justice Judge so poignantly and pointedly referred becomes a reality:

> If murder cannot be proved, the conviction cannot be safe. In a criminal case, it is simply not enough to be able to establish even a high probability of guilt. Unless we can be sure of guilt the dreadful possibility always remains that a mother, already brutally scarred by the unexplained death or deaths of her babies, may find herself in prison for life for killing them when she should not be there at all. In our community, and in any civilised community, that is abhorrent.[19]

[19] *R v Cannings*, at para 179.

A sentence in the penultimate paragraph of the judgment in *Cannings* contains a resonance from the judgment in *Nicholls* a quarter of a century before, its brevity in contrast to the immensity of its implications for future prosecutions of this kind.

> ... in cases like the present, if the outcome of the trial depends exclusively or almost exclusively on a serious disagreement between distinguished and reputable experts, it will often be unwise, and therefore unsafe, to proceed.[20]

CODA: OVERLOADING THE JURY

> For of all the institutions that have been created by English law, there is none other that has a better claim to be called 'the privilege of the Common people . . .
> Trial by jury is the lamp that shows that freedom lives.

Sir Patrick Devlin. *Trial by Jury*.[21]

It is almost certainly the case that of all the institutions of the English law none is more revered than the jury. Any attempt to change the law by limiting the scope of its availability in criminal trials can stimulate fierce opposition. The right to trial by jury is perceived as fundamental to the idea of freedom under law; it is seen as the warranty that is given by the state to its citizens that none, no matter how serious the crime of which they stand accused, shall be condemned save by the judgment of a dozen of their peers who will have listened to the evidence and brought to bear upon it that highly prized intellectual commodity otherwise known as common sense. The deliberations of the jury are nowhere held to be more essential to justice than in a trial for murder, since the extreme gravity of that crime is mirrored in its penalty.

When Devlin delivered his Hamlyn Lectures on trial by jury, the penalty for murder was death. The substitution of imprisonment for life, though capable of moderation in a variety of ways, remains something to be feared by all save those few mentally aberrant offenders for whom anything beyond the present, or its immediate vicinity, has no reality. The 'life' sentence, though it may not come to mean life-long incarceration, nevertheless proffers a prospect of seemingly endless time in which days follow each other into weeks, weeks into months and months into years, such that time itself may seem to stand still. Added to the corrosive *ennui* that is the common characteristic of long-term imprisonment, is likely to be added a gnawing sense of guilt amplified by the knowledge that the life taken can never be brought back. It is small wonder that those convicted of murder and sentenced to life imprisonment are normally considered to be at risk of suicide in the early months of their time in prison.

---

[20] *R v Cannings*, at para 178.
[21] Sir Patrick Devlin, *Trial by Jury* (London, Stevens & Sons, 1956). This is the published version of his Hamlyn Lectures.

It is for these reasons, and possibly others, that those who stand trial for murder, believing themselves to be innocent of the crime, while they may hope for much within the trial process, place their final trust in the jury to deliver a true verdict.

1066 AND ALL THAT

The jury, no less than Parliament and the institution of monarchy, has a history that is long and complicated, the true narrative often bearing little resemblance to the substance of popular belief. The assumption that trial by jury can be traced to Magna Carta is erroneous; that moment in history simply confirmed the political principle of 'one baron, one vote'. The jury, and its close relative, the Coroner's inquest, have undergone substantial change in the course of that history. In the Middle Ages, various devices were employed to determine the truth or otherwise of complaints of crime; trial by battle, by ordeal, and by jury. Trial by ordeal—being precipitated into water or made to carry a red-hot iron, the latter test during the celebration of the Mass, was effectively abolished by a decree of Pope Innocent III in 1215.[22] By the twelfth century the jury had come to consist of twelve, or some other number of jurors[23] fixed by the court, according to circumstances, who were called upon to swear, not to the facts of the case, but that from their knowledge of the accused, his word was to be believed. These jurors, termed 'compurgators', would attest to the oath of innocence taken by the accused being 'clean' or founded in truth, thus purging him of guilt. Over time, the judges ceased to play an inquisitorial role, assessing the weight of the evidence themselves, leaving this task to a new kind of jury that developed in the thirteenth century, whose verdicts came to be accepted as unquestioningly as the outcome of the ordeal.

Though the jury was to emerge in relatively modern times[24] as an essential component part of the system of criminal justice, the idea that those indicted for crime would be judged by their peers was by no means consonant with the social reality. Until adult suffrage became the basis for the selection in the 1960s, eligibility for jury service depended upon possession of some title to real property.[25] It was therefore more likely that until the property qualification was abolished,

---

[22] In the Fourth Lateran Council.
[23] The term derives from the Latin *jurare*; to swear or take an oath.
[24] ie post-1500.
[25] In 1951 a person was qualified for jury service if he or she was:

   (i)   aged between 21 and 60
   (ii) a registered local government elector
   (iii) either, (a) a resident beneficially possessed of £10 p.a. in real estate or rent charge, or £20 p.a. in leaseholds held for not less than 21 years or determinable on any life or lives, or, (b) a householder residing in premises of rateable value of not less than £30 p.a. in the counties of London and Middlesex or £20 p.a. elsewhere in England and Wales.
In 1951 most manual workers needed to work 60 or more hours each week to take home more than £10 in wages.

a large proportion of offenders were judged, not by their peers, but by those superior to them in social status. A Victorian or Edwardian jury, drawn from a comparatively affluent middle class, would have been likely to have distinct views about morality—and certainly the lack of it—among offenders who were identified as belonging to the lower orders of society.

OBJECTIVE JUDGMENT-GUARANTEED

The task with which the modern jury is charged is to determine whether or not the prosecution has made out its case and in so doing, to entertain no reasonable doubt as to its own judgment. Jurors will have heard an outline of the prosecution case and the testimony of its witnesses. They will have heard those witnesses cross-examined by the defence and the testimony of defence witnesses, in their turn cross-examined by the prosecution. They will have had the benefit of a summing up of the evidence by the judge and, in a trial for murder, a careful statement of the law, enabling them to test what they decide are the established facts against it. All this will have occupied many hours and demanded considerable and continuous concentration on the part of the jury.

It is presumed that, being ordinary citizens randomly drawn from the local community, their approach will be determined by a realism deriving from their experience of ordinary life. The remainder of the cast of the courtroom drama who have the speaking parts, professional lawyers all, are, in contrast, generally believed to be more distant from the world inhabited by ordinary people. To some extent this is true, given their generally privileged social background, but they are not as socially remote as their critics often portray them.[26]

The contemporary requirement of a civilised system of criminal justice is now expressed in Article 6 of the European Convention on Human Rights; a fair trial before an independent and impartial tribunal conducted in public. These are the primary criteria against which the jury system must itself be judged. Each of these is self-evidently met, save for the issue of impartiality. For it is not that we have reason to believe that juries *are* partial; rather, that because they conduct their deliberations in private, there is simply no way of knowing how objectively each member of the jury approaches the task. Because the jury room is literally closed to outside scrutiny, even to the most professionally conducted research, we have nothing upon which to rely except for anecdotal accounts of what may have transpired. If the jury does experience difficulty, part of the problem arises from the circumstances in which juries have to deliberate when perhaps none except the foreman has had any experience either of jury service, or indeed, of the criminal justice system.

---

[26] Times have moved on since it was possible for a judge seriously to inquire as to what a 'bikini' might be. One senior judge is recently reported to have thanked the jury at the end of a trial by employing the language of text messaging by mobile telephone—'thanx'.

Before 1965, when both rational selection and training were introduced into the lay magistracy,[27] a large part of the business of the criminal courts was conducted by people who had never been trained to view matters judicially. To 'think' a defendant was guilty, or to be 'pretty sure', never mind speculate on the nature of the facts beyond what was disclosed by the evidence, would, nowadays, be recognised by every new magistrate as no basis upon which to establish a criminal conviction. Justices came to recognise that while the details of the law were not their direct problem, assurance for the standards laid down in *Woolmington* was very much their responsibility. Jurors, in contrast, who by definition are likely to be called upon to deliberate in substantially more serious cases than lay magistrates, receive no training; only encouragement to do their best.

Assuming an effort on the part of each juror to set aside his or her own feelings about the evidence in a homicide case and their natural reactions as human beings, to what further pressures may they be subjected? The essential virtue of the jury is that it is encapsulated in the collective view of 12 ordinary citizens having the ability jointly to determine the guilt or innocence of the accused, using a commonplace experience of human behaviour. Cases of homicide, which instinctively arouse the deepest concern of the community because of the violence employed and the resultant grief of the victim's family, are particularly susceptible to adjudication by an admittedly amateur body whose members have knowledge of the ways in which most people live their lives. Selection on the basis of a universal adult suffrage, though it may not always produce the kind of random sample necessary to social science research, is nevertheless more likely to provide a deep reservoir of relevant social experience. When the criminal trial is primarily concerned with assessing eyewitness evidence the jury is a very suitable body to undertake the task.

Since most cases of murder and manslaughter are committed within the compass of domestic relations—victims killed by strangers are comparatively rare— jurors can easily identify the patterns of social behaviour that lie behind the homicidal event. The shortcomings of the modern jury system relate much less to the identity of the jurors and their varying abilities, but rather to the nature of the tasks with which they are sometimes presented.

The modern criminal trial before a jury, in contrast to its historical counterpart, has become more protracted and more complicated. A murder trial that forty years ago might have occupied a matter of days is now likely to require weeks. Given the sheer volume of evidential material—sometimes much of it given by experts on abstruse medical matters—the average juror is at risk of suffering what is nowadays known as 'information overload'. At the end of the trial so much will have been said that it would be hardly surprising if a person unused to receiving information in this way did not experience some degree of confusion, not to say mental exhaustion.

---

[27] One of the reforms actively propelled by the enthusiasm of Gerald Gardiner.

Stripped of the complexities of the modern criminal trial for murder, there is no reason to tinker with the system. We conclude that our proposals will reduce some of these pressures and expectations, and in fact remove many of the complexities that have questioned the propriety, if not the viability of trial by jury.

6

The Past Revisited: When Memory Lifts the Latch

Every man, whoever he may be, and however he may have fallen, requires, if only instinctively and unconsciously, respect to be given to his dignity as a human being. The prisoner is aware that he is a prisoner, an outcast, and he knows his position in respect to the authorities, but no brands, no fetters, can make him forget that he is a man. And since he is a human being, it follows that he must be treated as a human being. God knows, treatment as a human being may transform into a man again, even one in whom the image of God has long been eclipsed.

Feodor Dostoevsky. *Crime and Punishment*. 1861

When Parliament came to abolish the death penalty in 1965 one might naturally have asked the question: what was to replace the mandatory penalty of death? Parliament baldly stated that the penalty of death should be replaced by that of imprisonment for life. Did it thereby do more than replace the physical ending of life by a concept of civil death? To understand our answer to that question today, it is necessary to explain the provenance of the alternative mandatory penalty, that of life imprisonment. Two issues emerge. First, there is a continuing and widespread belief, assiduously promoted by Government ministers, that at the time of the 1965 Act there was a compact of some kind, whereby, as a *quid pro quo* for abolition, life imprisonment would have the meaning of incarceration for an exceptionally long time. This has variously been described as 'the pact with Parliament', a 'pact with the people', or an arrangement entered into 'on faith'. Those who believe the 'compact' was indeed made insist that it must be honoured today; therefore, they hold, that in order to reflect the (supposed) bargain between abolitionists and retentionists there can be no abandonment of the mandatory life sentence for murder. We consider that belief to be profoundly mistaken. Erroneous though it is, it cannot be lightly put aside, since such is the tenacity with which it is now held that it has the effect of inhibiting any rational discussion of the mandatory life sentence. Those who challenge that belief, do so at the risk of being regarded as infidels in the realm of the political history of the last 40 years. If we seem to return to it more than once in the course of our arguments, it is because it represents so great an obstacle to innovative and progressive thinking about the sentencing of those guilty of criminal homicide.

Secondly, following abolition in 1965 and until the mid-1980s, the understanding was that arrangements for the custody and discharge of life sentence prisoners would essentially continue the pattern of procedure and practice of the Home Office with regard to prisoners who were reprieved from the death sentence before 1965, or sentenced to non-capital murder post-1957. Things changed dramatically, however, with the policy, first pronounced by Mr Leon (now Lord) Brittan when Home Secretary in October 1983, fixing what was to become known as 'the tariff'—namely, the period to be served to satisfy the presumed need for retribution and deterrence before a life sentence prisoner could be released from custody.

THIRTY YEARS ON: A DEAL, CURIOUSLY REMEMBERED

One of the arguments advanced by the opponents of reform of the mandatory sentence of life imprisonment, is that when the death penalty was abolished it was conceded by the promoters of the 1965 Act that the mandatory life sentence should be retained, and that to change the law now would be a manifestation of bad faith towards those retentionists of the time who had accepted it as a compromise. In1996, in a first leader highly (and in our view unfairly) critical of the judges,[1] *The Times* newspaper lent its authority to the re-affirmation of what has fast become one of the most sedulously promoted myths about the historical origins of the present mandatory penalty of life for those convicted of murder.[2] In fairness, it must be said that *The Times*, in fact, did no more than echo a passage in the First Report of the Home Affairs Committee, published in December 1995, which had referred to the 'pact' with Parliament.[3] Referring to the consensus for abolition, the Committee asserted

> . . . to abandon the mandatory life sentence would betray those who voted to abolish the death penalty in 1965 and 1969, as well as those who vote against its re-introduction on the understanding that the life sentence for murder will continue to be mandatory.[4]

The myth that abolition was secured at the price of the mandatory life sentence is repeated in the report by *Justice*.[5]

---

[1] "IN THE DOCK: judges, not ministers, should mend their ways" *The Times*, 31 July, 1996.

[2] 'When the death penalty was abolished Parliament made a compact with the people that their representatives would have the right to insist on the basement for sentences in certain capital crimes.' *Ibid*.

[3] House of Commons. Session 1995–96, 111. Home Affairs Committee, *Murder: The Mandatory Life Sentence*, First Report, 13 December, 1995, para 53.

[4] HC Home Affairs Committee, Session 1995–96, First Report, *Murder: The Mandatory Life Sentence* (London, HMSO,13 December 1995) para 54.

[5] *Sentenced for Life: Reform of the law and procedure for those sentenced to life imprisonment* (1996) at.4.

A myth is to be distinguished from a conscious or deliberate untruth, which it is not; rather, it is an essentially structured social fiction, frequently based upon a highly plausible account of how things *might* have been; a device which nevertheless encapsulates a belief which its promoters seek to portray as a truth which can be the foundation of action; or in this instance, inaction. The more often it is repeated, the more firmly rooted it becomes and the less likely to be subject to critical scrutiny. It comes to assume the character of a given fact.[6] There is a very real and present danger of the mandatory penalty for murder assuming the status of an inalienable principle, beyond any question of challenge, let alone abolition. It is a short distance in rhetoric from the notion of 'trust betrayed'—the clear implication of the passage in the First Report of the Home Affairs Committee in 1995—to the use of such terms as 'on faith', in turn suggestive of a trust which has become vested with the quality of the sacred. To challenge the sacred is heretical.

Both the present writers were actively involved in the campaign against the death penalty throughout the period 1950–1965 and knew a number of those in Parliament who were similarly involved. Initially, we were perplexed by this novel account, which seemed to bear no relation to our own recollection of events which we had ourselves closely followed. But recognising that memory, however well exercised, can sometimes play tricks, we decided to discover what evidence there might be from the period that would give substance to the claim. To this end we initially examined two sources of data:

1. The reports of the Parliamentary debates in both Houses on the 1965 Bill, and
2. The Cabinet Papers for the period, by this time in the Public Record Office (now the National Archives) at Kew.

Neither of these sources yielded a scintilla of evidence suggestive of any 'deal', 'compact', nor 'bargain' that had been struck, either in public debate or in the privacy of Cabinet, with respect to a *quid pro quo* whereby abolition would proceed in return for the retention of the mandatory penalty. We published our findings[7] in the hope (if not expectation) of comment or rejoinder but none was forthcoming. By 1998, however, another source of data became available, in the form of the private papers of the late Lord Gardiner which had been deposited in the MS Department of the British Library.[8]

---

[6] It is not uncommon for important events in history that are sufficiently momentous as to have relevance long after their time; perhaps the most outstanding example is that of the *Magna Carta* of 1215, that some have argued to be the well-spring of modern democratic government. In fact, it was more limited in scope, constraining the abusive exercise of power by the Crown, notably guaranteeing that no subject should be kept in prison without trial and judgment by his peers. *Habeas Corpus* of 1679 had a broadly similar objective.

[7] Terence Morris and Louis Blom-Cooper [1996] *Criminal Law Review*, 707–17.

[8] 56461 A. *Gerald Gardiner Papers*, volume VII Pt 1 (ff ii+150) [Correspondence and papers of Gardiner as Lord Chancellor concerning the passage of the Murder (Abolition of Death Penalty) Bill 1964–1969]. 56461 B. *do.* Volume VII Pt 11 (ff.108) [Drafts and amendments to the Murder (Abolition of Death Penalty) Bill; 1964–1965]. 56462 A. *do.* Volume VIII Pt 1 (ff.126) [Speakers' notes for Parliamentary debates on the abolition of the death penalty; 1965–1969].

What the documentary material reveals is that not only were the relative roles of the judiciary and the executive, in determining the minimum period to be served by life sentence prisoners, the subject of debate in considerable depth, but that there was also substantial support in the Lords for the judges to have power to pass discretionary life sentences. Save for a change of mind by the then Lord Chief Justice, Lord Parker of Waddington, in withdrawing his successful amendment to that end, the mandatory sentence might have disappeared 40 years ago. Close scrutiny of the private papers of Lord Gardiner has similarly disclosed no evidence of any such bargain.

How, then, has the myth of the 'compact' acquired such importance as a source of authority that it has been quoted across what passes for the political spectrum; from the Conservative chaired[9] Home Affairs Committee of the House of Commons in 1995, to a New Labour minister[10] in debate on the Criminal Justice Bill in the Lords in October 2003? An examination of the chronology, gestation and development of the myth is highly revealing.

1995: THE YEAR OF REVELATION

After the publication of the First Report of the Home Affairs Committee of the House of Commons on the mandatory penalty for murder we were concerned that the Committee should have relied so uncritically—and in our view so mistakenly—upon the recollections of Lord Shepherd[11] of the debates on the 1965 Murder Abolition of Death Penalty) Bill.[12] Lord Shepherd, who had been the Government Chief Whip in the Lords at the time, first made these recollections public in 1995. The occasion was the debate on an amendment[13] that had been put down by Lord Ackner to the Criminal Appeal Bill then before the House. The distinct impression he gave, and which was subsequently to be accepted as credible evidence by the Commons Select Committee later in the year, was that a 'deal' was done between abolitionists and retentionists, in which the 'price' of abolition was the retention of the mandatory penalty.

Reading the speech of Lord Campbell of Alloway, and particularly the intervention of Lord Shepherd, it is possible to discern the way in which the myth of the compact concerning the mandatory penalty began to assume the shape in which it is still, almost a decade later, presented by the opponents of reform. Lord Campbell, who in the debate went on record as being abolitionist with regard to the mandatory penalty, stated:

---

[9] Sir Ivan Lawrence, QC, MP.
[10] The Baroness Scotland of Asthal, QC.
[11] Malcolm Newton Shepherd PC, 2nd Baron Shepherd of Spalding (1918–2001)
[12] Hansard HL, 26 June 1995, Col 536.
[13] The amendment (which was rejected) would have provided for appeal against a judicial recommendation made under s 1 (2) of the 1965 Act.

It is claimed that the disparity between the respective sentencing regimes—the manda-tory and discretionary life sentences—is unjustifiable, illogical and anomalous. Such is not the case. Such disparity was part and parcel of a deal reflected in Section 1 (2) of the 1965 Act and but for which this Bill would not have passed this House. Such dis-parity was in continuance of the concept that the unique gravity of murder demanded a sentence disparate from other offences to mark the gravity of the offence.

As to the compromise which enabled the Bill to pass, to which I referred at Committee stage, my understanding is based on the information given to me by the noble Lord, Lord Shepherd. . who, as Government Chief Whip, was present when the deal was made. He will correct me if I am wrong, but I believe it was founded on the concept of unique gravity which demanded a disparate sentencing regime to mark the gravity of the offence, and that recommendations from the judiciary could be made as to the minimum term to be served before release for the consideration of the Home Secretary in the exercise of his unfettered discretion as to the date of release. I hope I have that right.[14]

The existence or otherwise of any 'deal' apart, it is beyond dispute that by s1 (1) of the Murder (Abolition of Death Penalty) Act 1965 penalty of death was substituted by the mandatory penalty of life imprisonment. It did no more, and no less. When, however, we come to examine in detail the content of Lord Shepherd's intervention, immediately following at that point, the opacity of its meaning appears to increase in proportion the closeness of the scrutiny to which it is subjected. In the light of its importance, we reproduce it in its entirety.

My Lords, the noble Lord is right in one respect. However, I do not believe, when the deal was done as he said, that any of those other matters applied in any of the minds of those involved in the discussions.

As it has been raised, the House may think it helpful for me to explain. As your Lordships know, it was a Private Member's Bill and the government of the day has no role in the way in which Private Members' Bills are taken through this House. There were splits in all the parties. There was a vote in the House of Commons with Conservatives, Labour Members and Liberals voting together both in support and against the Bill. The situation was similar in this Chamber.

It was at the end when there was a real risk that the bill could be lost—it related to the anxiety that a life sentence would not be severe enough, that it would not be long enough in terms of a prisoner who had committed a specifically vile sort of crime—that a deal was reached between he opponents and proposers of the Bill. The only part that the Government played in that matter was to provide the amendment to meet the wishes of both parties. Therefore, it was not a political deal. We provided services only and never considered the ramifications of what was being proposed.[15]

As to the statement that this was a Private Member's Bill and the Government had no role in the determining the way in which it went through the House, this is true, inasmuch as this was not *officially* a Government Bill which in the

---

[14] Hansard, HL,vol 565, col 535.
[15] *Ibid*, cols 535–36.

normal course of events would be introduced by a Minister and in due time voted upon under the scrutiny of the Whips. The sponsor of the Bill in the Commons had been a Private Member, Sidney Silverman[16] but finding a sponsor in the Lords was not initially straightforward. The Gardiner papers contain a letter dated 27 July 1965 from the Archbishop of Canterbury, Michael Ramsey, to Gerald Gardiner indicating that he had been approached to introduce the Bill in the Upper House, but expressing substantial doubts as to his competence to do so, not least his lack of experience in guiding a Bill through its various stages. It is clear from the letter that he had been in conversation both with Sydney Silverman and also the Earl of Longford (a Government Minister closely associated with the penal reform movement)[17] on the subject. In the event, the Bill was introduced into the Lords by a life peer, the Baroness Wootton of Abinger.

Though Silverman's conversation with Longford is scarcely surprising, it is curious that Ramsey, who was not in the penal reform 'loop', should have thought it proper to write to Gardiner if this were indeed a Bill in which the Government stand was one of neutrality as Lord Shepherd would seem to have had us believe in 1995, benign only insofar as;

> We provided services only and never considered the ramifications of what was proposed.

The Gardiner archive contains material that suggests otherwise. Gardiner's commitment to the cause of abolition was well known and his enthusiasm for wide ranging law reform, like that of Elwyn Jones, was a matter of common knowledge. In the archive we found a list, compiled presumably for, or by him in November 1964, of all the Members in the Commons, grouped by Party, with an indication of their stance on abolition. More significantly, there is correspondence at this time between Gardiner and Silverman on the subject of the introduction of an abolition Bill and its scope. The tenor of this correspondence suggests something rather more than a 'provision of services'. Indeed, when Lord Shepherd's contended that it was a Private Member's Bill in which the Government had no role, he would seem to have forgotten that although it had undoubtedly been introduced in the Commons by Sydney Silverman and not a Government Minister, it had nevertheless been included in the list of forthcoming Bills in the Queen's Speech for the Session 1964–5.

---

[16] Silverman had been at the forefront of the campaign to abolish capital punishment and had played a major part in the attempt to include abolition in the Criminal Justice Bill of 1948.

[17] In 1963, shortly before the election of the Labour administration of 1964, Frank Longford had been appointed by Harold Wilson to chair a study group on criminal justice which included Gardiner (who became Lord Chancellor), Elwyn Jones (who became Attorney General), and Alice Bacon (who became a Minister of State at the Home Office) as well as a number of other experts. See Terence Morris, *Crime and Criminal Justice since 1945* (Oxford, Basil Blackwell, 1989). In 1964–65 Longford was in the government as Secretary of State for the Colonies and afterwards became Leader of the House of Lords.

The papers, many of which consist of handwritten personal letters, reveal that in November 1964 there were exchanges between Gardiner and the Scottish Secretary, William Ross, and Sir Frank Soskice, the Home Secretary, on the subject of the defence of diminished responsibility[18] to a murder charge. Gardiner's view, expressed in a letter to Soskice (who had also been in correspondence with his opposite number in Scotland) dated 16 November 1964, was that he wanted rid of this provision from the 1957 Homicide Act, and that if it were not abolished, then it ought to be applied to all crimes. The correspondence contains a revealing phrase:

> We are not so much concerned with the merits of the proposals as for the smooth passage of the Bill.[19]

indicating that already Gardiner's anxieties that nothing should impede the implementation of abolition were among his urgent concerns. There is also a copy of a letter dated 14 December 1964 from Sir Frank Soskice to the Lord Chief Justice, Lord Parker of Waddington objecting, among other things to the idea of the court being empowered to specify the minimum term to be served in the case of a life sentence. We can be certain, therefore, of two things: that in late 1964 there was a degree of anxiety in the abolitionist camp concerning the safe passage of the Bill and the roles of the judiciary and the executive in relation to whatever sentence should take the place of death were already under discussion. Clearly, a great deal was going on.

Lord Shepherd was, of course, strictly correct when he maintained in 1995 that the Bill was not a Government Bill. What all the evidence from the Gardiner papers indicates is that a number of Government ministers, including the Home Secretary and the Law Officers, who had a direct interest in the outcome were very closely involved in the comings and goings behind the scenes. Nor was that interest noticeably neutral. In the penumbra of supporters around the Wilson government, which was perceived as a radical administration that would become an engine of social and legal reform, support for the abolition of the death penalty was at the very epicentre of concern. The notion that the Government

> . . . provided services only . . .

must, therefore, be treated with some scepticism, given the often agitated correspondence going in and out of the Lord Chancellor's office, but, ironically, Lord Shepherd is only too correct in the concluding part of his intervention when he recalls that

> (We) . . . never considered the ramifications of what was being proposed.

---

[18] Introduced by s 2 of the Homicide Act 1957.
[19] Gardiner Papers, 56461 A Volume VII Pt 1.

With a brevity that is almost epigrammatic, those ten words identify the Achilles heel of the campaign against the death penalty that was mounted with such apparent success in the second half of the 1960s. By paying so little heed to the inherent danger of accepting the simplistic substitution of the mandatory life sentence for the brutal penalty of hanging, that failure to look beyond the immediate situation to what the future might portend, has made possible, unwittingly, a return to a punitive approach to the penalty for murder. It is now the case that, for a growing number of those guilty of what the law still defines as murder, the penalty is not simply 'life' but 'life until death'. From the Home Affairs Committee in 1995 down to the participants in the debate in the House of Lords on an amendment to the Criminal Justice Bill in 2003[20] on 14 October 2003, Lord Shepherd's recollections have, explicitly or implicitly, been regarded as an unimpeachable authority on the existence of the 'pact'. Could Lord Shepherd have been the victim of his own imperfect recollection? Given the lapse of 30 years it must surely be a possibility that cannot be entirely discounted. There are few left among those who were at the heart of the action who could, from their own memories, corroborate or contradict the Shepherd testimony.

Effectively, therefore, in the absence of oral evidence, we are driven to rely upon the written source material. It can, of course, be objected that the printed material of the Parliamentary debates is imperfect; in public places speakers are given to being careful as to what they say, though a lack of clarity of meaning can at times conceal what is going on informally. But it is also the case that in the printed material the various proposals and the evaluation of them are publicly presented. It is when we come to the private material of letters and memoranda,[21] in handwriting that gives an impression of both immediacy and authenticity, that we can approach closer to the events of 1964–65. Though more formal in style, they are the rapidly exchanged emails of their day.

HALF A COLUMN OF HANSARD ON A SUMMER AFTERNOON

The comparatively brief passages of debate in the context of Lord Ackner's amendment to the Criminal Appeal Bill on 26 June 1995 have been of immense importance in informing the views of those who wish to maintain the mandatory character of the life sentence for murder. Yet close examination of what was said, initially by Lord Campbell and subsequently by Lord Shepherd,

---

[20] Moved by Lord Lloyd of Berwick to amend s 1(1) of the Murder (Abolition of the death penalty) Act 1965 to substitute the word 'liable' for the word 'sentenced'. That is, a person convicted of murder shall be *liable* to imprisonment for life.

[21] In his autobiography, published when he was 93, Lord Shawcross recalls some fascinating background material from 1948 (when as Sir Hartley Shawcross he was Attorney-General) contrasting the debates about abolition with the issues raised in the Lords in 1995: *Life Sentence*, (London, Constable & Co, 1995) 167–70. His frank—and at times amusing—account sheds considerable light on events of the time which can be cross-referenced from printed sources.

reveals that clarity was not always in evidence. Lord Campbell began by referring to the disparity between mandatory and discretionary life sentences and
went on to say:

> Such disparity was part and parcel of a deal reflected in Section 1 (2) of the 1965 Act
> and but for which this Bill would not have passed this House. Such disparity was in
> continuance of the concept that the unique gravity of murder demanded a sentence
> disparate from other offences to mark the gravity of the offence.

Section 1 (2) of the 1965 Act was concerned with the provision whereby the trial
judge could, having sentenced a defendant to life imprisonment for murder,
make a recommendation as to the minimum term to be served before release on
licence should be considered. It is by no means clear how this section, section 1
(2) could be a reflection of the 'deal' when the deal was supposed to be a straight
exchange between the abolition of capital punishment on the one hand and the
imposition of the mandatory life sentence on the other, provided for by section
(1) The provision for a minimum judicial recommendation had no bearing on
the mandatory character of the sentence for murder.

When Lord Shepherd intervened, re-affirming the information he had apparently given to Lord Campbell on a previous occasion about the existence of a
'deal', he went on to say, in his second sentence:

> I do not believe, when the deal was done as he said, that any of those other matters
> applied in any of the minds of those involved in the discussions.

Those 'other matters' must surely refer to the distinction between the discretionary and mandatory life sentences; if not, it is difficult to guess what else he
had in mind.

When he goes on to say that,

> It was at the end when there was a real risk that the Bill could be lost—it related to the
> anxiety that a life sentence would not be severe enough, that it would not be long
> enough in terms of a prisoner who had committed a specifically vile sort of crime that
> a deal was reached between the opponents and proposers of the Bill.

this is only part of the story. The fact of the matter is, as we know from the
Gardiner papers, that, given the contentiousness of the issue in both Parliament
and the country, anxieties were running high more than six months before the
debates in the Lords of July 1965 and there was already another, separate issue,
reflected in correspondence between the Home Secretary and the Lord Chief
Justice about what judicial input there might be in the determination of releases
on licence. The strong impression we gathered from reading the exchanges of
1964–5 is that the view, in both the Home Office and the Lord Chancellor's
Department, was that it should be a close to zero as could be arranged. As we
shall show when we come to discussing the events of the summer of 1965 the
anxiety at that stage derived from two, interconnected things. On the one hand,
Lord Parker had put down two amendments, the first of which had been carried
by two votes, which would have given the judges discretionary sentencing

powers in respect of murder. On the other was the fact that the Summer recess loomed uncomfortably close. Parker's amendments, never mind the intrinsic objections that might be made to them, could well have the effect of impeding the smooth passage of the Bill. If it were not safely through the Lords by time the House rose and headed back to the Commons, who could say what delays might arise in the new Session, never mind what potentially fatal pitfalls it might encounter.

Could Lord Shepherd have been the victim of his own imperfect recollection? It is certainly a possibility, given the elapse of time. When we examined the Gardiner papers we checked carefully to establish the nature of his involvement in the comings and goings behind the scenes as the Bill was on passage through the Lords.

Contained in the papers[22] are letters from Shepherd to Gardiner dated 29 July 1965 and from Gardiner to Lord Stonham, the Joint Parliamentary Under Secretary of State at the Home Office, dated 30 July, drawing the latter's attention to Shepherd's letter of the previous day. Gardiner's papers deal not only with the passage of the Bill in 1965, but also with its final stage by which abolition became permanent in 1969. These include drafts and amendments to the 1965 Bill and the speaking notes that he used in the course of the Parliamentary debate. In all this substantial body of material these two brief letters are the only instances in which Lord Shepherd's name occurs. As Chief Whip in the Lords, one would have expected him to be close to the management of those issues in which important figures such as the Lord Chancellor, the Home Secretary and the Attorney General had a close interest. The fact that Shepherd's name appears only twice, and then only at the end of July 1965, does not appear to us to be persuasive evidence that Shepherd was as closely involved as a generation later it is accepted that he was. This does not, of course, preclude the possibility that they may have spoken on the topic, but the tenor of the correspondence between Gardiner and other members of the Government indicates that the conventional practice was to exchange a great deal in the form of handwritten memoranda in a very short period of time, rather in the way that nowadays emails go back and forth within the hour. Given the gravity of any *quid pro quo* on the subject of the mandatory penalty becoming, as it were, the 'real and valuable consideration' necessary to complete the 'contract' that would ensure abolition, it seems inconceivable that there is not the least hint of it in the papers.

What the Gardiner note to Stonham does, however, make clear, is that there was a serious issue arising from the amendment tabled by the Lord Chief Justice, Lord Parker of Waddington, which was designed to give the judges the power to impose discretionary life sentences for murder. This had been carried by a margin of only two votes, but Parker was subsequently to withdraw it, for reasons we shall discuss later. The issue, however, was not focused on any 'deal', whereby abolition would be bought by a guarantee of the mandatory life

---

[22] Above note 19.

sentence, but ranged about a more diffuse anxiety that it would generate the kind of discussion that could have the eventual effect of killing the Bill. Perhaps more importantly, it would not have escaped Gardiner's mind that the Parliamentary session was drawing towards the close of the Summer recess.

If Shepherd was indeed mistaken in his recollection of what happened 30 years before, and the evidence would suggest that he was, then how did this come about? We suggest that it did so in the following way.

The Parker amendments, the first of which was so narrowly carried, and would have given the judges discretion in sentencing, caused alarm in the abolitionist camp. In any event, Gardiner was hostile to the idea in principle, for reasons which we shall discuss shortly, in the course of our account of the 1965 debates. The second amendment provided for the judicial recommendation as to the minimum term to be served; thereafter release would be at the discretion of the Home Secretary, there being at the time no Parole Board. It was this resolution of a difficulty, a potential impediment to the Bill's subsequent smooth passage through the remainder of its Parliamentary stages, regarding the provision of judicial input to the management of mandatory sentence while preserving the long established role of the Home Secretary in such matters that is surely the source of the myth of the 'compact'. It had nothing whatever to do with abolition *per se* being conditional on the provision of the mandatory sentence in section 1 (1).

THIRTY YEARS ON: THE COMMONS DELIBERATE

By the mid-1980s the climate of penal policy was undergoing a profound change. The broad political ideology that was enshrined in Reaganite policies in America and reflected in those of Thatcherite Britain had revived old anxieties about crime and generated new popular demands for authoritarian remedies. One consequence of the introduction in 1983 of the Brittan guidelines on the tariffs for mandatory lifers was a stimulus to litigation on the part of prisoners. Between December 1984 and March 1995[23] there were no fewer than 14 actions involving 20 prisoners seeking relief in the domestic courts. In the same period there were five cases involving six prisoners who sought relief elsewhere, four before the European Commission of Human Rights and one in the European Court of Human Rights. In this period the numbers of prisoners seeking relief from various actions on the part of the Home Secretary in relation to their release on licence accelerated. The issue of the mandatory life sentence began to assume a prominence that was matched by a growing political sensitivity on the part of Home Office Ministers, not least as the judges were perceived as being no longer the compliant legitimators of the *status quo* determined by those in

[23] Full details of each of these cases appear in the appendices of minutes of evidence taken by the Home Affairs Committee and are published in the *First Report* in December 1995.

political power, but, when occasion demanded, the independent intellectual critics of ministerial actions.

In turn, successive incumbents of the office appeared to rely upon the argument that the implementation of policy needed to accord with the responsibility of the Government, both to maintain public confidence in the administration of the criminal justice system, and to be accountable to Parliament. Thus on 4 August 1995, the then Home Secretary, Mr Michael Howard QC, wrote to the Chairman of the Home Affairs Committee (Sir Ivan Lawrence QC), amplifying his earlier evidence of 29 March.

> While the Court of Appeal or the Lord Chief Justice could of course issue guidelines of their own [in relation to tariffs] these would not be binding on judges—and unlike the Home Secretary of the day, the judiciary are certainly not accountable to Parliament for whatever guidance they formulate.

As befitting a careful lawyer, Mr Howard was perfectly correct in suggesting that any such guidelines would not be binding on any individual judge, and in reminding the Committee that while the Home Secretary is accountable to Parliament, the judges are not, he was right to observe, constitutionally flawless. It is when he goes on, in reference to the executive determination of tariffs, to say,

> Under the present arrangements, these important decisions are taken by the Home Secretary of the day, who is accountable to Parliament and democratically responsible for maintaining public confidence in the criminal justice system. In my view the "Brittan guidelines" provide an important safeguard, and I believe there would be considerable public concern and disquiet if that safeguard was lost. I would invite the Committee to consider this further reason for retaining the mandatory sentence for murder.[24]

that we discern at this point in 1995, more clearly perhaps than hitherto, the drift of thinking on the part of politicians in relation to what has been throughout our modern history, one of the central elements in constitutional affairs. Politicians, holding themselves to be the guardians of democracy, can be tempted in their perception to conflate public confidence with the expression of the public will. But when the democratic process is reduced to little more than the implementation of populist demands it is not always the case that the resulting policies are those of the greatest utility, never mind whether they meet the minimal requirements of justice. What, then, ought to be the proper balance between the provision of penalties for crime in statutes that emerge from the legislative process and the imposition of sentences on convicted offenders? The independence of the judiciary is a long established safeguard of the liberties of individual citizens against the actions of those in power. The purpose of judicial review is to establish whether or not a Minister or other public authority has

---

[24] Full details of each of these cases appear in the appendices of minutes of evidence taken by the Home Affairs Committee and are published in the *First Report* in December 1995.

acted in a way that is outwith the authority granted to him. It is concerned less with the substantive issue, than with whether the minister or public authority acts with procedural regularity and legally. Thus in the case of *Findlay and Others* in 1984, the first challenge of the Brittan guidelines, the relief sought was the quashing of the policy. It was clear that, within the composition of the court, there were those who could understand that the appellants felt aggrieved that the policy was less than fair to them; but that was not the issue. The issue was whether, in acting as he did; the Home Secretary had exceeded the powers he was entitled to exercise by authority of Parliament.

What almost every Home Secretary and Home Office minister from Michael Howard onwards has done, is to argue that any profound change in the nature of the penalty for murder would undermine public confidence. However, we have no satisfactory definition of what constitutes public confidence. Nor do we have any way of knowing whether any politician in office has ever hesitated before implementing some change, speculating upon the possible consequences of public unpopularity.

When the Home Affairs Committee began its deliberations towards the end of almost 20 years of unbroken Conservative rule, it did so against a background of popular concern about crime in general and some disquiet in political circles about what seemed to be the adoption of an increasingly critical stance with regard to ministerial powers on the part of the judges. The mandatory life sentence, and ministerial control over its administration seemed to serve as a symbol of a relationship that was becoming increasingly uneasy. The Committee was charged with an important task, and it is understandable that it should seek to identify a benchmark for its deliberations.

As a guide to the complex events of July 1965 from which abolition was to emerge, the passages from Columns 535 and 536 of the record in Hansard of what transpired in the Lords on the afternoon of 26 June 1995, were shortly to be regarded by the Home Affairs Committee in their deliberations on the mandatory penalty in the manner of navigators reliant upon an Admiralty Pilots' Guide, additionally possessed of its latest monthly corrections. In our view, it was no such thing, not so much the equivalent of a hydrological authority out of date as an *ignis fatuus* leading to error highly damaging to, and, in the last analysis, effectively fatal to their arguments.

If the comparatively brief passages in the Lords had been characterised by a lack of clarity, nor was all of what the Home Affairs had to report completely clear as to its meaning. Paragraph 54 of the First Report is central to understanding the Committee's position on the mandatory penalty, and we reproduce it in full.[25]

> It is sometimes argued that it was to a certain extent part of the consensus which led to a political majority for the abolition of the death penalty, that it should be replaced

---

[25] Passages in italics are the emphases of the present authors; those in bold type are those of the Report as published.

with a penalty which would be of a severity to mark the seriousness with which the crime was viewed, and that the life sentence was the only sentence which could do this.[26]

Consequently, it may be said that *to abandon the mandatory life sentence would betray those who voted against the death penalty in 1965 and 1969*, as well as those who vote against its re-introduction on the understanding that the life sentence for murder will continue to be mandatory. One witness[27] accepted that this was true in certain cases but queried whether substitution of a maximum life sentence for murder would in fact provoke a significant number of former opponents of the death penalty to vote in future for its restoration. *We recognise that as a sentence of life imprisonment does not mean and has never necessarily meant imprisonment for life*, such a pact was never enforced; we also recognise that the retention of a unique punishment for murder has not necessarily succeeded in deterring would-be murderers. Nevertheless, there is no doubt that to abolish the mandatory life sentence for murder would risk sending a signal to the public at large that causing the death of another person was in some way less seriously regarded than previously. **We would not wish the abolition of the mandatory life sentence for murder to suggest that there was any downgrading in the severity with which society views the crime of murder.** (Original emphasis)

The first sentence refers to the 'pact' as recalled by Lord Shepherd. Why the Committee should have chosen to say 'It is sometimes argued', when not only was it confidently argued and the argument went unchallenged, is puzzling. Were there some members who doubted the accuracy of the 'Shepherd Recollection'? But it is when we turn to the statement that 'such a pact was never enforced' (on account of the fact that life imprisonment does not mean and has never necessarily meant imprisonment for life) that meaning becomes elusive. A pact, in this context would have been a political agreement, having as its object a consensual resolution of an otherwise protracted dispute; it could never have been enforceable since it was not a justiciable contract. By what device or procedure, then, would enforcement have been possible? Any idea of there arising a potential cause for judicial review must surely be fanciful. If there was indeed any 'pact' it could only be founded in what has later been identified as 'faith'.[28] The reader is left with the impression that the Committee had, in its collective thoughts, somehow amplified the status of the alleged 'pact' but had not considered what were the implications of their own assertions. The pact allegedly encompassed the acquiescence of those in favour of retaining the death penalty to the abolition Bill, in return for an undertaking that the penalty for murder would be the mandatory imposition of life imprisonment. It had nothing to do with whether or not life imprisonment meant imprisonment for life; only that murder should be recognised as a uniquely heinous offence by the imposition of the most severe penalty available.

---

[26] At this point the Committee cites Lord Shepherd's recollections in the Lords on 26 June 1995.

[27] Mr Paul Cavadino, a witness for the Penal Affairs Consortium, Q 209.

[28] The Baroness Scotland of Asthal on 14 October 2003 in the debate on the Criminal Justice Bill, Hansard HL, Vol 653 No 149, at Col 837.

It is in the final sentence of Paragraph 54, printed in bold type, that contains the Committee's most significant conclusion; the equation of the abolition of the mandatory sentence with a suggestion that it would constitute a suggestion of a 'downgrading'; in the severity with which society views the crime of murder. No signal would be sent to the public that would precipitate a lack of confidence in the administration of criminal justice. Perhaps more significantly, the Committee's signal could be interpreted in another way, with which not only Michael Howard but also his successors, Jack Straw and David Blunkett would prove to be in perfect accord, namely; that as far as the mandatory sentence was concerned 'this correspondence was now closed'[29]. As to the role of the Home Secretary in determining the tariff, that battle was one in which the cause of the executive was doomed, and in 2003 the decision in *Anderson*[30] brought to an end that particular exercise of executive power.

---

[29] *See* Annex 6.
[30] [2003] 1 AC 837. Exceptionally, seven Law Lords sat on the appeal.

7

On the Dealing Floor of the Lords: Rewind to 1965

————◆————

> I cannot see why . . . the powers of a judge should be different just because
> the conviction is one of murder. If capital punishment is abolished, I think
> a judge should have the power to pass a determinate sentence if he thinks
> that is right.

Who, among the reforming spirits of 1965, their radical approach to law reform
emboldened by the social climate of the day, could have entertained such a
thought, given public utterance in the House of Lords in the course of the
debates on the Murder (Abolition of Death Penalty) Bill? Given everything that
has been subsequently averred and regurgitated on the subject of the 'deal'—
abolition, but only in return for the mandatory life sentence—such a *credo*
would, no doubt, have received short shrift in the last decade in both the press
and the Westminster village.

The identity of the speaker may well come as a surprise to many and be the
source of baffling disappointment to perhaps some others, for the speaker was
none other than the formidable Viscount Dilhorne, the immediately preceding
Conservative Lord Chancellor and earlier, holder of the office of Attorney
General. Sir Reginald Manningham-Buller, QC had long practised at the criminal Bar. More importantly, as a law officer in the Macmillan administration, he
had played a critical part in the reform of the law of murder, which was embodied in the Homicide Act 1957.[1] That Act, as we have indicated earlier, could be
most generously interpreted as a fundamentally flawed attempt to limit the
extent of capital punishment. Professor Sir Leon Radzinowicz, a member of the
Royal Commission on Capital Punishment, recalling it some 40 years later was
to write:

> Sir Reginald Manningham–Buller, the Attorney General and Viscount Kilmuir, the
> Lord Chancellor (formerly Sir David Maxwell Fyfe) took charge of [the Bill]. I had no
> hesitation then, nor do I hesitate now, to endorse the characterisation of the Bill by the

---

[1] Some lawyers could not resist the quip of referring to it as the 'Reggie-cide Act' (itself a pun on
the Regicide Act of Charles II which provided for the trial and capital punishment of those who had
been his father's judges in 1649).

Archbishop of York and the Bishop of Chester as 'morally shocking'. But I would supplement it by saying that to moral shabbiness the epitaph of professional incompetence should be added.[2]

If its critics had identified it as a botched work at the time, by 1965 all the deficiencies of the 1957 Act were embarrassingly transparent, even to the firmest adherent of capital punishment. It says much about Dilhorne's intellectual and jurisprudential integrity that he recognised, and acknowledged with such clarity,[3] that the proper direction of reform ought to be inclusive of judicial discretion.

He could in no sense be identified with the reformist zeal, so prominent at the time. But that he held to his new view, is indicative of the extent to which the man of law, experienced in its time honoured practices and ways of thinking, could draw upon the pragmatism that characterised the successful man of politics. Recognising that the pressures for reform were irresistible, he had shifted his stance on capital punishment in 1957 and by 1965 was persuaded that movement on judicial discretion in sentencing was the appropriate course, now that the 'doomed ship', as Leon Radzinowicz had described the 1957 Act, was about to founder and capital punishment to disappear with it.

Dilhorne's comments have another significance, which, to the best of our understanding has remained unrecognised by those who either promote or accept the notion of the 'pact'. Had such a proposal been at issue, it seems inconceivable that he would not have expressed a view on it in the same forceful terms. Yet the myth seems almost ineradicable and as recently as 2002 the Court of Appeal (Criminal Division) interpreted s 1(2) of the 1965 Act as follows:

> The provision in Section 1 (2) was made . . . in order to assuage public concern about the possible release date of those convicted of murder who would probably have been sentenced to death.[4]

The Parliamentary debates indicate that section 1(2) came about as a consequence of the Parker amendments; a very different source. One is tempted to speculate upon the meaning of the words in *Mason and Sellars*;

> . . . would *probably* [our italics] have been sentenced to death.

As far as the death sentence for those convicted of murder was concerned, before 1957 it was characterised not by probability, but by absolute certainty. There was no other sentence available to the court. Likewise, between 1957 and 1965 for those convicted of capital murder, there was the same certainty attaching to the pronouncement of the death penalty. It was the mandatory penalty for capital murder; no other sentence was available. In contrast, for non-capital

---

[2] Leon Radzinowicz. *Adventures in Criminology* (London and New York, Routledge, 1999) at 271.

[3] See p 116 below, *passim*. During the 1965 debate.

[4] Lord Justice Clarke giving judgment in *Mason* and *Sellars* [2002] 2 Cr App Rep 497 at 500–01.

murder, the death sentence was statutorily unavailable. One can only assume that the phrase should really have been formulated not as 'probably sentenced to death', but rather as 'probably executed'.

Had the climate of social thought not changed in the decade of the 1970s, towards an altogether harsher and less tolerant approach to the ways in which society dealt with all its offenders, there might now be a substantial body of case-law and sentencing practice enabling the courts to deal equitably with offenders convicted of a whole range of homicidal offences. As a despairing 'nothing works' approach degenerated into various expressions of enthusiasm for what became known as 'social incapacitation', so the public clamour for more repressive legislation against crime and more overtly punitive sentencing, increased in volume. The political responses to the clamour resulted in a competitive approach to what became known as 'law and order'.[5] Every political party became sensitised to the need to be seen by the electorate as having 'robust' and 'realistic' policies in relation to crime. This was the time of the discovery of The Victim whose claims were to be seen as paramount in contrast to the offender's right to just and humane treatment. Not, that in reality, all victims came to clamour for a negative approach to penal policy and it is a characteristic of many articulate victims that they express a desire for restorative rather than retributive justice.

Perhaps nowhere was penal reform more effectively put into reverse than in respect of mandatory life sentence prisoners. Those whose offences were the most grave could be readily identified as those with minimal, or even non-existent desert. Myra Hindley, throughout her more than 30 years in prison was first regarded as the probably redeemable follower of her co-defendant Brady,[6] then reviled and ultimately demonised as the archetype of feminine wickedness. In the nearly 40 years that has elapsed since the 1965 Act, a generation of politicians have grown up, for whom the period is utterly remote. It is not merely that the passage of the years has removed many of those active at the time; the seismic shift in the approach to penal policy that occurred in the late 1970s has acted like some impermeable membrane constricting the possibilities for ideological continuity. Among those now on the political stage it is likely that there are some for whom the possibility of moderating the presently mechanistic arrangement for sentencing of homicidal offenders, certainly in any way which could be construed as lenient, is perceived as little better than a form of electoral suicide. The period of great reform is now far distant and its progressive penal philosophy perceived as irrelevant, politically controversial, and thereby potentially disastrous. The mandatory penalty cannot, it is argued, be abolished.

Stated in sum, the past is history. All that the contemporary world needs to know about the 1965 Act is that it abolished capital punishment in return for the mandatory penalty. Lord Shepherd said so; and he was there.

---

[5] It is a comment on our times that so few, if any, commentators have reflected upon the philosophical and not least the jurisprudential issues arising from this slick conjunction of concepts.

[6] A view certainly taken by the trial judge, Mr Justice Moreland.

JUST BEFORE THE DAWN

We have discussed in an earlier chapter[7] some part of the history of abolition in England, though most of that consisted of various attempts to limit the extent of capital punishment by means of categorising murders by means of which that end might be achieved. None succeeded in being either practical or intellectually convincing, and nothing of any consequence happened until the passing of the Homicide Act 1957.

Before 1957 the penalty was remarkably uncomplicated. On conviction for murder a defendant over the age of 18 was subject to a single mandatory penalty, that of death, no matter what the circumstances of the criminal event. Any mitigation of the penalty was achieved by an ancient device known as the Royal Prerogative of Mercy, originally exercised by the sovereign as an act of grace, and, after 1837,[8] by the Secretary of State for the Home Department acting on the sovereign's behalf, after reflecting upon any representations made to him by interested parties and consulting with the trial judge. The exercise of the prerogative was a crude and often erratically deployed device which saved from the gallows many—but by no means all—of those whose mental state had failed the so-called 'M'Naghten test' of insanity and some—though again, by no means all—of those whose hanging would, on account of their age or physical infirmity,[9] have offended public susceptibility. Additionally, there were those convicted of murder in which the circumstances of the particular criminal event disclosed considerable mitigation or uncertainty, however the jury may have found or the trial judge expressed his own view of the matter. As a device for

---

[7] Chapter 2.

[8] This constitutional change arose from the avuncular concerns of the Prime Minister of the day, Lord Melbourne, for the supposed sensitivies of his newly ascended Queen, the 17 year old Victoria. Hitherto, decisions about the exercise of the Royal Prerogative had been made in by the sovereign in the Privy Council. George IV had gone against ministerial advice on at least one occasion in granting mercy. Melbourne, who was immensely protective of the young queen, thought the subject altogether unfitting for her consideration. In more recent times it is known that individual Home Secretaries approached the task with a great sense of the awesome moral responsibility laid upon them. RA (later Lord) Butler would apparently immure himself in the case papers of condemned prisoners, to the exclusion of other Home Office business for up to two days when considering a reprieve. *See* Anthony Howard, *RAB: The Life of R A Butler* (London, Jonathan Cape, 1987) at 253–4. In the 1930s Sir John Simon had written above the permanently framed card that was placed on his desk listing the names of those awaiting execution a line from Juvenal: *Nulla unquam de mortis hominis cunctatio longa est.* (You can never hesitate too long before deciding that a man must die.)

[9] In March 1958 Mrs Mary Wilson was convicted of the murders *seriatim* of her second and third husbands, each of whom had died within a few days of the wedding and in whose bodies were found traces of phosphorous (a common ingredient of rat poison). Aged 66, she was sentenced to death for capital murder, but reprieved. She died in Holloway prison in January 1963, aged 71. In December 1954 Mrs Styllou Christofi, an illiterate Greek Cypriot (who may have had mental health problems in the past) was hanged for the murder of her daughter-in-law whose body she subsequently burned in the back garden. She was aged 53. She had been acquitted of the murder of her mother-in-law when she was 25, the killing having equally bizarre features involving fire.

maintaining public confidence that the administration of the criminal law, while firm, was not devoid of common humanity, it was a device with considerable merit. By the end of the nineteenth century, its procedures had become well established and while acknowledging its imperfections, there is little to suggest that it was other than a humane backstop to capital punishment. Those reprieved were normally sentenced to penal servitude for life,[10] the successor to transportation for life.[11] As a distinctively spartan prison regime, penal servitude with 'hard labour' had largely fallen into desuetude by the early 1930s and was eventually abolished by the Criminal Justice Act 1948.

After 1957, the law of murder became complicated by the innovatory distinction between capital and non-capital murder, the introduction of the new defence of diminished responsibility, the extension of provocation to include provocation by words, and new provisions for dealing with the survivors of the suicide pacts. The sentences available to the court remained limited and largely inflexible, consisting of death in the case of capital murder and mandatory life where the conviction had been one of non-capital murder. Only in respect of convictions for manslaughter consequent upon the new defences introduced by the Act did the court have any significant latitude with regard to sentence.

Until 1957 the role of both the trial judge and the Home Secretary had been very limited. The numbers of those reprieved were not large since the cases generated by the Prerogative tended to be limited to those which manifested the most extenuating circumstances, frequently falling into that class of domestic killings in which there was neither a significant history of other criminal activity. In contrast, those offenders whose cause excited little public sympathy, tended to end their lives on the gallows.[12]

THE DAY OF ABOLITION COMES: OR THE HANGMAN'S P45
(HAD HE NOT BEEN AN INDEPENDENT CONTRACTOR)

The Homicide Act 1957, in distinguishing between capital and non-capital murders, did little to facilitate the task of the Home Secretary in recommending

---

[10] Perhaps the most notable exception being that of Dudley and Stephens convicted in 1884 of the murder of the cabin boy following the wreck of the ocean-going yacht *Mignonette*. Reprieved, they were sentenced to six months imprisonment. See: AWB Simpson, *Cannibalism and the Common Law: The Story of the Tragic Last Voyage of the Mignonette and the Strange Legal Proceedings to which it Gave Rise* (London and Chicago, University of Chicago Press, 1984) at 240 *et seq.*

[11] Whether such a penalty should have been regarded from the outset as a *discretionary* life sentence, in that it arose from the exercise of that discretion vested constitutionally in the Home Secretary as the Crown's adviser in the context of the Prerogative is an interesting point, but to our knowledge, it remains unargued. If that proposition were to be established in the affirmative, it would have a significant bearing upon the proposition that the life sentence served by murderers even if based on S1 (1) of the 1965 Act is to be regarded as *sui generis*, and distinguishable from other life sentences deriving from Statute.

[12] For a definitive account of the situation before 1957 see Royal Commission on Capital Punishment 1949–53. Cmd 8932 (Commonly known as the *Gowers Report*).

the grant of reprieve by means of the Royal Prerogative. Most of the capital murderers were those who had killed in the course or furtherance of theft and included young and incompetent burglars as well as sophisticated armed robbers. Nor were all those who killed with firearms hardened and professional criminals. The distinction was one against which the Royal Commission had counselled, describing the search for it as 'chimerical'.[13] The distinction between capital and non-capital murders aroused such hearty disapproval among the judiciary that it propelled many judges to support outright abolition. Nor, in any way, did the Act address the establishment of criteria that might be employed by the Home Secretary in deciding upon the appropriate point at which a convicted murderer, whether sentenced to mandatory life or reprieved from the gallows, might be released on licence. The establishment of the Parole Board was to come some ten years after the 1957 Act.

The pressure to amend the law on murder in 1957 had been building steadily over the preceding decade, significantly stimulated by a number of cases in which popular notions of justice and humanity had been substantially violated.[14] It is important to note, however, that the concerns of abolitionists in the post-war era were not with reform of the law of murder *per se*, and certainly not with the more general question of the law of homicide; the focus was extremely narrow. In a not dissimilar fashion, the popular concern had been not with the death penalty, *per se*, but with its infliction in cases in which, for a variety of reasons, it appeared manifestly unreasonable, unjust, or lacking in common pity. It was also with what would today be readily identified as possible miscarriages of justice. Recognition of the fact that the wrong of an unsafe conviction that had taken the defendant to the gallows could never be righted this side of eternity served to extend the support for abolition.

The primary motive of those who supported the Bill to abolish the death penalty in 1965 was to remove it from English Law once and for all and conclude what had been a very long running campaign. A Private Member's Bill brought by Sydney Silverman MP, a veteran of the 1948 attempt at abolition, was backed by the Wilson administration, and the Lord Chancellor, Lord Gardiner, was determined to see it through.[15] Notwithstanding that the question of how the arrangements for the release on licence of a much larger population of life

---

[13] The Royal Commission which had been established to examine ways of restricting the death penalty said: 'We began our inquiry with the determination to make every effort to see whether we could succeed where so many have failed and discover some effective method of classifying murders so as to confine the death penalty to the most heinous . . . We conclude with regret that the object of our quest is chimerical and that it must be abandoned.' Para 534 at 189.

[14] Notably those of Timothy Evans, hanged in 1949, only for it to come to light that John Christie (hanged in 1953) who had been living in the same house had been a serial killer since 1943; Derek Bentley, hanged in 1953 when his 16 year old accomplice, Christopher Craig, who had fired the fatal shot was too young to hang, and Ruth Ellis, hanged in 1955 for the shooting of her lover. For a fuller account of this period *see* Terence Morris, *Crime and Criminal Justice Since 1945*, at 71–88.

[15] As Gerald Gardiner, QC he had been a prominent member of the National Campaign for the Abolition of Capital Punishment founded by Victor Gollancz; *see* Ruth Dudley Edwards, *Victor Gollancz* (London, Big Fat Books, 1989) 632–47.

sentence prisoners were to be managed, and that there were those who considered that the mandatory life sentence would present difficulties, all attempts in the House of Commons to address these matters by way of amendments to the Bill were brushed aside. It was therefore left to the House of Lords to consider the arguments for and against empowering the judiciary to sentence at their discretion, or for the provision of a mandatory sentence, the nature of which would be the subject of the subsequent exercise of discretion by the executive in the person of the Home Secretary.

What abolition was to bring in its train was a serious management problem. When all that limited the death penalty was a reprieve following the exercise of the Prerogative, it was the case that those serving life sentences were predominantly numbered among the least dangerous and often more pitiable of offenders. The perverted, the vicious and the few who were multiple killers went speedily on their way to the gallows. The defences available under the Homicide Act 1957 meant that among those sentenced on a discretionary basis following conviction for manslaughter were some that almost certainly would have hanged, but for the Act. Yet even after 1957, there were few indications, and even fewer criticisms, that the established practice regarding arrangements for release on licence, albeit modified to meet the new situation, was working other than satisfactorily. We know that in the closing months of 1964 both Gardiner and Soskice, the Home Secretary, were opposed to any fundamental change, certainly any in which the judges would have a discretionary power. In particular, Gardiner held that the mandatory sentence offered the greatest degree of flexibility, and that flexibility was the essential quality that should be evident in a sentence for murder.

Some anxiety was expressed in the Commons about the judges being precluded from deciding how long a convicted murderer should stay in prison before release on licence. The Home Secretary proclaimed the official view that this was a matter best left to the Home Secretary. There can be little doubt that his influence on the Commons was considerable in maintaining the discretionary power of his office to determine the time and conditions of release.[16] The Cabinet Minutes for the period indicate clearly that Government support for the Bill was conditional on the exclusion of any possibility of negotiated amendment on this point: it was to be all or nothing.[17]

The Gardiner papers provide evidence that there were two things in the Lord Chancellor's mind as the Bill made its way through the Lords in the summer of 1965. His immediate concern was that nothing should hold matters up, and it seemed as if this might be the outcome if the first of Lord Parker's amendments, providing for judicial discretion in sentencing were to remain. The second was a matter of penal policy. His notes make it clear that he regarded murder as a

[16] Hansard HC Debs Vol 704 Col 930.

[17] That nowhere in the cabinet papers of the period dealing with the Bill is it possible to find any reference to either of the Parker amendments suggests that involvement by Government managers would have been on an entirely informal basis.

'crime apart', almost *sui generis* in that it frequently involved those who had no other connection with criminal activity and was often associated with mental aberration of various kinds. His notes for the Second Reading debate on 19 July include the following:

> I can assure the House that in all types of case where there is any possibility of a danger to society, my Right Honourable and Learned Friend, the Home Secretary does not, and will not release a murderer from prison, even if that means detaining him for a very long period indeed; if necessary, for life.[18]

The element of uncertainty of outcome, which could not be assessed with any degree of confidence or certainty at the time of trial, was one reason why, in arguing against the first Parker amendment that would have provided flexibility in sentencing he maintained that the life sentence was the most flexible of all sentences. Should the offender be sentenced to a fixed term, the Home Secretary would have no power to detain, nor any to recall the prisoner in order to ensure public safety.

As to the second Parker amendment, Gardiner liked it no better. In his view

> . . . most people, and notably the prisoner himself [would regard the minimum term to be served as specified by the trial judge] as equivalent to a determinate sentence.[19]

His notes reveal much more, and in particular his view on the relationship between the judiciary and the executive in relation to the life sentence:

> . . . the Lord Chief Justice may argue that his amendment is constitutionally more appropriate, since it gives to the judiciary and not to the executive, the primary control over the length of an offender's detention. But this is not a matter of rigid principle. Everyone accepts that there are some cases where the courts must impose a life sentence, and the courts have made increasing use in recent years of their power to impose a life sentence for such offences as wounding with intent and rape. All that Parliament would be doing in the bill as at present drafted is to say that in the case of murder this need for an indeterminate sentence is likely to arise so frequently and in cases which cannot be identified at trial that it would be wise to have an indeterminate sentence in every case.[20]

The issues for Gardiner, both political and penal, were essentially pragmatic.

During the Committee stage of the Bill on 27 July, the Lord Chief Justice, Lord Parker of Waddington, had tabled two possible replacements to the mandatory life sentence for which the Bill provided, in the form of two amendments. The first embodied the discretionary life sentence, which had the support of Lord Dilhorne. The second provided for the device of the 'minimum recommendation' that would allow the judge, on passing the mandatory life sentence on the murderer, to recommend the term of years of imprisonment which should be served before consideration of release on licence. At that stage, the

---

[18] Gardiner Papers, 56462 A.
[19] *Ibid.* 56461 B.
[20] *Ibid,* 56461 B.

first amendment succeeded and the second was not even moved. The Government response, expressed by Lord Stonham, was uncompromising:

> Now, since our last vote Parliament has virtually abolished capital punishment for murder, no major difference exists between us except the method of achieving our common objective, namely, to ensure the protection of the public . . . .. Unfortunately, we strongly disagree with the Lord Chief Justice about the means of achieving this objective . . .[21]

Whereas many of the present arguments about the tariff to be served, and the Home Secretary's obligation to assuage public opinion, are driven by a predominantly retributive approach to sentencing, in 1965 a more objective concern for the protection of the public occupied an equal place with considerations about deterrence. The views of Lord Stonham, for the Home Office, were broadly in accord with those of the Lord Chancellor, who, as we have noted, was decidedly unenthusiastic about the idea of the judges being involved in determining how long life should be. Arguing that murder was a 'crime apart', partly at least because it was so often the product of a 'diseased mind', he added.

> People like that may get better, on and off. A judge knows very little about the man in front of him. He sees him for a couple of days. He may or may not go into the witness box at all. No doubt, if a man has a record, the judge knows the bare bones of his record. But this is quite different from the Home Secretary. I have become persuaded that the right time to decide when somebody ought to be let out is when a man's whole record is being considered; and that cannot be done by any man, however able, ten or twenty years in advance. The Home Secretary has all the reports from the prison officers who see the man every day and get to know him well, reports of prison doctors and prison governors. The modern Home Secretary, and I dare say, former ones, goes round the prisons and meets a number of life prisoners.[22]

Viewed in the context of our own time, there is, perhaps, a certain naiveté in these comments. Although individual Home Secretaries undoubtedly varied in both their abilities and interest in the details of penal regimes, there was a culture of humane civility most marked in the prison administrators of the day, but by no means absent among the permanent officials of the Home Office. If any of them cast a figurative glance over their shoulders towards the public prints, it would more likely have been in the direction of Printing House Square rather than what were then the less esteemed parts of Fleet Street. In the 1960s it was still possible to perceive the presence of a generally benign body of Platonic Guardians.

In the upshot, Lord Parker's first amendment was successful by the narrow margin of 80 votes to 78. A week later, on 5 August, Viscount Dilhorne returned to the subject, noting that Lord Parker's amendment had been

---

[21] Hansard HL Debs Vol 268 Cols 1219–20
[22] Hansard HL Debs Vol 268 Col 1240. His views would hardly survive the Human Rights Act 1998 which he would, of course, have keenly supported.

. . . widely supported, and supported, be it noted, by many in favour of the abolition of the death sentence.[23]

He went on to say:

I am sure that the whole House was impressed by the arguments for the amendment which were advanced by the noble and learned Lord. Everyone knows that a life sentence does not ordinarily mean a man spending the rest of his life in prison; and the general impression (which is, I think, supported by statements made by the Home Secretary which I have already quoted) is that ordinarily a life sentence means something of the order of nine years, unless the prisoner would on release be a danger to society. In view of this belief the passing of a long determinate sentence is, I think, on some occasions likely to prove a more effective deterrent. Logically there is no reason, once capital punishment has been abolished, why a judge's powers, when a man who has murdered is found to be of diminished responsibility, should differ from his powers when the murderer has not diminished responsibility. Logically there is no reason for judges, when sentencing for murder having different powers from those they have when sentencing for attempted murder. The difference between the two cases is simply that in one the victim has died and, in the other has survived.

Dilhorne's argument in favour of judicial discretion was clearly linked to the notion that if the average life sentence prisoner were released after only nine years, the availability of a long determinate sentence would be an option worth having at the court's disposal. On this point he was not as well informed as he might have been. On 12 June 1961 Mr Edward Gardner, QC, MP, had written to the then Home Secretary, R A Butler on the subject of life imprisonment for murder. This correspondence we had ourselves published in 1964.[24] Gardner, who was a staunch advocate of the death penalty and still supporting it during the various attempts at limited restoration by amendments attached to other criminal justice legislation during the time of Margaret Thatcher, was correct in his assumption that for murder committed before 1957 that was the average time served. Gardner disliked the indeterminate sentence, arguing that,

. . . the weakness of an indeterminate sentence is not its ultimate length or brevity, but its *uncertainty*. [His italics] What has a killer to fear if he can kill believing that if he is caught and convicted he may spend less time in prison than a thief?

In the course of his reply of 4 July, Butler emphasises that,

. . . no prisoner . . . is released unless the Home Secretary is satisfied that that there is unlikely to be a risk of his repeating his offence or being a danger to the public. One person released in the last five years has been detained for 20 years and among the . . . prisoners now detained are two who have served 16 years and two who have served 13 years. Successive Home Secretaries have not hesitated to use [the power of recall] in the interests of public safety.

---

[23] Hansard HL Debs Vol 268 Col 1240, Vol 269 Cols 405–6

[24] Terence Morris and Louis Blom-Cooper, *A Calendar of Murder* (London, Michael Joseph, 1964) 369–72.

It is evident from the rest of Dilhorne's speech, and later contributions, that the attention of the House was sharply focused on the need for a proper system for reviewing the arrangements for release on licence, whether they were for murder or any other type of offence—a prelude to the parole system introduced in 1967. Whether his enthusiasm for judicial discretion was that he saw it as a way of judges ensuring that those convicted of murder served longer terms and with greater certainty, than under a system of Home Office controlled indeterminacy is unclear. It is a distinct possibility.

Lord Parker's explanation for withdrawing his successful amendment and for substituting the alternative of a minimum recommendation by the trial judge (which was not part of the sentence) had nothing to do either with appeasing the retentionists or supporting the abolitionists. His object was simply to ensure some effective role for the judiciary in a system which was exclusively executive-driven:

> That [first] amendment was carried out in your Lordships' House, albeit by a small majority. I still think that it is right in principle and indeed, logical. But, as it was carried, I did not have the opportunity of moving an alternative Amendment which would, I think, meet many of the criticisms of those who were against the Amendment which was carried—there were really three criticisms, or fears. One was that murder was still a unique offence and should be marked by a unique penalty, in this case life imprisonment. Secondly, there was a fear, I think exaggerated, that judges might give what some people thought were inordinately long sentences, and that there is at the moment no machinery for review. Thirdly, and I think this was the point which largely influenced those who voted against the Amendment—that there might be cases in which the Home Secretary would have to release a prisoner who has served a determinate sentence, less his remission, when though he might feel that it was unsafe to do so.[25]

Dilhorne was clearly disappointed and expressed his feelings very directly:

> I am sorry that the Lord Chief Justice has taken the course of cancelling his amendment. I think the Amendment today is not nearly so good.[26]

Re-reading the debate after nearly 40 years, one cannot be other than struck by a sense of the ironic. Among the supporters of the idea of judicial discretion were those of the view that licences might come too soon, and the deterrent consequences of conviction for murder would be thereby eroded. It would be the politicians and their civil servants who would be tempted towards liberality; the judges, on the other hand, could be trusted to understand the sentiments and anxieties of society. For the remainder of the century, the balance was to be progressively reversed. It would be the politicians who would seek to impose longer terms, including 'whole life' tariffs. The judiciary, on the other hand, increasingly informed by the European jurisprudence and latterly having to take

---

[25] Hansard HL Debs Cols 418–19
[26] *Ibid*, Col 409.

account of the Convention principles now enshrined in domestic legislation, would make progressive inroads into the exercise of those executive powers that had once been characterised by considerable latitude.

What seems to have been overlooked was the potentially wide range of outcomes made possible by the minimum recommendation. Not only could it ensure that long periods of imprisonment were imposed on the most dangerous killers; it could also make possible the comparatively early release for those at the other end of the scale of moral culpability. As Lord Stonham observed:

> . . . the court could recommend anything from a very short sentence to a very long one.[27]

The Home Secretary, Sir Frank Soskice QC, said the same thing in the House of Commons.[28] It is a remarkable fact that there is no record of any recommendation for a 'very short' sentence. It is highly doubtful whether the imposition of a 'very short' sentence—whatever that might mean—was ever seriously entertained by the judges.[29] Any sense of retributive or deterrent tariff fixing was absent from their minds: 'dangerousness' was their exclusive concern.

Whatever was intended by the sponsors of the Bill and by ministers, those peers who debated Lord Parker's two amendments must have been envisaging some substantial input by the judiciary into the system for dealing with mandatory life sentence prisoners. That has turned out not to be the case, neither before nor after the establishment of the Parole Board in 1967. The Advisory Council on the Penal System in its report on Maximum Penalties noted that during the first eleven years in which the power to make a minimum recommendation had been available to the courts, judges had used it in only 78 out of 938 cases of persons sentenced to mandatory life, a mere 8 per cent. It commented:

---

[27] Hansard HL Debs, Col 421.

[28] Hansard HC Debs Vol 718 Col 379.

[29] The notion of a recommendation for a 'very short' minimum period was largely a flight of fancy entertained by contributors to the debate such as Lord Stonham whose comments were often less than profound. In 1973 the Court of Appeal indicated in *Flemming* (1973) 57 Cr App Rep 524, that no recommendation should be for a period of less than 12 years. What is interesting about the 12 year minimum established in *Flemming* is that the question before the court was whether it had been lawful for the trial judge to make a minimum recommendation in the case of a Young Person sentenced not under s 1 (2) of the Murder (Abolition of Death Penalty) Act 1965, but on a conviction of manslaughter for which a sentence of detention at Her Majesty's Pleasure under s 53 (2) of the Children and Young Persons Act 1993 was a discretionary option. Thus the 10-year recommendation of the trial judge was set aside, not on the grounds of it being inappropriate, but because it was, by definition, unlawful. The recollection of the judges concerned, Lawton and Scarman, LJJ. and May J, in response to a query by present authors in 1996 is that the figure of 12 years arose from a discussion among senior judges initiated by the then Lord Chief Justice, Lord Widgery. There is no appeal against a minimum recommendation made by a trial judge, *Aitken* [1996] 1 WLR 1076. The decision was re-affirmed in the Court of Appeal in 1995 in *Leaney* by Lord Taylor CJ, Mantell and Keane JJ [CLR 1995 at 669–71.] An attempt to amend the Bill to provide such a right failed during the passage of the Criminal Appeal Bill in 1995.

The introduction of this provision in the 1965 Act was at the time an acknowledgement that judges should have some effective say in the length of time that convicted murderers should spend in prison, and it is clear from the reports of the Parliamentary proceedings that the intention of Ministers was that the courts should be able to recommend anything from a very short to a very long sentence. It is clear that the use now made of the provision is not in accordance with the original intentions of Ministers and in view of this, as well as for the reasons below, we consider it should now be repealed.[30]

It referred to the Twelfth Report of the Criminal Law Revision Committee[31] which expressed the view that the merit of minimum recommendations was that they were made exceptionally and not as a matter of routine. Contemporaneously, a committee in Scotland, under the chairmanship of Lord Emslie, which had considered the position there had, however, suggested a course precisely to the contrary; that a minimum period should be recommended in every case.[32] The Advisory Council took the view[33] that:

... such a recommendation would no longer be an indication of either strong mitigation or strong aggravation, circumstances sufficient to warrant a public indication of the time the judge considered should be spent in custody, and it would be a very short step to conferring the power to pass a determinate sentence in those cases where indeterminacy was considered inappropriate. If, on the other hand, recommendations by the judiciary continue to be conceived as an appropriate method of expressing particular public revulsion, it is difficult to see why the use of the recommendation is so apparently inconsistent. No recommendations were made, for instance, in such notorious cases as the Moors murders,[34] or those originally convicted of the M62 coach bombing, or the Birmingham bombing, while in the Guilford public house bombing in 1975 formal recommendations were made in the case of two offenders, but in the case of the acknowledged leader there was only an informal indication that "life should mean life".[35]

UNFINISHED BUSINESS

There was no 'pact', deal', 'contract', whatever term may be used to describe the supposed *quid pro quo* of 1965 that secured abolition of the death penalty. In

---

[30] Advisory Council on the Penal System, *Sentences of Imprisonment: Review of Maximum Penalties.* (HMSO, 1978), paras 258, 260 at 114–15. The incidence of minimum recommendations has not significantly changed since 1978.

[31] Criminal Law Revision Committee. Twelfth Report, *The Penalty for Murder*, Cmnd 5184, (1973), paras 31–33.

[32] *The Penalties for Homicide.* Cmnd, 5137 HMSO (1972) para 92.

[33] Advisory Council on the Penal System, above n 266, para 259 at 114.

[34] In the case of Myra Hindley, although the trial judge had expressed the view that she was not entirely beyond hope of redemption, she was eventually to receive no fewer than three tariffs, each longer than the one previously imposed, the final decision being that she should serve 'whole life'. She began what was to prove a protracted course of litigation contesting its lawfulness and might well have been on the threshold of success when she died, still a prisoner.

[35] All the convictions in these cases have subsequently been quashed.

our view, it is now incumbent upon those who take the contrary view to produce other evidence than that comprised by the recollection of the late Lord Shepherd, if only to corroborate it. We have searched diligently but have found none, but in the manner of those who in another context have failed to find 'weapons of mass destruction' we must admit that simply because our search has proved fruitless, it does not follow that nothing is there.

It is our view that the myth of the pact has arisen, not as a fiction, deliberately inserted into the historical record, but from a misunderstanding of what actually took place. We know that Gardiner and the other Law Officers were (a) concerned to ensure that the window of opportunity presenting itself should not be lost and (b), were therefore anxious lest any secondary issue, such as the relative positions of the judiciary and the Home Secretary with regard to the release of prisoners sentenced to mandatory life, should complicate matters and produce a fatal delay in meeting the legislative timetable. We know too, that Gardiner and Soskice, the Home Secretary, were opposed to the idea of judicial discretion. Soskice had no reason to believe that the previous experience of the Home Office in deciding when to release would not continue to be used to good effect. Gardiner, for his part was clear in believing that an indeterminate sentence in murder was penologically preferable to a determinate one, in which he foresaw all manner of difficulties. When we come to what we might term the 'lawyers' it is the case that while the objectives were clear, the motivation was sufficiently opaque for us only to be able to hazard a guess as to its nature. It is clear that Parker, as Lord Chief Justice, considered that the judicial role could be usefully extended by providing for discretion in sentencing, a view that was endorsed in the House, but by what was an insubstantial margin of two votes. It is clear that, reflecting upon the constitutional aspects of that fact, he subsequently withdrew his amendment. If there was any element of compromise, and it may well be that this is, indeed, the source of the myth of the 'pact', it was that the proposal for a judicial recommendation as to the minimum term to be served eventually emerged into law as section 1 (2). His most vocal supporter was undoubtedly the former Lord Chancellor. Dilhorne's reasoning that it was illogical for judges to have discretion in sentencing in attempted murder, but not in murder itself, can scarcely be faulted. Indeed, judicial discretion can be seen as a mark of judicial independence, certainly from the executive if not entirely of the claims of the legislature. In our view, he was a pragmatist who saw not only that the compromise of the 1957 Act had been a disaster, not least in having attracted almost universal criticism and increasing hostility, but that the days of the death penalty itself were now numbered. What moved these two important participants in the discourse to adopt the positions which they did? As far as Parker was concerned it is clear that he saw an extension of the judicial role as both logical and legitimate, but his motivation was less clear. In Dilhorne's case it is possible to argue that in this instance he was wearing his political hat rather than his lawyer's gown. He was a Conservative lawyer in the traditional mode and inhabited much the same world as Sir Edward Gardner;

both were equally committed to the retention of the death penalty. But we know from Gardner's correspondence with Butler little more than four years earlier, that there were concerns about how long or, more accurately, how short were the actual periods in which life sentence prisoners were spending in custody. Butler's liberal stance with regard to penal affairs generally was not celebrated in all sections of his party and there was a suspicion that the Home Office officials were inclined to undue lenity in their approach. Allowing the judges freedom to sentence as they thought fit could certainly provide the means of ensuring that convicted murderers, now that they would no longer hang, spend a longer time in prison than perhaps would be the case if their periods of actual incarceration were within the control of the Home Office. The determinate sentence, taking into account remission, could ensure that. Both Parker and Dilhorne, whose years at the Bar exempt him from the criticism that his experience of politics was greater than that of the law, came to professional maturity in a world that was dominated by figures like Rayner Goddard,[36] whom Parker[37] succeeded in 1958 and Gordon Hewart.[38] Whereas none could argue that Hewart was an outstanding lawyer, equally, none could doubt his undisguised reactionary approach. Goddard, on the other hand combined the qualities of a highly competent lawyer and scholar with an equally undisguised commitment to severity in sentencing that old age seemed not to mellow.

Forty years ago, the phrase 'trusting the judges' would have implied confidence in their handing down sentences of undoubted severity and it is perhaps no coincidence that the period of the 1960s was one in which sentence length in cases held to be of exceptional seriousness began to be passed on such offenders as those convicted of the Great Train Robbery, the Richardsons and their associates and the spy George Blake.[39] If a Home Office presided over by a liberally minded Conservative like Rab Butler was a source of anxiety to those who sought to ensure that, should the hangman become redundant, the alternative would constitute a deterrent not to be lightly set aside, it was as nothing compared to the prospect of a government on the Left that had clearly taken to itself many of the values of the world that became known as the 'Swinging

[36] Lord Chief Justice from 1946 to 1958. Born in 1877, he lived until 1971.

[37] Parker was in many senses, a transitional judge between a period dominated by Victorian and Edwardian values and modern times. He was certainly possessed of a sense of humour and the *Observer* newspaper of 12 March 1961 credited with having said, 'A judge is not supposed to know anything about the facts of life unless they have been presented in evidence and explained to him at least three times.'

[38] Lord Chief Justice from 1922 to1940 and generally regarded as one of the least satisfactory holders of the office. Born in 1870 he died in 1943. He had been a member of the court that had set aside the conviction of Reginald Woolmington; significantly, the judgment was delivered by the Lord Chancellor, Lord Sankey.

[39] Blake was sentenced to 42 years (a three-fold multiplier of a 14 year maximum) the longest known determinate sentence to have been passed in modern times. He subsequently escaped from Wormwood Scrubs, precipitating the Mountbatten Report on prison security and lived out his days in Moscow. The train robbers were sentenced to periods of up to 30 years and the Richardson's periods in excess of 20.

Sixties'[40]. Once the Bill passed into law it was characterised by a major omission. Nowhere did it offer any statutory definition of life imprisonment. Draftsmen and legislators alike had appeared to think that it needed none, not least since it was a case of 'If you seek a definition, look about you', that is to say, it has been happening to those convicted of murder who have been reprieved from the gallows and those sentenced for non-capital murder since 1957. It was, of course, recognised at the time by the supporters of the Bill, that there would be instances where in the interest of public safety, it would be necessary to detain an offender indefinitely, maybe until the end of his days. But such life-long detention was predicated solely upon the question of potential dangerousness; at no point was it ever suggested that such protracted detention constituted a punishment embodying an estimation of the offender's moral desert. No one, even among the staunchest opponents of abolition articulated the notion that if the death sentence were to go then it should be replaced by the equivalent of being immured alive within the confines of a lawful prison. The introduction of the executive determined tariff, though denied to be a re-sentencing exercise, was to have precisely this effect when it was modified to extend to 'whole life'. Myra Hindley, at trial perceived as the follower of Brady, but for whom redemption was yet a possibility, metamorphosed into the independent archetype of evil, symbolic of betrayal of all that was virtuous, caring and feminine. The argument that the progressive increases in her tariff were to accord with the legitimate demands of public policy could be readily mistaken for a barely encoded admission to the effect that if she were to be released there would be a degree of public outrage that would tax the skills of even the most subtle practitioner of political management. *Vox populi* was generally less inhibited. There were those yet unborn in 1966 who could nevertheless proclaim her to be an evil woman who deserved to rot in Hell, if not Holloway. Yet it is this notion that has found contemporary favour and provision for it is to be found in Schedule 21 of the Criminal Justice Act 2003. History, and the history of the criminal law is no exception, is replete with instances of policies and laws which, had their authors given thought to their long term, as distinct from short or medium term consequences, might not have been the source of future difficulty.

The Offences Against the Person Act 1861, though it assumed the common law definition of murder that has subsequently proved to be the dubiously valuable legacy of Sir Edward Coke, nevertheless statutorily declared the penalty for murder as death. It must be admitted that the death penalty has the advantage

---

[40] Gardiner, whose great love was the theatre, was an opponent of censorship, as was the Attorney General, Elwyn Jones. In 1961 Penguin Books had been prosecuted for the publication of *Lady Chatterley's Lover* and entrusted their defence to Gerald Gardiner. Mervyn Griffith-Jones, counsel for the prosecution in his long remembered address to the jury in which he assumed that they employed servants, embodied the conservatism that characterised the legal establishment of the day. The trial judge, Mr Justice Byrne, expressed his concern for the moral welfare of young factory girls who might read this book.

of being clear and unambiguous. The term 'death' in this context would seem to mean that the offender would lawfully be put to death; no more, no less than that. When it comes to seeking a statutory definition of life imprisonment the search is fruitless; there is none. In contrast, there are two alternative, interpretative, possibilities. The first is that the offender is subject to a period of incarceration from which he may be released, but being subject to recall is thereby subject to the possibility of spending other periods in custody that could extend until the end of his natural life. The sentence in that sense, is a sentence that has currency until he breathes his last. The second is that life imprisonment means exactly that, and the prisoner is thereby subject to life-long incarceration. Should he be released on licence, that is not a recognition of right but a mercy; an expression of undeserved benevolence donated *ex gratia* on the basis that he might no longer constitute a risk to society.

When Myra Hindley was in the Court of Appeal in 1998 Lord Bingham of Cornhill, CJ, said:

> One can readily accept that in requiring a sentence of imprisonment for life on those convicted of murder Parliament did not intend 'sentence' to mean what it said in all, or even a majority of cases, but there is nothing to suggest that Parliament intended that it should never (even allowing risk considerations aside) mean what it said.[41]

Lord Justice Judge specifically agreed, adding;

> The language of the statute is clear . . . . *The sentence* [his italics] is life imprisonment. In my judgment the possibility remains that for purposes of deterrence and punishment alone the criminal culpability involved in some cases of murder may lawfully permit imprisonment for life in accordance with the actual sentence pronounced by the trial judge.[42]

Simplicity in the phraseology of the Parliamentary language there certainly is, but of clarity of meaning and purpose there is none. The purpose of the Act, so unambiguously stated in its title, was the abolition of the death penalty, not a change in the nature of life imprisonment. This is not to say that incarceration for life has never been in the mind of a trial judge. In the case of one, Skingle,[43] who was convicted at Reading Crown Court of the particularly brutal murder of a policeman, Mr Justice Stephen Chapman informed the convict that the words imprisonment for life would have their 'awful, terrible meaning', but this was not something which other judges were inclined to do, even in the gravest instances of homicide. The remedy for the present uncertainty, we would argue, is both simple and readily to hand in the formulation of a definition of life imprisonment that takes into account all its current features.

---

[41] [1998] QB 751, confirmed on appeal by the House of Lords. [2001] 1 AC 410. And see p 161 *infra*.

[42] *Ibid.*

[43] An unreported case.

8

The Starting Points:
where do they end?

'You mar all with this starting'[1]

AN UNHAPPY LOT

It is to the wit of W S Gilbert that we owe the memorable phrase:

When constabulary duty's to be done,
The policeman's lot is not a happy one.[2]

Although Mr David Blunkett, during his tenure of the office of Home Secretary, may not have been greatly troubled in the course of discharging his responsibilities in the field of policing, the same cannot be said of his relationships with those in other part of the criminal justice system. It can scarcely have gone unnoticed that his personal and public reaction to certain judicial decisions suggests that, to use the demotic idiom, they have given him 'grief'. Future historians of the relationship between the law and politics may well identify his time at the Home Office as a period in which the frequent expressions of frustration on the part of the Home Secretary with those determinations of the judiciary that held his decisions to have been in excess of his statutory powers, as one characterised by a growing rift between the executive and the judiciary.

Indeed, a casual observer might even have been tempted to wonder whether these unelected judges were participants in some conspiratorial scheme to ensure that whatever Parliament—or, more realistically—whatever the course a benevolent Government had determined upon for the promotion of the public good—would encounter some immoveable legal impediment. Thanks to a recalcitrant judiciary, could the irreproachably worthy intentions of Government, which of course had the warm and enthusiastic support of the populace, be thus rendered nugatory? Was this spectacle of an unelected judiciary succeeding in overcoming the legitimate aspirations of democratic government tolerable? Against a background of widely held misconceptions

---

[1] Macbeth, Act V ll 42–3, Lady Macbeth speaking.
[2] W S Gilbert. *The Pirates of Penzance.* Act 2.

about their undue lenity in sentencing, that serve only to encourage a general denigration of judges and magistrates, the idea that somehow those in judicial office have recently metamorphosed into the enemies of the Common Man is understandable; but egregious nonsense nonetheless. One thing, however, is certainly clear; that as far as dealing with the judiciary is concerned, the lot of the Secretary of State has recently been far from a happy one.

ENDING THE 'EXECUTIVE' TARIFF: THE LEGISLATIVE RESPONSE

On 25 November 2002, the Home Secretary, as a result of court decisions,[3] was finally stripped of his power to fix the minimum term—the 'tariff'—of a mandatory sentence of life imprisonment which a convicted murderer should serve before he or she could be released from prison on licence. The Government response was a combative—some considered minatory- retort of Parliamentary action. It seemed as if, frustrated yet again, the Home Secretary was determined to retain the *status quo*, or perhaps go one better, by legislation that would consign the outcome of that litigation into the long grass. Parliament would deal with things.

The vehicle for this supposed triumph of the democratically elected executive over the unelected judiciary was to be the Criminal Justice Act 2003, which would, in addition to many other matters affecting other parts of the criminal justice system, address the effect of the life sentence[4]. The assumption that was widely made in advance of the publication of the relevant parts of the Bill was that they would result in a substantial reduction in judicial autonomy. In the 'worst case scenario' the judiciary would, where the life sentence was concerned, be reduced to little more than automata, identifying the relevant legal prescriptions that Parliament had determined and translating them into sentences.

The insertion, late in the day, of Schedule 21 into the Criminal Justice Act 2003 (the new form of the mandatory life sentence) in practice surprisingly confirms the judiciary's practice of exclusive tariff fixing, while at the same time still being denied the power to pass determinate sentences of any length as an alternative to a maximum life sentence, or to impose non-custodial penalties, including hospital orders. The mandatory life sentence, established in 1965, remains intact.

A NOISY BARK, BUT AN OUTCOME LESS MORDANT THAN EXPECTED

The Executive threat to judicial independence has proved to be much less draconian than expected, and with the exception of 'whole life' orders, the

---

[3] *R v Secretary of State for the Home Department ex parte Anderson and Taylor.* [2003] 1 AC 387.
[4] Criminal Justice Act 2003, especially s 269 and Sched 21 to the Act.

exercise appears to be convention-compliant. Our conclusion, that the result, while seriously flawed, is not unpleasing to any penal reformer, requires some explanation. For all the build up, the realities of those parts of the 2003 Act that address the life sentence for those convicted of murder are actually quite different. If the judges perceived that the statute might be putting handcuffs on them (though not of the golden variety) they may be swiftly disabused of the notion of any such manacling.

Section 269: *Effect of Life Sentence* indicates, *inter alia* how the minimum term (the 'tariff') is to be determined. The court must consider the seriousness of the offence and in so doing have regard to both the principles set out in Schedule 21 and any guidelines relating to offences in general which are relevant to the case and not incompatible with the provisions of Schedule 21. The court must also give reasons, in open court and in 'ordinary language' (*sic*) for having decided upon the order made and, in particular, indicate which of the 'starting points' in Schedule 21 it has chosen and its reasons for doing so, as well as reasons for any departure from the starting point. We set out the 'starting points' below.

4 (1) If —
  (a) the court considers the seriousness of the offence (or the combination of the offence and one or more offences associated with it) is exceptionally high, and
  (b) the offender was aged 21 or over when he committed the offence, the appropriate starting point is a whole life order.
(2) Cases that would normally fall within sub-paragraph (1) (a) include:
  (a) the murder of two or more persons, where each murder involves any of the following:
    (i)   a substantial degree of premeditation or planning,
    (ii) the abduction of the victim, or
    (iii) sexual or sadistic conduct.
  (b) the murder of a child if involving the abduction of the child or sexual or sadistic motivation,
  (c) a murder done for the purpose of advancing a political, religious or ideological cause, or
  (d) a murder by an offender previously convicted of murder.

If the case does not fall within paragraph 4 (1) but the court considers that the seriousness of the offence (or the combination of the offence with one or more offences associated with it) is particularly high and the offender was 18 or over at the time of the offence, the appropriate starting point in determining the minimum term is 30 years. Cases which would normally fall within this category are identified as including: (a) the murder of a police or prison officer in the course of his duty, (b) murder using a firearm or explosive, (c) murder done for gain (such as murder done in the course or furtherance of robbery or burglary, done for payment or done in the expectation of gain in the event of the death), (d) a murder intended to obstruct or interfere with the course of justice, (e) a murder involving sexual or sadistic conduct, (f) the murder of two or more persons,

(g) a murder that is racially or religiously aggravated by sexual orientation, or (h) a murder falling within paragraph 4 (2) committed by an offender who was under 21 at the time of the offence, the appropriate starting point in determining the minimum is 15 years. If the offender was aged under 18 at the time of the offence the starting point is 12 years.

Having identified these various 'starting points', Schedule 21 continues, in prose embodying elephantine precision, the aggravating and mitigating factors which the trial judges should take into account, to the extent that allowance has not been made for them in the choice of the 'starting point'. *Detailed consideration of these aggravating or mitigating factors may result in a minimum term of any length (whatever the starting point)*, [our italics] or in the making of a whole life order.[5]

Aggravating factors

These are listed as follows. (a) a significant degree of planning or premeditation, (b) the fact that the victim was particularly vulnerable because of age or disability, (c) mental or physical suffering inflicted on the victim before death, (d) the abuse of a position of trust, (e) the use of duress or threats against another person to facilitate the commission of the offence, (f) the fact that the victim was providing a public service or performing a public duty, and (g) concealment, destruction or dismemberment of the body.

Mitigating factors

These are identified as (a) an intention to cause serious bodily harm rather than to kill,(b) lack of premeditation, (c) the fact that the offender suffered from mental disorder or mental disability which (although not falling within Section 2 (1) of the Homicide Act 1957), lowered his degree of culpability, (d) the fact that the offender was provoked (for example by prolonged stress) in a way not amounting to a defence of provocation, (e) the fact that the offender acted to any extent in self-defence, (f) a belief by the offender that the murder was an act of mercy, and (g) the age of the offender.

One might be forgiven for thinking that as far as these criteria of aggravation and mitigation are concerned, the most that they do is to introduce a welcome element of consistency into what is an essential component of the life sentence, namely the determination of the tariff for the purpose of retribution and deterrence. They are unlikely to present many surprises to those experienced judges who conduct trials for murder. What however the list does contain is a

---

[5] Criminal Justice Act 2003, chapter 7. Especially s 269 and Sched 21. 9.

recognition, albeit oblique, of what is perhaps the most patent absurdity in the substantive law of murder.[6]

The first of seven mitigating factors is the murderer's *intention to cause serious bodily harm rather than to kill*. [Our italics] Since a high percentage, perhaps as great as 80%, of those convicted of murder do not exhibit any intention to kill, presumably those whose intention was no greater than to cause serious harm will, at a stroke of the penological pen, have departed from whatever starting point judicially chosen. Hey-presto, for the run of the mill murderer, the tariff is at large. Will, incidentally, judges seek a special verdict from the jury on finding the accused guilty of murder, in the form of asking what the jury thought the accused's intention to have been? Or will the task of answering this question be left to the judge, who alone is responsible for sentencing? And that is not all. Mitigating factors include any mental disorder or mental disability that 'lowered (the offender's) degree of culpability', though outwith the statutory defence of diminished responsibility. Likewise provocation including such things as 'prolonged stress', though in a way not amounting to a defence of provocation is also identified as a mitigating factor. Self-defence and the age of the offender are on the list. So too is 'a belief by the offender that the murder was an act of mercy'. Since the mercy killer intends to kill, this humane provision sits uneasily in a scheme designed to create clear water between the two classes of specific intent.

Judicial manoeuvrability through the thickets of detailed tariff-fixing seems assured. We shall have to wait and see how the senior judges who try murder cases (all the High Court Judges in the Queen's Bench Division and a few senior Circuit Judges in the Crown Court) will deploy their newly-constructed freedom. The area of discretionary tariff-fixing may not be unfettered, but it is sufficiently ample to rectify any present defects in this aspect of sentencing, placing the matter squarely in the lap of the judiciary. So much for Mr Blunkett's supposed aim of shackling the judges.

But the end result remains still well short of the satisfactory solution of leaving the judges to decide on sentences for murder, as they do with every other crime (including manslaughter, which is often indistinguishable from murder in terms of the degree of culpability). If there can be relief at the outcome of some fortuitous draftsmanship in Schedule 21, that cannot be said of Schedule 22 which deals with the transitional cases of those existing life sentence prisoners—presently some 700 in number—convicted before the Criminal Justice Act 2003, whose tariffs have yet to be determined by the judges). Their fate must be decided by reference to Schedule 22 of the Act which comprises no fewer than 18 paragraphs (compared to 12 in Schedule 21) wherein the judges will, no doubt, find much by way of enlightenment.[7]

---

[6] That is that to prove murder it is only necessary to prove an intention to do serious harm, in contrast to proof of attempted murder where the prosecution must demonstrate an intention to kill.

[7] The first determination under Schedule 22, paragraph 3 of the Criminal Justice Act 2003 for setting a minimum term was given by Mr (now Lord) Justice Hooper in the case of Mohammed Riaz on 26 January 2004, [2004] EWHC 74 (QB).

Schedule 21 had necessarily to fix a point of departure on its penal journey, because to have alighted upon a fixed point, without judicial adjustment to suit the individual case, would have fallen foul of the European Convention of Human Rights. What the Home Secretary has been able to do is to retain his power, in conjunction with the Parole Board, to engage in the other part of the life sentence—namely, an assessment of risk if and when the prisoner is to be released back into the community. Dangerousness, however, is itself, a dangerous concept, for which judicial review is required. Even the opprobrious starting point of 'whole life' cannot be guaranteed to apply to those convicted of the most heinous murders, since the judges need not open the door even to that iron cage of vengeance. And although the Convention is now incorporated within domestic law, Strasbourg remains as a long-stop.

What must surely concern us most is that the Act of 2003 gives legitimacy to the expression of a view that ought to be repugnant in any civilised society; it is the view that it is acceptable to sentence a person to what constitutes entombment for life, a literal immuring within prison walls, on the ground, not of credible public danger, but imputed moral desert. No matter that the offender may have the capacity for change or may do so, no matter that the passage of years and physical degeneration may render the offender's condition no different from that of any other elderly person who is in need of long term personal and nursing care; for that offender the prison door is as surely shut as if it had been bricked up, leaving no more than an aperture through which a coffin might pass.

Is it not inhumane treatment to say of anyone that he or she will never leave prison alive? Civil death is the prescription of populist politics. The reformer's plea, though it may at times be drowned in the clamour of those who would, one suspects, be not averse to the return of the gallows, must be that for a straightforward penalty for murder, determined appropriately by the trial judge, with a maximum of life imprisonment, the sentence to be subject to review on appeal to which offender and prosecutor would have equal and unfettered access.

9

Corporate Killing

⟶•⟵

> They [corporations] cannot commit treason, nor be outlawed, nor excommunicate, for they have no souls, neither can they appear in person.[1]

> The businessman does not regard himself as a lawbreaker . . . he does not think of himself as a criminal because he does not conform to the popular stereotype of the criminal . . . Business leaders are capable, emotionally balanced and in no sense pathological. We have no reason to think that . . . US Steel has an Oedipus complex or that the Armour Company has a death wish or that Du Ponts desire to return to the womb.[2]

The absence of any soul or attribute of the human being is no longer a bar to corporate liability, civil or criminal. But if companies or other corporate organisations have been subjected, by way of statutory control, to stringent health and safety regulations, they have largely escaped the ultimate criminal responsibility for deaths resulting from corporate activities. Prosecutions for corporate manslaughter have been singularly unsuccessful, the reason being the requirement to identify the directing mind of the corporate body.[3] If there is no conceptual legal difficulty in that exercise, the stumbling block is the need to establish, by clear evidence, guilt of an identifiable human individual. This is because the corporation's criminal responsibility depends crucially upon some individual person's actions supplying the corporation's guilty mind.[4] In their report in 1996 the Law Commissioners recommended a new of offence of 'corporate killing' broadly comparable to killing as a result of gross negligence on the part of an individual. Corporate liability would ensue if a management failure by the corporation resulted in a person's death and such failure constituted conduct falling far below what could be reasonably expected of the corporation

---

[1] Sir Edward Coke, in the case of *Sutton's Hospital*. (1612) 10 Co Rep [23a] at [32b]: 77 ER 573.

[2] Edwin Sutherland. 'The Crime of Corporations', a lecture to the Toynbee Club at DePauw University, Indiana in the Spring of 1948. Published in Albert Cohen, Alfred Lindesmith and Karl Schuessler (eds) *The Sutherland Papers* (Bloomington Indiana, Indiana University Press, 1956).

[3] *See: Legislating the Criminal Code: Involuntary Manslaughter*. Law Commission. Report No 237 March 1996.

[4] *Attorney-General's Reference* (No 2 of 1999) [2000] 3 All ER 182. A point underscored by the Law Commission report.

in the circumstances. Such prosecutions should only proceed in the Crown Court and on conviction the court would have the power to impose an unlimited fine and make an order to remedy any cause which had been identified.

In Coke's day, corporate bodies of the kind with which we are familiar today were in their comparative infancy. Apart from the Church and such charitable institutions as schools, the universities and almshouses, corporations that were devoted wholly to commerce were few and often had a relatively short span of commercial life. Thus merchants would collectively finance a specific trading voyage and divide up the profits on the ship's return.[5] It was not until the establishment of modern systems of banking at the end of the seventeenth century facilitated the fiscal infrastructure that modern corporate enterprise began to develop on a significant scale. If the criminal law had any interest in them it was largely in relation to such malfeasance as fraud and forgery. The idea of a corporate body having liability for criminal homicide was not at issue. The Industrial Revolution in turn gave rise to the enterprise which raised its capital through the medium of the transferable share and cognate devices, resulting in the emergence of the limited liability company. But again, such legislation as developed was directed towards the maintenance of standards of commercial and financial probity rather than other aspects of corporate activity. The origin of legislation dealing with the welfare of those whose lives might be affected by the activities of corporations lies elsewhere, in the area which we nowadays term 'health and safety'.[6]

WELFARE AND HUMANITARIAN LEGISLATION

Commencing with the first Factory Act in 1833, which limited the hours of work for women and children, Parliament progressively enacted legislation that limited the extent to which employers could pay little or no heed to the welfare of their employees. With the increasing complexity of steam driven machinery, industrial accidents resulting in death and serious injury increased. In the course of the civil engineering works associated with the building of railways in which large numbers of illiterate or semi-literate labourers were employed, the casualties were many; men were blown up by the careless use of explosives, fell from bridges and viaducts, or died, or were injured in other violent ways. On the high seas the loss of life was, if anything worse, since the number of vessels trading, particularly on the North Atlantic in winter, had increased while standards of

---

[5] The origin of the term 'When my ship comes in.'

[6] In the latter part of the 19th century, when statutory legislation relating to health and safety was becoming more widespread, many police forces opted to list breaches of them as 'quasi-crimes'. The application of the concept of strict liability to such offences, and a correspondingly limited emphasis upon *mens rea*, seems a plausible explanation of why such offences were, and largely remain, unvisited by the more diffuse sanctions of public obloquy that normally attach to crime.

maritime safety remained unchanged from those of earlier centuries.[7] Until Samuel Plimsoll MP, introduced legislation in 1876 establishing what became known as the 'Plimsoll Line'[8], ships whether seaworthy or not, might be freighted to whatever depth the owners pleased, irrespective of the inherent danger.[9]

The key area of corporate liability in the period from 1850 onwards, extending beyond the epicentre of commercial activity, was in relation to various forms of what might broadly be termed 'industrial accidents'. The railway system continued to provide such instances, well after the actual lines had been constructed, notably in the form of people being struck by trains,[10] being on the track for whatever reason, and train crashes. In 1864, for example, the London and North Western Railway made payments in settlement of personal injury claims in no fewer than 15,185 cases, though this reduced in the following year to 9,920.[11] It is not without significance that these issues of liability were rehearsed not in criminal trials but in the course of civil actions, nor that the litigants tended to be passengers who were likely to be more affluent than railway 'servants' (as they were termed) who might have been injured. Where the criminal law was employed, it was in respect of railway servants, such as engine drivers and signalmen, who by their action or inaction had brought about serious incidents involving death and were prosecuted for the crime of manslaughter. This practice continued well into the twentieth century. There is thus a distinction to be observed between the liability in tort of the corporation for all forms of loss, including personal injury, and the criminal liability of its employees in instances of death.

DEATH IN QUIET WATER

On the evening of 6 March 1987 the 7,951-ton 'roll on-roll off' vehicle and passenger ferry *Herald of Free Enterprise* left the Belgian port of Zeebrugge, bound for Dover. There was a light easterly breeze and the sea was easy. With a crew of 80 and 459 passengers she carried in addition a cargo of 81 cars, 3 buses and

---

[7] The exception being the provision of efficient lighthouses around the British and Irish coasts.

[8] More accurately, 'Plimsoll *lines* in the form of a series of marks indicating the depth to which a ship might lawfully be loaded, depending upon the conditions in which she would sail. The highest mark is "WNA"' (Winter North Atlantic).

[9] Seamen, who were 'signed on' for each individual voyage, were not slow to discover the more cynical among the shipowning community who took the view that the loss of a ship and its cargo might well be offset by the insurance. Mortality among the crews of sailing ships in the last of the days of sail was such that, like railway navvies, they were in a sense 'expendable'. Seamen also termed some vessels as 'coffin ships'.

[10] It was an irony of fate that William Huskisson, President of the Board of Trade was struck by a train at Parkside at the opening of the Manchester and Liverpool line in September 1830 and died from his injuries.

[11] R W Kostal. *Law and English Railway Capitalism 1825–1875*, (Oxford, The Clarendon Press, 1994).

47 trucks. Immediately beyond the inner harbour entrance at Zeebrugge the water is comparatively shallow. As the *Herald* passed the outer mole she gathered speed. Like all modern vehicle ferries, to enable cars and trucks to be speedily loaded and unloaded, the *Herald* had doors at each end of the ship giving access to a main vehicle deck and two suspended car decks at each side. But unlike some other ferries, the *Herald* had been built with doors of the 'clam shell' type. The difference is best explained by reference to domestic garage doors. Houses in the 1930s had garages with a pair of doors that opened in the horizontal plane, like French windows; it is this pattern that the 'clam shell' design resembles. Other ferries had single section doors like the modern 'up and over' garage door, save for the fact that they went 'up' but not 'over'. The distinction was important in this case since, being hidden from the bridge, it was impossible to see whether the clamshell was open or closed; on the other ships it was impossible to miss the massive section of bow towering above the fo'c'sle head when the door was open. The vehicle ferry, unlike any other type of large vessel, has a large uninterrupted space from bow to stern for virtually the entire width of the ship; constructed otherwise it would be impossible to drive vehicles on at one end and off at the other. But this is their Achilles heel, since in the absence of bulkheads to contain any excess water safely within a limited space, the sudden ingress of any mass of water cannot be contained and will slop from end to end or side to side with the movement of the ship. It is the doors that constitute the ferry's first and last defence against any such disastrous event.

Shortly after leaving the harbour, the *Herald* began to take on vast amounts of water through her still open bow doors. In less than two minutes she had heeled over and was lost, and 189 people with her. Most died inside the ship from hypothermia in the frigid water and many others had been injured as the ship fell on her side. The death toll was the greatest for any British passenger vessel in peacetime since the loss of the *Titanic* in April 1912.[12]

---

[12] It was to be followed two years later in August 1989 by the sinking of the Thames pleasure boat *Marchioness* in a collision with the dredger *Bowbelle* with the loss of 51 lives. In addition to a Marine Accident Investigation, the matter was before more than one Coroner's court, and on more than one occasion was to involve the High Court. The immense distress experienced by the relatives, who were not allowed to view the recovered bodies and discovered later that in some cases (without their permission) hands had been removed to assist identification, led to great anger. These various procedures were protracted over a period of a decade. The tragedy of the *Marchioness* was an echo of a Victorian disaster in London River. In September 1878 the *Princess Alice*, carrying almost 800 excursion passengers, mainly women and children, was returning in the dark to the Pool of London after a day trip to Gravesend and Sheerness when, on the bend in the river at Woolwich she was cut in two by the collier *Byward Castle*. The loss of life in the *Princess Alice* (some 640 passengers and crew) was proportionally of the same order as the loss in the *Titanic*. The collision occurred largely as a consequence of the ambiguity of the regulations governing steering orders (originally established for sailing ships). Although the ensuing Board of Trade Inquiry recommended that rudder orders be used instead of helm orders, it was not for 54 years, in January 1933, that a new regulation came into force.

'It has to be somebody's fault'—or does it?: the Inquiry

Examination of the causes of disasters generally reveals that nothing is quite so simple as it at first seems, and the loss of the *Herald* was no exception. It was evident that she had left her berth with the bow doors open. They ought to have been shut. Why were they not shut, and how was it that no one noticed?

A Court of Formal Investigation pursuant to the Merchant Shipping Act 1894, before the Commissioner of Wrecks, Mr Justice Sheen, opened in London in April 1987 and concluded some two months later.[13] In addition to investigative powers, the Court had power to suspend or remove a Merchant Navy officer's Certificate of competency, and to determine who should contribute to the cost of the inquiry. It had no others.

What were the known facts? As a modern ship, the *Herald* had two vehicle decks and to facilitate loading at Dover and Calais there were two separate ramps, one higher than the other. At Zeebrugge there was only a single ramp, and this necessitated the vessel's height in relation to the ramp being achieved by means of ballast tanks, which trimmed the ship up or down. When the *Herald* left Zeebrugge on the fatal night not all the water had been pumped from the ballast tanks at the bow, with the result that she was three feet down by the head. This would have brought the incoming water closer to the main vehicle deck that was exposed by the fact of the doors being still open. It was the task of the Assistant bo'sun to close the bow doors. He had opened them on arrival at Zeebrugge and then supervised some maintenance work. When he was released from this work by the Bo'sun he went to his cabin where he fell asleep and was not awakened by the public address call to crew for 'harbour stations' as the ship prepared to leave. The Bo'sun himself left the vehicle deck at 'harbour stations' to go to his assigned station elsewhere. It was not one of his tasks either to close the doors or ensure that anyone else was there to do so. Meanwhile, the Chief Officer who was in charge of vehicle loading, remained on the vehicle deck until he saw—or thought he saw—the Assistant bo'sun threading his way through the parked vehicles to the door control panel. He then went to his assigned station on the bridge. As the *Herald* headed out towards the open sea, down some three feet by the head and with her doors wide open, she gathered speed and with it hundreds of tons of seawater. It was only a fortuitous turn to starboard in her last moments, grounding her on her side, that prevented her from sinking completely in deeper water.

---

[13] Department of Transport (UK) *MV Herald of Free Enterprise*. Report of the Court of Admiralty No 8074: Formal Investigation by the Hon Mr Justice Sheen, Wreck Commissioner, 29 July 1987 (London, HMSO, ISBN 0 11 550828 7).

What is meant by a 'cause'?

The *Herald of Free Enterprise* sank and people in her died because a sudden onrush of 'free water' caused her to become fatally unstable. The doors were open because the Assistant bo'sun had not closed them. He had not closed them because he was asleep in his cabin. It was not the task of the Bo'sun to close them and the Chief Officer was under the impression that the Assistant bo'sun was on his way to the door controls when he went to his assigned station on the bridge. No-one on the bridge, including the master, had any way of being alerted to the fact that the doors were still wide open as the ship headed for the open sea.

The immediate 'cause' of the sinking was the ship's sudden and fatal loss of buoyancy, but that approach is but the beginning of a 'for want of a nail' type of explanation. What of the management practices of the company, and the absence of 'fail-safe' procedures and devices, including provision of a light on the bridge indicating the open or closed position of the doors? At the Inquiry it emerged that two years earlier, the Master of a similar vessel in the Company had requested the installation of a warning light following an incident in which the bow doors had been left open, but at management level this request had not been treated with any seriousness. Mr Justice Sheen's wider criticisms of management were considerable:

> All concerned in management, from the board of directors down . . . . are guilty of fault. From top to bottom the body corporate was infected with the disease of sloppiness . . . The failure on the part of management to give proper and clear directions was a contributory cause of the disaster.

DEATH IN A RAGING SEA

The question of how ferries are operated is not new. On 31 January 1953 the British Railways ferry *Princess Victoria* was lost in the North Channel of the Irish Sea on passage from Stranraer to Larne. The weekend of 31 January to 1 February 1953 was visited by exceptional weather conditions, namely; an unusually high Spring tide, an unusually low Atlantic depression passing over the British Isles and the North Sea resulting in a raising of the sea level at high water still higher, and a severe north-westerly gale. Fishing boats off the Hebrides were overwhelmed and on the night of Saturday/Sunday the wind and tide drove down the North Sea, flooding vast areas of the Netherlands, Lincolnshire, Norfolk and Suffolk and inundating Canvey Island in the Thames Estuary. From the North Channel to the North Sea, many hundreds of lives were lost. The *Princess Victoria* had sailed with a crew of 49 and 125 passengers (though certified to carry 1515) among whom all the female and child passengers were lost. The *Victoria*, a much smaller vessel than the *Herald of Free Enterprise*, had a large car deck loaded through stern doors which was a 'weather' deck from which excess water taken aboard would drain out through scuppers. The tremendous violence of the sea broke open one pair of doors, damaged its mechanism so that it could not be re-fastened and then took the other pair of doors. The inadequacy of the design whereby the excess water could flow off the weather deck was such that, taking on more and more water, she finally capsized.

From 1 March to 9 May a formal investigation into her loss was conducted at Belfast. The report was damning. It found that the ship was unseaworthy by reason of the inadequacy of the stern doors, which had yielded to the sea, and that of the clearing arrangements for the water, which accumulated on the freeboard deck, which had resulted in her developing an increasing list to starboard. The owners (The British Transport Commission) and the managers (British Railways) were held in default for:

(a) failing to provide stern doors sufficiently strong to withstand the conditions reasonably expected to occur from time to time in the North Channel,

(b) failing to provide adequate freeing arrangements for seas that might enter the car space,

(c) failing to take precautionary steps after an incident in November 1951, and

(d) failing to comply with the provisions of Section 425 of the Merchant Shipping Act 1894 insofar as the incident in (c) was not reported.

The shipping forecast had been for severe gales[14] in the relevant sea areas and even in the relative shelter of Loch Ryan between Stranraer and the open sea it had been necessary to fit additional lashing to secure the cargo. Ought she to have sailed at all in these conditions, given that she was apparently unseaworthy? Completed in 1947 at the Dumbarton yard of William Denny Bros., the most experienced British shipyard for this type of vessel, she had been constructed under the rules and inspection of both Lloyd's Register and the Ministry of Transport. The crossing from Stranraer to Larne is the shortest of the Irish Sea passages and a substantial section of it is within the comparatively sheltered waters of Loch Ryan. In spite of being constructed to Lloyd's and MOT standards, the Ministry seems to have had some misgivings about the seaworthiness of the *Princess Victoria* since it refused an extension of certification of plying from the more southerly ports of Holyhead and Fishguard for much longer crossings in waters notorious for being subject to the effects of Atlantic weather in the Western Approaches. Yet as a distinguished naval architect, KC Barnaby, observed some years later

---

[14] A severe gale is rated at 9 on the Beaufort Scale, immediately below storm Force 10. The *Princess Victoria* had sailed at 0745 and was abandoned at 1354. Given the development of the weather pattern that day, allied to the unusual Spring tide, by the time she was lost, and the parlous condition of the ship, any distinction between 9 and 10 on the Beaufort Scale would have been academic.

This was a curious decision as it seems doubtful if the maximum sea conditions between Fishguard and Rosslare are any worse than when a north-west gale is driving in through the North Channel.[15]

In other words, if there was doubt about her fitness for sea on the southern routes, ought not the same question to have been posed in respect of her plying the North Channel which, though a shorter crossing, could be subject to ferocious seas caused by a north-west gale or storm driving down the narrow channel between the coasts of Scotland and Ireland and indeed, into the north-west facing entrance to Loch Ryan? He makes more general observations on the problems of vehicle ferry design that have an eerie resonance, given that they were written some twenty years before the loss of the *Herald of Free Enterprise*.

> It is undeniable that ferries with enclosed car decks are subject to special risks that do not apply to normal passenger and cargo ships. These are due to the necessary requirement of a very large undivided space carried so near the waterline. Dealing . . . with risks due to stress of weather or to collisions, it is obvious that the safety of such vessels is entirely dependent on the strength and integrity of the large loading ports or doors. Should a side port, or an end door, be stove in by either heavy seas, or by a collision, or burst open by shifting cargo when the ship is in heavy weather, then her fate seems inevitable if the car deck extends from side to side and all fore and aft. The sequence of events will follow the sad pattern set by the *Princess Victoria* on her last voyage.[16]

Barnaby had in mind the traumatic events of storm or collision that would be beyond the abilities of ship and crew to withstand. The idea that a ship could put to sea with her bow doors wide open is not a matter he considers.

The loss of the *Princess Victoria* in 1953 and the *Herald of Free Enterprise* in 1987 produced improvements in the design, equipment, and ship operation that increased safety. Yet these practical responses, important though they are, do not address those issues which are nevertheless of great importance to the public, namely; the identification of justiciable responsibility for the events which have led to tragedy and the application of appropriate sanctions where necessary. In this process the distinction between individual and corporate liability makes for difficulty.

OFF THE RAILS: THE SAME QUESTIONS ARE ASKED

In 1953, the loss of the *Princess Victoria* occasioned no strong public reaction against any public or corporate body. The tragic events of that entire weekend were somehow accommodated within the insurer's curiously archaic category of 'Acts of God', although, ironically, many of those whose homes were destroyed by flood and loved ones lost had no insurance. Even after the public

---

[15] KC Barnaby. *Some Ship Disasters and Their Causes* (London, Hutchinson, 1968) at 202.
[16] *Ibid*, at 203.

inquiry, whose findings may well in the circumstances have been somewhat harsh, there was no great outcry against British Rail or the Transport Commission. By the time the *Herald of Free Enterprise* was lost the public was not only more critical of those it perceived to be 'in charge' but also its knowledge and perception of events was shaped by infinitely more sophisticated mass media of communication. While the public only saw monochrome newsreel film of the wide ranging damage and distress resulting from the extraordinary weather conditions of that winter week-end much later in the cinema, the wreck of the *Herald* was visible in colour on every live domestic television screen.

While the *Princess Victoria* was owned and managed publicly, by the 1980's the Thatcher government had liquidated the ferry operations of British Rail and cross-Channel sea traffic was in the hands of private companies. The *Herald* had been built for the Townsend Thoresen ferry company, but shortly before her loss, Townsend Thoresen had been taken over by P & O.[17] While neither public nor private operation can guarantee total safety in the face of the worst that nature can show, safety procedures and safe operation ultimately depend upon the competence and policies of management, and human error, though it can never be completely eradicated, can nevertheless be virtually eliminated by scientific and technologically devised risk management. Where there is a single, identifiable managerial 'spine', it is arguably more straightforward for safety procedures to be monitored along with the quality of such work that is performed which has a bearing upon them. When structures are fragmented and particular units regularly contract work out—which may in turn be subcontracted—matters are more difficult to scrutinise.

One of the last acts of 'privatisation' of the 18 years of Conservative government was that of the railways. British Rail was swept away and in its place instituted an authority known as Railtrack which had charge of the physical infrastructure—the stations, buildings, permanent way and signalling—and a series of train operating companies who were responsible for the provision of rolling stock and its motive power. In many instances several train operating companies used the same track signals and stations. The railway companies that had survived from the nineteenth century had been amalgamated in 1923 into four; Great Western, London Midland and Scottish, London and North Eastern, and Southern. At the outbreak of war in 1939, all four had been brought under the single control of the Ministry of War Transport for their greater efficiency, and in 1947 formally brought into public ownership to be administered by the British Railways Board. The break-up of British Rail, as it was by then known, was not a particularly popular privatisation, not least since the public perception of the new system was substantially negative, both with respect to the cost of travel and the quality of service provided. The frequent

---

[17] The Peninsular and Oriental Steam Navigation Company. Incorporated by Royal Charter in 1840, the P&O had been the principal passenger line for travel to India, the Far East and Australia since the 19th century but turned its attention to the short sea routes as long distance passenger traffic to the Orient and Antipodes declined to the point of extinction.

industrial disputes and resulting strikes of the 1970's had done nothing to improve the negative aura of railway travel, and matters were not improved by the widespread public knowledge that the railways as a whole had been the subject of substantial under-investment for many years.

In public relations terms, the railway system had little by way of margins of goodwill, and the train crashes at Southall, Ladbroke Grove and Potters Bar became the focus of both public disquiet and anger on the part of bereaved relatives. The negative perception of the railway system was not diminished by the fact that establishment of civil liability, let alone criminal responsibility had become an extraordinarily difficult task. Back in the nineteenth century, as we have seen from Kostal's study of the London and North Western Railway, when one company operated everything there could be but one corporate defendant in any civil action, a state of affairs that subsisted throughout the period of public ownership. But what was the position when trains operated by different companies collided and when the signals and points had been operated by a third? When maintenance of the permanent way was involved, specialist civil engineering firms might be contracted to do work that would have formerly been done 'in house' by British Rail.

Establishing civil liability is difficult enough; in this context the question of corporate criminal liability approaches the realms of the impossible.[18] Public disquiet may be more difficult to assuage when the operation is a commercial one and when profits must be made to satisfy the legitimate demands of shareholders; this is in contrast to the situation of public ownership where the profit motive is not readily perceived as the primary objective if it indeed is recognized at all. At its most simplistic level, the matter is perceived thus: it is suspected that private companies, hungry for profit, will cut corners and thereby compromise the safety of passengers. This was a sentiment that could be discerned in some comments on the loss of the *Herald of Free Enterprise* on the Internet. There is undoubtedly a contrast between the individual operatives, the seamen, the engine drivers and the like, who are vulnerable to prosecution for the crime of manslaughter, unlike corporate bodies who, in Coke's phrase, 'have no souls'. The response to competitive commercial pressures cannot reasonably be compared to those of the unregulated days of the nineteenth century when purveyors of rotten food and quack medicines abounded, shipowners sent leaking and overladen vessels to sea, and mine owners and factory magnates regarded their workforce as no more than an expendable factor of production. Rather, the good name of a company is considered a major asset, a long-term investment to be protected and not recklessly to be put at hazard in the hope of short-term gain. Human error in particular operations can be increasingly insured against by technological means; thus warning lights on the bridge of the *Herald of Free Enterprise* would have made it clear that the bow doors were open. But in other

---

[18] *See Attorney General's Reference (No 2 of 1999) above note 3.*

situations, including those where much depends upon routine maintenance and inspection, managerially determined protocols are of critical importance.

As far as health and safety issues are concerned there is no significant problem. The lessons of disasters, certainly those of recent marine disasters, have been translated into the establishment of new standards and procedures. If there is an impediment, it lies largely in the area of arranging adequate inspection and enforcement. But there remains the important issue of assuaging the perfectly proper public demand that the shortcomings of corporate bodies, where they result in situations that would result in criminal prosecution in the case of individuals, should be treated on a comparable basis. This, not unreasonable demand is underscored by the knowledge that though they have, in Coke's words, 'no souls'—nor, for that matter, any 'minds'—they make decisions by, as it were, borrowing the minds of individuals who do. A corporate decision does not issue like the disembodied voice of the Delphic Oracle from some equivalent of a fissure in the rock—a crack in the boardroom panelling, perhaps—but from the resolution of individual human beings gathered round the table. The question that is likely to bring up any prosecution for corporate manslaughter, all standing, is that of identifying the 'mind' within the body corporate. Hence the identification of an individual dimension to corporate criminal responsibility may be the pursuit of yet another *ignis fatuus*.

For several years Government has pondered over reform of the law, prompted by successive failed prosecutions and by a report in 1996 of the Law Commission, to which the Government responded favourably in 2000.

There is clearly a mood for change in the existing law, but the task is far from straightforward. Unsurprisingly, many ordinary people find it difficult to accept that in terms of moral responsibility for conduct, which is reflected in the criminal law, there is a distinction to be drawn between individuals and corporate bodies. Corporate responsibility, so far as it can be identified, is essentially a socio-legal construct that has emerged in the long process of development whereby the law has come to accommodate the requirements and realities of economic activity. The legal reification of corporations, which are nevertheless capable of conduct, may encourage a form of anthropomorphism on the part of the lay observer for whom such concepts present a perplexing contrast to the realties of everyday life. Yet as far as the criminal law operates, there is also a necessary distinction drawn between the conduct of individual employees and that of the corporation itself.

The question is how to bring about a helpful change in the law. In our view the approach should be, as it ought to be with the control of crime generally, to ensure prevention and control rather than to concentrate on attempting an estimate of moral opprobrium and for that to be reflected in a punitive response.

How far ought liability to criminal prosecution extend to other, non-corporate undertakings? And should there be a form of secondary liability on particular individuals involved in the failure of corporate management?

We think there is no difficulty in imputing to large undertakings a corporate liability for homicide. Economic activity is performed increasingly by them, and their potential for causing physical harm to the work force, to customers and to the general public who are affected by their economic activity is manifest. The courts have expressed just such a view. Mr Justice Turner, in the failed prosecution against P&O in 1987 following the loss of the *Herald of Free Enterprise* said:

> A clear case can be made for imputing to corporations social duties, including the duty not to offend all relevant parts of the criminal law.

The twin elements of corporate killing would be that a failure in management was the cause, or one of the causes, of a person's death, and that failure would reflect a competence falling far below what could reasonably be expected of the corporation. The key is management failure. We think that the law should provide that every corporation be required to nominate one of its executive directors as directly responsible for health and safety aspects of its corporate activity. In that way the corporate state of mind would be readily identified through that of the nominated director.

The Government appears to favour the extension of the new offence to non-corporate 'undertakings', and by that they mean 'any trade or business or other activity providing employment'. This proposal is rendered topical by the decision of the Crown Prosecution Service in February 2004 to prosecute Barrow Borough Council for manslaughter over the deaths of seven people from Legionnaires' disease. One of the local authority's employees, a design services manager, is likewise being charged with the allied offence of 'gross negligence' manslaughter. But is this move wise, and will it give any inkling to the prospective liability of the extended offence?

Fatalities do not arise solely from incorporated commercial activities. Schools, hospitals, police forces, prison establishments, partnerships and unincorporated identities can all fail to install proper preventive measures against incidents involving fatal or serious injury. Even two-person businesses are singled out for potential inclusion, in which case financial penalties might be disastrously punitive.

The purpose of the extension is superficially commendable. It is to avoid inconsistencies that would arise depending on the fact of incorporation. Organisations within the NHS—trusts and hospital authorities—have as much potential (perhaps more since they engage directly in the cause of human life and limb) as any large commercial organisation. We think this extension to be misguided.

No doubt a failure in hospital management in the treatment of patients, or shortcomings by the police in exercising proper control over the crowd at a football match, can be equiparated with the privately owned company failing to improve the permanent way of our railway system. But whereas the latter is not within public sector control, responsibility for the former are under systems of direct political control and statutory regulation. Management systems can be effectively imposed by public authority and do not need the criminal law to underscore responsibility. Even if the penalties for corporate killings were to be confined to fines and remedial orders, their extension to small undertakings with only a few individuals in employment or the workplace would be unnecessarily harsh. Such secondary liability should not, in our view, arise in connection with corporate killings.

The Government gave no reason for departing from the Law Commission's stance that a new form of corporate liability, arising irrespective of any individualised responsibility, should be synonymous with organisational failure. There is every reason and good sense why the homicidal offence caused by an incorporated body should be free-standing, unencumbered by individual criminality, either in a primary or secondary capacity.

The *leitmotif* of the proposed crime of corporate killing—we envisage the offence being easily subsumed under the rubric of criminal homicide—is to underline the public insistence on standards of safety by large commercial undertakings outside of the public sector.

10

Motorised Killing

As the familiar sound broke forth, the old passion seized Toad and completely mastered him, body and soul. As if in a dream he found himself,
somehow . . . in the driver's seat. . . . and, as if in a dream, all sense of right
and wrong, all fear of obvious consequences, seemed temporarily suspended . . . he was only conscious that he was Toad once more, Toad at his
best and highest, Toad the terror, the traffic queller, the Lord of the lone
trail, before whom all must give way or be smitten into nothingness or ever-
lasting night. He . . . sped he knew not wither, fulfilling his instincts, living
his hour, reckless of what might come to him.

Kenneth Grahame, *The Wind in the Willows* (1908).

DEATH ON THE ROAD

Thus, in the early years of motoring, Grahame captured with unerring accuracy
a vision of the psychology of a delinquent driver; in Toad's case guilty of unlawful taking, besides reckless driving. Fortunately, neither death nor injury was the
outcome. In court Toad received 12 months for the theft, three years for the furi-
ous driving and fifteen years for cheeking the rural police officer who arrested
him. Absurdity apart, what is reflected here is a mindset from Edwardian
England that identified challenging behaviour as a serious threat to social order,
not to say life and property, besides an insight into that intoxicating excitement
that may be the forerunner of recklessness behind the wheel. There is little
doubt that the aggressive, anti-social driver remains deeply unpopular, and,
while it is recognised that not all drivers involved in road traffic incidents are
equally culpable, those who are deemed to be seriously so would appear to be
increasingly the subject of public concern. For of all forms of violent and potentially unlawful death, that on the road is probably the most familiar.
Fortunately, it is only a minority of people who are brought face to face with the
reality of those homicides that are termed 'murder' by the present law. While
what are deemed 'murders' are numbered in hundreds, deaths on the road—
though not all of them the subject of criminal prosecution—are counted in thou-
sands. And of all forms of violent death there are perhaps none, save for those

arising from railway or shipping disasters in which corporate liability may be at issue, where those who are left to grieve, nurture, and often with good cause, a greater sense of the law's inadequacy in providing justice.

When the charge has been one of careless driving alone (though a death has been involved) many relatives have immense difficulty in understanding how mention of a death does not form part of the prosecution evidence. In proving such offences the Crown is required to demonstrate that the driving has been without due care; the outcome of such driving is irrelevant to the matter of proof and can have no logical bearing upon the charge, the danger or lack of care being prior in time to the outcome. Indeed, it is a frequent complaint that not all instances of road death become the subject of prosecution for causing death, being limited to charges of driving dangerously or without due care. Our view is that in any road traffic incident, where there is *prima facie* evidence of a death having been the result of some unlawful action involving recklessness or gross negligence, a charge of criminal homicide ought invariably to be brought. Since these are the constituents of manslaughter there is no reason to do otherwise. If conviction should follow and there is mitigation in respect of the particular circumstances of the event, then this can be accommodated at the time of sentence.

THE BLAMEWORTHY 'ACCIDENT'

Until the coming of road vehicles propelled by the internal combustion engine at the end of the nineteenth century, if, as a result of their actions or omissions, those in charge of the man-made means of transport, whether ships, railway trains, or horse drawn vehicles, brought about a death, they could be charged with the offence of manslaughter. The same remains true today. The exception to this general rule in practice is the driver of the motor vehicle. Motor manslaughter is obsolescent.

The exponential growth of the motor vehicle between 1920 and the present day has changed the nature of economy and society. But it was not until the 1930s that Parliament began seriously to address the hazards involved, addressing such matters as third party insurance, the construction and maintenance of vehicles and the competence of drivers.[1] Until 1956, where it was alleged that a driver had caused a death unlawfully, the charge was one of manslaughter, but juries were frequently reluctant to convict. Whether this was because—consciously or unconsciously—they identified with the driver, since so many people now owned motor cars and adopted a 'there but for the grace of God' approach, is difficult to say. Anecdotal evidence suggests that they may have been hesitant on account of the fact that a manslaughter conviction could be visited with a long term of imprisonment, including life. The Road Traffic Act 1956 estab-

---

[1] The Road Traffic Act 1930 was followed by the Motor Vehicles Construction and Use Regulations in 1934. Driving tests were introduced at about the same time.

lished a separate offence of causing death by dangerous driving and set a maximum penalty of five years.[2] The sentencing pattern that developed was characterised by custodial sentences for periods severely skewed towards the lower end of the tariff.

A change in approach to sentencing

In the years following the Road Safety Act 1967, public attitudes toward drinking and driving underwent a remarkable change in that, whereas in previous times a drunken driver who was prosecuted was often thought to have been 'unlucky', drink-driving became increasingly regarded as 'disgraceful' behaviour and attended with public obloquy. There can be little doubt that deaths on the road that arise from circumstances in which it is evident that the driver has behaved irresponsibly are similarly regarded.

There are indications that recently the courts are beginning to adopt a sterner approach in certain cases. In February 2004, Heather Thompson, a mother who had reportedly driven at speeds between 70 and 80 mph, overtaking a line of other vehicles on a bumpy country lane, crashed her car killing her daughter and a school friend. She entered a guilty plea and was sentenced to two years' imprisonment at Lincoln Crown Court. She had clearly suffered enormous distress at having killed the children, and the trial judge stated in open court that he had received communications from the general public urging that he take a lenient course, on the ground that she had 'suffered enough'.

Earlier, in February 2001, a vehicle with a laden trailer whose driver had allegedly dozed at the wheel, plunged over an embankment on the M62 motorway to the main railway line below. Moments later it was struck by an early morning passenger train. A further collision with a laden coal train coming in the opposite direction ensued. Six passengers and four railway staff died and a large number of others (between 70 and 80) were injured. The driver, Gary Hart, who had had little sleep before he had begun his journey, was sentenced to five years imprisonment at Leeds Crown Court, having been convicted on ten counts of causing death by dangerous driving. He pleaded not guilty at his trial and his later appeal against conviction was subsequently dismissed. The consequences of this event were to involve his insurers having to pay out a very substantial sum, in excess of £22m by way of compensation.

The case of *Hart* may be compared with the more recent case of *Travers*. The defendant, a 21-year-old barman pleaded to two counts of causing death by dangerous driving, to driving with excess alcohol and without having either a licence or third party insurance. He had given a lift to three young girls in a car that he had borrowed and driving at high speed in a 30 mph zone lost control and crashed the vehicle, which rolled on to its roof. One passenger, Natalie McCabe (20) died at the scene and Victoria Browne (19) died a month later in

---

[2] The maximum has been progressively increased from 5 to 10 and recently to 14 years.

hospital. The third passenger Becky Fish (20) survived, but had to have part of her leg amputated. Travers denied failing to stop and that charge was subsequently withdrawn. It was said that he had earlier had an argument with his girl friend and had been driving in an 'agitated manner'. Tests revealed him to have been one and a half times over the legal limit of alcohol. At Lewes Crown Court in March 2004 he was sentenced by Mrs Justice Rafferty to a total of imprisonment for five and a half years and disqualified from holding a licence for five years. Her words to the defendant left little doubt of the impression his behaviour had made on the court.

> Your driving was an exercise in arrogance.
> Like a petulant child you indulged your temper, but you did so using that most dangerous of weapons, a motorcar. It's not accurate to say you have ruined three lives, those of your victims, since you have blighted many more.

In the Hart case 10 people died and between 70 and 80 were injured, while in the Travers case two died and one was injured. Yet both received similar sentences. This might initially appear to reflect a highly variable approach to sentencing in motorised homicide, but it also draws attention to the fact that in such circumstances—and they apply in all such cases—it is the initial decision to drive in a particular manner in which the essence of culpability is to be found. The precise nature of the outcome, including the ultimate tragedy of death and serious injury, while the driver ought to be able intellectually to appreciate such possibilities, cannot be certain. But if probability is uncertain, the possibility cannot be ignored.

A case in June 2004 in Scotland, which also involved multiple deaths and driving under the effect of alcohol, concluded with a sentence substantially more severe than that imposed in *Travers*. Dean Martin, 23 had spent a night drinking whisky and lager as well as taking the drug 'ecstasy. Next morning he took his mother's car and drove through a housing estate at estimated speeds of up to 75 mph. Losing control of the vehicle, he killed a mother and her eight-year old daughter as well as another five-year-old child whose mother was seriously injured. After hitting the pedestrians, the car struck a wall and Martin drove on, later abandoning the damaged vehicle. He was charged with culpable homicide rather than causing death by dangerous or drunken driving and sentenced to 11 years imprisonment and disqualified from driving for life. Martin expressed immense remorse after the event and pleaded guilty. The trial judge, Lord Brodie, told the defendant that had he not done so the sentence would have been longer.

Those bereaved by Martin's actions, like the relatives of Travers' victims, have made it clear that they consider the sentences passed to have been unduly lenient.[3] However, if we contrast *Martin* with *Travers* we note that (albeit in a

---

[3] Natalie McCabe's mother is quoted as saying: 'As far as I am concerned we should be looking at manslaughter' *London Evening Standard,* 4 May 2004. It is reported that they have gathered some 7,000 signatories to a petition calling for a change in the law; for more severe penalties for causing death by dangerous driving and for proof of licence and insurance to be displayed on vehicle windscreens. The father of one child victim is reported as saying: "It is disgraceful that it is only 11 years. Is that what my son's life amounted to, and the other two lives? Eleven years is nothing".

Scottish court rather than in the south of England) while the case also involved driving at high speeds in a built up area having consumed substances known to impair driving skills, concluding with multiple deaths and serious injury, the sentence in *Martin* was twice that imposed in *Travers* and the period of disqualification life as opposed to five years.

These cases provide some suggestion that the *quantum* of sentence may be moving upwards in what are undoubtedly serious cases, and other courts in the United Kingdom may possibly follow, not least in respect of substantially longer periods of disqualification. Presently, lifetime periods of disqualification are rare and it may be that it is the insurance companies, rather than the courts, that more often restrict the lawful driving of serious offenders, either by increasing premiums to unaffordably high levels or refusing to provide any cover at all.

Nevertheless, what cannot be ignored is the common feature in such cases, namely, the dissatisfaction felt by those bereaved at what they perceive to be the comparative lenity of the penal consequences of criminally irresponsible behaviour. It is a view likely to be widely shared among those who have been bereaved and are left to grieve. For some reason there is a tendency to sanitise them by employing the term ' road traffic accidents' whereby, quixotically, the offences identified are in the vast majority of cases prosecuted under road traffic legislation and not as serious infringements of the criminal law relating to unlawful killing and the infliction of criminal injuries. Yet, in the real world, remarkably few crashes involving motor vehicles and their occupants or other road users (including pedestrians) are 'accidents' in the true sense of happening by chance or being otherwise unavoidable.[4] Given that these are situations in which those concerned have a general duty of care, there is a temptation to assume that the actions of defendants involved in motorised homicide need be assessed only by objective standards that are exemplified in the driver equivalent of the passenger on the Clapham omnibus. But here, as in every instance of criminal homicide, the moral culpability of the defendant, as distinct from his criminal responsibility, is neither uniform nor absolute. It is the level of culpability which varies, and enormously so. We have no hesitation in arguing for a change in the law whereby road deaths identified *prima facie* as being unlawful would be prosecuted as instances of criminal homicide. Where conviction followed, the penalty would be at large.

Death on the road raises a number of issues that the present law does not adequately reflect. First, although the driver will not have deliberately driven with the intention of killing or seriously injuring the dead person (or the charge would be murder) the effect of the death may be no different from that of any other homicide. The person will be dead and his family stricken with grief. The death may have disastrous long-term consequences of a financial and or

---

[4] In common parlance roads are often described as 'dangerous'; though empty of traffic they constitute no threat of harm. The 'danger' arises from the behaviour of those who use them, whether from simple lack of skill, error, or irresponsibility.

psychological nature. There is therefore a problem of matching the objective consequences of the event with the degree of culpability demonstrated by the offender's behaviour.

Secondly, this is a 'conduct' crime in that the essence of the offence is contained in the driver's behaviour prior to any consequential result. No doubt every driver faced with the fact of having caused death would wish to have behaved otherwise than he did. Is it possible, or indeed reasonable, for the offender to bear a penalty that is commensurate with consequences he did not directly foresee? In the case of *Lawrence*[5] Lord Diplock addressed the question of liability in a case of careless driving and in defining it suggested that all that was needed by way of *mens rea* was that the prohibited physical act done by the accused was directed by a mind that was conscious of what the body was doing, it being unnecessary to show that the mind was also conscious of the possible consequences. That decision is now regarded as too narrow and forensically unhelpful.

Notwithstanding that what might be termed 'motorised homicide' has, by the effects of road traffic legislation been separated out from the mainstream of jurisprudential thought concerning homicide, there is no reason why it cannot be brought back there. Our proposed new offence of criminal homicide would be that with which drivers, now prosecuted for causing death by dangerous or drunken driving, would be charged. It would not, in our view, present any serious problem, not least since many offences presently charged with manslaughter arise out of similar situations in which it is the conduct of the accused which constitutes the kernel of the offence and the result may well have never been foreseen, let alone intended. It is in the recklessness or negligence that the epicentre of culpability is to be found.

A person who drives a motor vehicle may be presumed to understand that, if it were to be driven in any way improperly, and that would include knowing that it was in an unsafe or dangerous condition, serious consequences, including the loss of life, could follow. It would not be enough for the accused to convince himself that taking a blind corner at a speed was acceptable, when he ought to have been aware of the possibility of there being a slow moving farm tractor or a group of cyclists, out of sight, but sufficiently close for him not to be able safely to slow down. More significantly, a driver who voluntary drinks before he drives knows that alcohol has the effect of impairing driving skill. Such a driver takes a deliberate risk. The question of estimating the *probability* of some catastrophic event, as distinct from the *possibility* of it is irrelevant. The application of a subjective test to the driver's conduct is clearly important in the context of assessing relative culpability for the purposes of sentence, but Lord Diplock was perhaps not, in one sense, so far from the mark when he suggested in *Lawrence* that the statute had created an 'absolute' offence in the sense in which the term is commonly used, although the term 'absolute' might be better

---

[5]   *R v Lawrence* [1982] 1 AC 510, 527.

rendered an offence of 'strict liability'. The driver must be held strictly liable with respect of driving in an incompetent manner.

While it would be unreasonable to make incompetence *per se* a crime—some people are incapable of driving competently and the driving test hopefully identifies them before they do any damage—deliberately to elect, as it were, to drive incompetently is a matter which ought to go to penalty, not least on account of the potential consequences that may result. The incompetence must be contextual, since even generally competent drivers are capable of lapses in their driving standard. That given, is there any good reason why a driver who has driven with what our proposed offence of criminal homicide identifies as 'recklessness' or 'negligence', should not be dealt with on the same basis as the youth who hurls a brick over a motorway bridge on to a stream of traffic below? He cannot be certain that his missile will strike any of the vehicles, or if it does whether it will do no more than damage the bodywork; but neither can he be certain that the brick will not go through the windscreen of a vehicle and strike the driver, either mortally injuring him or causing him to crash and die as a consequence—or worse—collide with other vehicles causing the death of their occupants too.

That there are millions of drivers of motor vehicles, most of whom do not indulge in the kind of driving that results in death, is no reason why the law should make special provision for them when others are harmed by their unlawful actions. Most train drivers behave in a responsible manner, but they are not similarly favoured by the law. If juries were, prior to 1956, reluctant to convict because of the possibility of sentences being imposed in excess of what they considered right—and there is only anecdotal evidence for that—they would have nothing to fear from our proposed change. The penalty for criminal homicide would be at large. The driver whose offence suggested that justice would demand a lenient rather than a condign punishment could expect to be treated mercifully; the hooligan behind the wheel, driving like Mr Toad, could receive the punishment he so richly deserved.

11

The Appellate Process

'If no appeal were possible . . . this would not be a desirable country to live in.'

Bowen LJ in *R v Justices for the County of London* [1893] 2 QB 492

Although our argument is for a fundamental change in the existing law relating to all homicides, and the abolition of the mandatory life sentence for murder, we would expect no legislative change in the present arrangements relating to questions of conviction. The question of sentence, however, raises issues of a very different order.

Presently, since a conviction for murder carries the fixed sentence of life imprisonment, it follows that there is no appeal against sentence. But if, as we would argue, the courts were to have the power to pass a range of sentences, appropriate to the culpability of the offender, taken together with other considerations of public policy that must form part of any rational approach to sentencing, neither the type, nor the duration of any particular sentence, may be deemed satisfactory by either party to the matter. The defendant may consider that the penalty is too harsh; the prosecutor too lenient. It may be that a particular sentence arouses strong public feeling which cannot sensibly be ignored. The present arrangements for appeals by the Crown against a sentence are limited by way of a reference by the Attorney General to the Court of Appeal (Criminal Division); they relate solely to the ground that the sentence has been unduly lenient. Our view is that the powers of the Court of Appeal in this respect are deserving of more ample application. While the Court should continue to address the issue of undue leniency as it is understood at present, it could be usefully extended to the appropriateness of a particular sentence. The term 'leniency', however, is capable of a variety of interpretations. It is essentially subjective. Upon whom you ask—the prosecutor, the convicted person, the family of the victim(s) of the homicide, the ordinary member of the local community, or public generally—will depend the answer you will get. The answers will rarely accord with one another.

We would not consider that sentencing at large for the proposed offence of criminal homicide should be confined within the sorts of 'starting points' that are enshrined in Schedule 21 of the Criminal Justice Act 2003, for the judiciary would, in due course, develop and establish patterns of sentencing that were appropriate. The review process, with its opportunities for the consideration of extensive argument, provides the appropriate forum of opportunity. While the trial judge would, no doubt, pass an appropriate sentence in the majority of cases, there would always be those in which closer scrutiny of the matter would be necessary. Given that the penalty for the new offence of criminal homicide would be at large, it follows that in many, indeed most cases, the Court of Appeal would deem the proper sentence to be one of a substantial term of imprisonment. In those cases where the future behaviour of the offender was difficult, if not impossible, to predict it would be likely that the court would consider the indeterminate sentence of life imprisonment to be the most appropriate penalty. We considered the proposition that defendant and prosecutor should both be equally entitled to an automatic right of appeal, but conclude that the present arrangement whereby a reference by the Attorney General to the Court of Appeal is available, on the ground of undue leniency, remains a simpler course. But because homicide is a matter of such gravity, it might well be necessary for special consideration to be given to sentencing in this instance since the term 'leniency' will need to be examined in the light of all the circumstances of a criminal event which, while its seriousness is in no way diminished, may vary in its details very widely indeed.

ACQUITTAL, QUASHED CONVICTION AND INNOCENCE

An outcrop from the spate of miscarriages of justice in murder prosecutions in the latter part of the twentieth century has been the voluble clamour by successful appellants (and accused persons acquitted by the jury) that they are innocent of the crime charged. The clamour stems from the undoubted principle that everyone accused of a crime is presumed innocent until proved guilty. But that principle is strictly evidential—that is to say, within the criminal process the burden of establishing the defendant's guilt rests throughout on the prosecution, and is displaced only if and when the jury brings in a guilty verdict. Outwith the criminal justice system, it has no application. But if the accused is acquitted, or his conviction is quashed on appeal, should there nevertheless follow, at least in certain circumstances, the conclusive proof of innocence?

Social policy can be ascertained from the state of English criminal procedure today. Section 2 (3) of the Criminal Appeal Act 1968, provides:

> An order of the Court of Appeal quashing a conviction shall, except when under section 7 below the appellant is ordered to be retried, operate as a direction to the court of trial to enter, instead of the record of conviction, a judgment and verdict of acquittal.

The successful appellant is, thus, in the same position as if he had been acquitted by a jury. He cannot be tried again for the offence of which he has been acquitted, or for any offence of which a jury could have convicted him on that indictment, subject to the very limited exception under the Criminal Justice Act 2003, that a person acquitted may be tried again only if there comes to light fresh and compelling evidence indicating criminal responsibility. The double jeopardy rule has been marginally modified.

According to a controversial passage in *Sambasivam v Public Prosecutor, Malaya*[1] Lord Macdermott, giving the judgment of the Privy Council, stated:

> The effect of a verdict of acquittal . . . is not completely stated by saying that the person cannot be tried again for the same offence. To that it must be added that the verdict is binding and conclusive in all subsequent proceedings between the parties to the adjudication. The maxim *res judicata pro veritae accipitur* is no less applicable to criminal than to civil proceedings.

Assuming that to be a correct statement of the law, it marks the limit of the effect of an acquittal: the acquittal is binding and conclusive *between the parties to the adjudication*, that is, between the prosecution and the acquitted person. It is not binding and conclusive between the acquitted person and anyone else, or between the prosecution and anyone else. If A has been acquitted of an offence, the prosecution may subsequently indict B for aiding, abetting, counselling or procuring to commit that offence and, at the trial of B, adduce evidence and prove A was in fact guilty of the offence of which he has been acquitted. A's acquittal is not admissible in evidence at the trial of B.[2] Where A and B are alleged to have conspired together to commit an offence, and there is evidence admissible against B, (for example a confession) which is inadmissible against A, the jury may properly convict B of conspiring with A while acquitting A of conspiring with B.[3] This is so whether A and B are tried together, or B is tried after A's acquittal.

Since a jury is invariably directed that it must not convict unless the jurors are sure of the accused's guilt, the only safe deduction from a verdict of acquittal is that the jury was not 'sure'. A jury which is satisfied only that it is more probable than not that the accused is guilty, or even that it is highly probable that he is guilty, will acquit so long as it loyally follows the direction of the judge, as it is strictly bound to do. So, in 1967 the Lord Chancellor's Law Reform Committee, having considered whether acquittals should be admitted in evidence, rightly concluded:

> So the acquittal, if admitted for 'what it is worth', would be worth nothing: not only would it have no effect on the onus of proof but it would be without any probative value.[4]

The Committee recommended that, on grounds of public policy, *defamation proceedings* should be treated differently, and that proof of an acquittal should

---

[1] [1950] AC 458, at 479.
[2] *Hui Chi-ming v R* [1992] 1 AC 34, PC.
[3] *DPP v Shannon* [1975] AC 717, HL.
[4] Fifteenth Report (1967) Cmnd 3391, para 15.

be conclusive proof of innocence. Parliament did not accept that recommendation; the law has remained as it was in *R v Loughrans Press*.[5] In that case the defendants stated that the plaintiff was guilty of a murder of which he had been acquitted, 20 years earlier. The defendants successfully pleaded the defence of justification, proving on the balance of probabilities that he had committed the offence. Since the law of libel now permits a public interest defence to an author who comments that an acquitted person is not instinctively innocent of criminal responsibility[6] there is no need for Parliamentary intervention.

It is the same when the Court of Appeal quashes a conviction as when a jury acquits. Until 1996 the Court was required to quash a conviction if it thought it was 'unsafe or unsatisfactory', and in any other case to dismiss the appeal. The fact that the Court quashed a conviction did not mean, however, that it necessarily thought the appellant was innocent of the crime. Quite the reverse, the Court may have been quite sure that he was guilty, but have held that the conviction was nevertheless 'unsafe or unsatisfactory' because of some defect in the trial or pre-trial proceedings. This was most strikingly illustrated by the case of *Algar*[7] where the Court quashed the conviction because inadmissible (but relevant and reliable) evidence had been admitted at the trial. The Lord Chief Justice, Lord Goddard, was reported to have said to the appellant who was present in court:

> Do not think we are doing this because we think that you are an innocent man. We do not. We think you are a scoundrel.[8]

To like effect was the judgment of the Court of Appeal (Criminal Division) in *R v Davis, Rose and AN Other*. Lord Justice Mantell ended the Court's judgment by saying that the quashing of the conviction did not mean that the appellants were innocent, 'far from it'.

The conclusion is that an acquittal, whether by jury or by the quashing of a conviction by the Court of Appeal, is of no value whatever in English law, except as between the Crown and the acquitted person.

In the Criminal Appeal Act 1995 Parliament accepted the view of the Lord Chief Justice, Lord Taylor of Gosforth, that 'unsafe' and 'unsatisfactory' could conveniently be expressed under the single rubric, 'unsafe'. By coalescing the two concepts—'unsatisfactory' relating to procedural irregularities in the trial process, and 'unsafe' relating to the impropriety of the verdict of guilt—the law obscures the case of the truly innocent from the case of the person acquitted on technical or procedural grounds.

In April 2004, in the case of *Mullen*,[9] the House of Lords comprehensively dispelled the notion that a miscarriage of justice (or an acquittal) inevitably

---

[5] [1963] CLY 2007 (QBD).
[6] *Reynolds v Times Newspapers Ltd* [2001] 2 AC 127.
[7] [1954] 1 QB 279.
[8] The *Times*. Law Report, 16 Nov, 1953.
[9] *R v Secretary of State for the Home Department (Appellant) ex parte Mullen (Respondent)* [2004] UKHL 18, (29 April 2004).

involves an assertion of innocence of crime. Lord Bingham of Cornhill observed that:

> The expression 'wrongful convictions' is not a legal term of art and has no settled meaning. Plainly the expression includes the conviction of those who are innocent of the crime of which they have been convicted. But in ordinary parlance the expression would, I think, be extended to those who, whether guilty or not, should clearly not have been convicted at their trials. It is impossible and unnecessary to identify the manifold reasons why a defendant may have been convicted when he should not have been. It may be because the evidence against him was fabricated or perjured. It may be because flawed expert evidence was relied on to secure conviction. It may be because evidence helpful to the defence was concealed or withheld. It may be because the jury was the subject of malicious interference. It may be because of judicial unfairness or misdirection. In cases of this kind, it may, or more often may not, be possible to say that he has been wrongly convicted. The common factor in such cases is that something has gone seriously wrong in the investigation of the offence or the conduct of the trial, resulting in the conviction of someone who should not have been convicted.

Lord Steyn interpreted the words, 'miscarriage of justice' in section 133 of the Criminal Justice Act 1988 (dealing with the right to compensation for wrongful conviction) to extend only to those acquitted who were 'clearly innocent'. Since the case of *Mullen* involved an abuse of executive power in breaching the principles of extradition, and hence was a factor external to the trial process in that the defendant had incontestably been convicted of terrorist offences, there was no conceivable basis for statutory compensation. All five Law Lords agreed that the case could not, in any event, fall within either meaning of 'miscarriage of justice'; the difference of approach taken by Lord Bingham and Lord Steyn remains unresolved.

We think that some regard should be paid to the popular (non-legal) view that an acquittal might be equated with innocence. There is a need to underscore public confidence in the working of the criminal justice system for there to be a clear indication of why the conviction has been set aside. Thus, on a conviction being quashed, the Court of Appeal should make clear whether in that case the successful appellant can properly claim that his acquittal is proof of his innocence for all purposes. Alternatively, it should indicate how some defect makes it necessary for the conviction to be set aside. Lord Bingham's list is comprehensive enough to provide a template for such statements. Lord Goddard's direct, if exasperated, language in addressing the appellant in *Algar*, is no doubt indicative of his awareness of the problem half a century ago. The problem persists.

It would not be desirable, or even practicable, for a jury in acquitting an accused, to state publicly why it had acquitted the accused even if it was required only to state briefly the grounds. The only possible amendment to the law would be for the appellate court to adopt the equivalent of the Scottish verdict of 'Not Proven', which we do not think would suffice to meet the clear distinction between complete innocence and a failed conviction. But the Court of Appeal is quite capable of articulating the precise reasons for quashing a conviction. It should start to do so, without being prompted by the legislature.

All the judges who staff the Court of Appeal (Criminal Division) would readily testify to the inordinate amount of time spent—both in and out of court—in pursuit of fine distinctions between murder and manslaughter, not to mention the problems associated with the partial defences of provocation and diminished responsibility. The cost in terms of judicial manpower and associated legal services at the Royal Courts of Justice is immense. That is not to overlook similarly needless exercises in the Crown Courts up and down the country where judges, lawyers and jurors wrestle with like problems at trial. The precise expenditure of public funds, whatever it may be, has never been quantified. But whatever the magnitude of the cost, the expenditure could be better deployed elsewhere in improving the efficiency and effectiveness of the criminal justice system. At the stroke of the legislative pen, our proposals would produce a huge saving in costs.

12

The Crime and the Penalty: Thinking Outside the Box

The noble Lord, Lord Stonham, held up his hands in horror at the fact that I was tending and intending to merge manslaughter and murder. Let me make it clear. Of course, as a matter of law, murder is a separate offence, and it is equally, perhaps the most serious offence. But . . . I dislike fine lines and technical distinctions.

I think that there is one offence of homicide, varying infinitely from the lowest degree of manslaughter up to the most intentional, deliberate and calculated true murder. Therefore, I think my argument is based on the anomaly which has been produced by the abolition of the death penalty.

The Lord Chief Justice, Lord Parker of Waddington, summing up in the House of Lords debate on his Amendment to the Murder (Abolition of Death Penalty) Act 1965.[1]

Forty years ago, Lord Parker had already adopted the view which we echo today. 'Let me make it clear', he begins. He could not have made it clearer. The 'fine lines' and 'technical distinctions' which he disliked had developed over the centuries, part of the increasingly anachronistic and unsolicited jurisprudential legacy of Sir Edward Coke. What he proposed could not have come closer to a common sense approach, whereby the ordinary and legal meanings of the word 'homicide' were at one. That his view was so readily cast aside at the time can be explained, as we have attempted to do earlier in this book. His argument was to be taken up again, a generation later, resonating in the judgments of Lord Mustill and Lord Steyn no less than in the Nathan and Lane reports, but it has if anything, been more stubbornly resisted. There are signs that, while those of a contrary view in 1965 were able readily to articulate their reasons, today we have what seems to resemble a dialogue with the political deaf.

[1] Hansard. HL, 27 July 1965, at Col 1241.

In 1969 the Murder (Abolition of Death Penalty) Act 1965 was finally approved by Parliament by resolution of both Houses. An attempt to delay, until 1973, the confirmation of the 1965 Act was rejected. Four years later, in 1973, the Criminal Law Revision Committee presented an interim report to Parliament on the penalty for murder[2] as part of a review of offences against the person. The report had been requested in March 1970 by the then Labour Home Secretary Mr James (subsequently Lord) Callaghan and presented to his Conservative successor, Mr Robert Carr. Its terms of reference were clear and straightforward:

> To review the law relating to, and the penalties for, offences against the person, including homicide, in the light of, and subject to, the recent decision of parliament to make permanent the statutory provisions abolishing the death penalty for murder.

The Report, which had taken the 14 members of the committee almost three years to produce, was, in the event, a concise document of no more than 24 pages containing some 43 paragraphs and one appendix comprising three tables of data on life sentence prisoners. The signatories to the report set out what has become the orthodox view on the penalty for murder, namely, that with one exception, it should be visited by the mandatory penalty of imprisonment for life. The sole dissenting voice was that of Professor Glanville Williams, who was opposed to the mandatory sentence in principle on the ground that the judge is thereby deprived of the power, which he possesses in all other cases, to distinguish between murders of different gravity by the sentences he imposes and since he cannot take into account any matters of mitigation. The exception to the mandatory sentence identified by the Committee related to what were considered to be

> . . . certain tragic cases of murder to which special considerations apply.
>
> Examples we have in mind are those in which a killing was done deliberately from motives of compassion . . . where a mother killed her deformed child or a husband terminated the agonies of his dying wife.[3]

In these instances the recommendation was that the trial judge should be able to make a hospital order, a probation order with a condition of psychiatric treat-

---

[2] Criminal Law Revision Committee, Twelfth Report, *Penalty for Murder* (London, HMSO, January 1973) Cmnd 5184. The CLRC had been charged with a broader remit than that of the committee set up by the Secretary of State for Scotland in September 1970, chaired by Lord Emslie and which reported ahead of its English counterpart in November 1972. (*Penalties for Homicide*, Scottish Home and Health Department. Cmnd 5137) Its terms of reference were; 'To review the law relating to the penalties for homicide in the light of the statutory abolition of capital punishment for murder and to report on the considerations that should govern any proposal for a change in that law'.

[3] *Ibid*, para 42.

ment, or order a conditional discharge where the sentencer was satisfied that it would be contrary to the interests of justice for the accused to serve any sentence of imprisonment.But this was no more than a sensitive, liberal suggestion for moderating the effect of the law, which would be seen to bear down unjustly upon those least deserving of public obloquy. At the core of the conclusions of the Criminal Law Revision Committee was a simple statement that the mandatory life sentence for murder should be retained, that the life sentence represented a greater deterrent than a determinate sentence, together with the implication that, since murder should remain a separate offence distinct from manslaughter, this should be reflected by a wholly different and more serious penalty. The Committee's argument on this point is worth stating in full:

> We first considered whether there should continue to be a separate offence of murder and, if so, whether the existing definition of murder at common law was satisfactory. It is sufficient for present purposes to say that, although it might be argued that by reason of the abolition of the death penalty for murder there was no longer the same need to draw a distinction in cases of homicide between murder and manslaughter, we are of the opinion that there should be a separate offence of murder. We believe that the stigma, which in the public's mind, attaches to a conviction of murder rightly emphasises the seriousness of the offence and have a significant deterrent value.[4]

This is a clear expression of the orthodoxy that has been rehearsed on every subsequent occasion when either the logic or the utility of the mandatory life sentence has been the subject of challenge. The essentials of this argument remain unaltered. Yet, as far as the public is concerned, there are homicidal offences, such as causing death by dangerous or drunken driving (which fall within the generic category of manslaughter) and which many—certainly the relatives of the victims—frequently consider to be the subject of woefully inadequate and lenient sentencing; likewise, in the public view, mercy killings of terminally ill patients are widely perceived not as crimes, but as acts of great humanity, certainly not to be visited by the mandatory penalty of life imprisonment should they be the subject of a subsequent conviction for murder.

In the early 1970s it was probably the case that those whose task it was to think about changes in the law were not always aware, or if they were, not entirely in sympathy with such views. But the same cannot be said to be true today. Some recognition of that is reflected in the recent increase in the maximum sentence for causing death by dangerous or drunken driving from 5 to 14 years, although not all defendants who are convicted are sentenced to custody, and among those who are, very few receive sentences approaching the maximum.

---

[4] *Ibid*, para 6.

A VIEW OF THE LIFE SENTENCE

In the early 1970s, it was still uncertain as to how the provision of the 1965 Act, whereby judges might indicate by way of recommendation (not sentence) the minimum term to be served, would develop. At that time, official thinking was far away from either the Rumbold doctrine, that held the life sentence to be precisely that, with release on parole constituting a 'mercy' of which the prisoner had no lawful expectation, or the later development of the Brittan doctrine that, by introducing the concept of the tariff conceptualised the life sentence as having within it, so to speak, a determinate portion necessary to satisfy the need for retribution and deterrence, ie, a punishment for a past misdeed. The Criminal Law Revision Committee was, however, quite clear in its understanding that;

> The essence of a life sentence is the *liability* to be detained for life; however long or short a period a life sentence prisoner has actually served before he is released on licence, he remains subject to recall for the rest of his life.[5]

When the Committee turns to the question of the judicial recommendation under section 1(2) of the 1965 Act there is an interesting and highly significant clue to its thinking about the purpose of the recommendation antipathetic to every official pronouncement over the last 30 years:

> . . . the trial judge may well not have sufficient information available to him at the time of trial to enable him to know what minimum period to recommend. If the trial judge were required to fix a minimum period in every case,[6] he might be put in a position of great difficulty in having to do so in circumstances in which he did not feel able to determine the appropriate period, this might be particularly so in a case in which there was evidence or suspicion of mental instability.[7]

The burden of this paragraph clearly *cannot* relate to any purpose other than that of estimating the minimum period for which, in the interests of public safety, it would be necessary to detain the prisoner. This is not 'tariff fixing'. Why else would there be reference to the 'suspicion of mental instability'? The theme is developed further in the succeeding paragraph. If the judicial recommendation had been intended to determine the minimum period required to satisfy the requirements of retribution and deterrence, then the trial judge would have all the requisite information at his disposal. The evidence of the trial would have clearly indicated the magnitude of the accused's desert with regard to retribution, additionally providing some guide as to how the recommendation might suitably mark the gravity with which the offence was viewed, and, other things being equal, the appropriate *quantum* for deterrence of others. That this is how the matter was viewed in the 1970s is underscored by a later passage in the Report:

---

[5] CLRC. Twelfth Report, *Penalty for Murder*, para 12.
[6] As the Scottish Committee chaired by Lord Emslie had recommended should be mandatory.
[7] *Penalty for Murder*, para 28.

In the most serious type of case, the trial judge may be inclined to doubt whether the prisoner can ever *safely* [our italics] be released.

In our view it would be undesirable in these circumstances for a judge to recommend that the prisoner should be detained for the rest of his natural life.[8] The effect of such a recommendation on the prisoner himself must be borne in mind. *Considerations of humanity suggest that it would be wrong to deprive a prisoner of all hope*[9] [authors' italics].

These opinions, on the nature of the life sentence and the purpose of the 'minimum recommendation' are substantially at variance with both the Rumbold and Brittan doctrines[10] and would seem to demonstrate with some clarity the degree to which the management of the life sentence became increasingly subject to development, not by way of court decisions, but rather, by way of political response to the presumed wishes of the public. Populism was readily translated into penal policy, unprompted by the dictates of justice in the criminal courts.

In sum, it can be said of the Report by the Criminal Law Revision Committee that, while on the one hand it accepted the long established concept of the crime of murder, distinguished from other, putatively lesser, homicides, on the other they embraced the well established liberal approach to the official management of the life sentence that had developed since the late nineteenth century. We think that the day of tariff fixing is over. Determinate sentencing itself will fully reflect the demands of punishment for criminal homicide. For the life sentence, when imposed, the minimum period of detention can be handled differently.[11]

THE ARGUMENT THAT DOES NOT GO AWAY

In 1989 a Select Committee of the House of Lords, under the chairmanship of Lord Nathan, reported on the subject of murder and life imprisonment.[12] It concluded that the arguments against the mandatory penalty were such that it should be abolished. The official response was to reject that position, and to reaffirm the belief that the unique crime of murder should be visited with the

---

[8] Although this was precisely the course adopted by Mr Justice Stephen Chapman in the case of *Skingle* (Unreported).

[9] *Penalty for Murder*, para 30. One signatory to the Report was Lord Justice (then Mr Justice) Lawton, (1911–2001) as he then was. Towards the end of his long life, throughout which he retained an acutely critical interest in the workings of the criminal law, he argued against the propriety of the 'whole life' tariff which was subsequently imposed on Myra Hindley, believing that the arguments for her eventual release could not be resisted indefinitely. The report of the Comittee does not appear to have been cited in Myra Hindley's case. (See p 123 *supra*.)

[10] The view of Lord Mustill expressed in *R v Secretary of State for the Home Department ex parte Doody and Others* [1994] 1 AC 531, was that while either of these doctrines is defensible, they cannot be applied at the same time.

[11] See below at pp 163 *et seq*.

[12] House of Lords, *Report of the Select Committee on Murder and Life Imprisonment*, HL 78–1 (HMSO, 1989).

unique penalty of mandatory imprisonment for life. In 1993, the Prison Reform Trust set up a Committee under the chairmanship of the former Lord Chief Justice, Lord Lane to consider the penalty for homicide, and, together with the mandatory life sentence, the arrangements for determining the period of actual custody to be served for murder under the present law, or a discretionary life sentence for manslaughter. Its unanimous recommendation was for the life sentence for murder to cease to be mandatory, but to become the maximum. The response of the Home Secretary in re-affirming that the arguments for the mandatory sentence were to be preferred was entirely predictable.[13]

Lord Lane had described the mandatory sentence as:

> . . . an anachronism and results in potential injustice.[14]

In summary, the Lane Committee argued the following case. The mandatory sentence for murder is founded on the fallacious assumption that murder is a crime of such unique heinousness that the offender forfeits for the rest of his existence his right to be free. The fallacy arises from the divergence between the legal definition of murder and that which the public believes to be murder. The common law of murder embraces a wide range of offences, some of which are truly heinous and others that are less so, some much less so; and it happens that the majority of murder cases fall into that category, though not those which receive the greatest publicity. The Lane Committee went on to advance three propositions:

> 1. that it is logically and jurisprudentially wrong to require judges to sentence all categories of murderer in the same way, regardless of the particular circumstances of the case before them.
> 2. that it is logically and constitutionally wrong to require the distinction between the various types of murder to be decided (and decided behind the scenes) by the Executive as is, generally speaking, the case at present.
> 3. that logically, jurisprudentially and constitutionally, the decision on punishment should be made in open court by the judge who passes sentence. He should be enabled to pass such sentence as is merited by the facts of the particular case, whether a hospital order, a determinate period of imprisonment, or, in the type of case which attracts most attention from the media, the wicked contract killings or those for gain, life imprisonment.

The second of these propositions is, of course, no longer relevant, since various decisions since 1993 have effectively stripped the Home Secretary of these powers, but the concerns of the Lane Committee about the involvement of the media were prescient:

> We are acutely concerned about the attitude of the public in general. Not unnaturally the general public base their views on the information which they receive from the media. The media focus attention upon the high profile murders; they are, generally

---

[13] See Annex 6.

[14] *Report of the Committee on the Penalty for Homicide* (London, Prison Reform Trust, 1993) at 1.

speaking, not concerned with the more humdrum, less newsworthy killings, many of which would not be regarded by the ordinary lay person as murder at all.[15]

The problem has perhaps become, if anything, more acute. The relationship between public perceptions of murder and presentations of it may have become symbiotic in the context of presentation and expectation. But although the tabloid sector of the media is frequently identified as the principal participant in the process, other sectors, notably television and the broadsheet publications cannot be excluded from the analysis. An important study by Professor Soothill of the University of Lancaster and his colleagues indicates that high profile cases can have a disproportionate effect on the public, though similarly, public memory can fade:

> 'mega-cases' contribute disproportionately to . . . the 'general knowledge of homicide'. Yet while it is likely that such cases will remain for some time in popular consciousness, not all 'mega-cases' reach 'iconic' status. . . . we can chart how killings become 'mega-cases' and how they either wane, or retain iconic status. Furthermore, while all 'mega-cases' are singular, unpleasant and demand that society is outraged and condemnatory, not all become the focus of moral panic.[16]

GUIDELINES OR TRAMLINES? THE ESSENCE OF THE ARGUMENT FOR CHANGE

Put simply, it is this. If the sentencing of offenders for the crimes of which they have been convicted is to be both rational and just, then the sentence must be both appropriate in character and proportional in magnitude, to the nature of the criminal event. If it is not this, then it can only be either entirely arbitrary or entirely mechanistic. As the German legal and social theorist, Max Weber, observed, for the rule of law to endure, it is essential that there be a balance between formal and substantive legal rationality.[17] Arbitrary forms of sentencing at their most extreme resemble something from the world of *Alice in Wonderland*, and are characterised by total unpredictability; at their least extreme they result in an inconsistency between one sentencing tribunal and another that likewise defies both predictability and rational explanation. We have long since moved away from a world in which judges and magistrates interpreted their powers to sentence at large in ways which often said more about the sentencer than the sentenced.

The use of 'guidelines' in the sentencing process is both proper and desirable, since it can demonstrate a degree of objectivity and rationality that evidently

---

[15] Above, at 6.

[16] Keith Soothill, Moira Peelo, Jayn Pearson and Brian Francis, 'The Reporting trajectories of top Homicide Cases in the Media: A Case Study of *The Times*' (2004) 43 *Howard Journal of Criminal Justice*.

[17] See the commentary on Weber by Professor Reinhard Bendix in David Sills (ed) *The International Encyclopaedia of The Social Sciences* (London, Collier Macmillan-Publishers, 1968) vol 16 at 499.

serves, rather than impedes, the processes of justice. For criminal justice to have the support of the public it must be seen to be just. A guideline is akin to the markings encountered on the highway, a line indicating the centre enabling the traffic to keep to its appropriate side, and lines at the side to indicate the margins of the road where necessary. While, as a general rule, the driver is expected to keep to the left of the markings down the centre of the road, he may, in certain circumstances cross to the other side, to overtake another vehicle or execute a right turn. Within the prescriptions of the Highway Code, the driver enjoys considerable latitude, enabling him to take account of road conditions and other factors as they present themselves. A 'guideline' is quite unlike a tramline or railway track. The latter has the effect of confining the vehicle to a particular track which cannot be varied, save by the operation of mechanical switches, only control over the speed of the vehicle being within the competence of the driver. The movement of a vehicle confined in such a way is predictable, but also inflexible; this is in contrast to the vehicle for whose driver the guidelines offer an indication, but no constriction. To pursue the comparison, while road traffic is highly varied in nature and complex in its movements—with variations in speed, type, and driver behaviour—fixed track vehicles operate largely within their own 'universe' (so to speak) which is characterised by far fewer variables. As far as sentencing in homicide cases is concerned, there is both variability and inflexibility. In sentencing for manslaughter, judges sentence as they consider fit, bearing in mind such guidelines as may have been set out by appellate decisions and practice directions. When it comes to sentencing for murder, the track runs straight and at its end is the terminus of imprisonment for life.[18]

There are two issues to be considered here. The first is that the distinction between murder and manslaughter defies rational explanation. Lord Mustill proclaimed it judicially in 1996. We have already discussed in an earlier chapter[19] the historical origins of the distinction, but it does not follow that what may have made good sense in the society of fifteenth and sixteenth century England is necessarily appropriate to the post-industrial society of the twenty-first century. It can easily slip from our analytical consciousness that the role of the prosecutor is critical in determining what charge shall be brought against a defendant in a homicide case. There may well, in consequence, be a significant gap between public expectation and pragmatism. It may result in homicides which appear to have, in the public mind, all the attributes of murder, being charged as manslaughter. Likewise, when the defendant to a murder charge is able to run a successful defence, be it provocation, self-defence or diminished responsibility, the public may, in its perplexity, come to the view that the accused has 'got away with murder'. Perhaps nowhere is this more common than in cases in which a defendant having committed a homicide of particularly

---

[18] How far the recommendation for the minimum term should constitute part of the sentence is still to be regarded as a matter of argument. So far Parliament has resisted making the minimum recommendation subject to appeal as a sentence. See p 151 *supra*.

[19] Chapter 2.

repellent character has been found guilty of manslaughter by reason of diminished responsibility. He is still considered, his mental health notwithstanding, to be a 'murderer'. The defences to murder may well allow the judge to pass a sentence other than one of life imprisonment, but that does not alter the public perception, which may well be one of arbitrariness.

The second issue is that while not all those offences determined by the trial process to be murder are like to each other, save that in each case death has resulted. The orthodox argument that has buttressed the mandatory penalty for so long is that murder is a uniquely heinous offence. In other words, once D has crossed the threshold of killing V, a mark of the most extreme moral obloquy follows, as night must follow day. That mark does not vary in its indelibility; it is impressed, with equal density and intensity, upon every person convicted of murder. It does not help that in common parlance, 'murder' is a term commonly employed as a synonym for killing, and 'killer' a term used to describe anyone who has committed a homicide. Yet not all homicides are regarded with the same social distaste. In September 1992, Dr Nigel Cox was tried at Winchester for the *attempted* murder of one of his elderly patients enduring excruciating pain in the last days, if not hours, of her life. His actions were widely perceived, far from those of one attempting a uniquely heinous crime, but as the actions of a caring doctor who sought only to alleviate his patient's suffering. He was convicted and sentenced to a suspended term of imprisonment of short duration, reflecting, no doubt, the view that although his action had been unlawful, it had been motivated by humanitarian concern. Had he been charged and convicted of murder, the sentence could only have been one of life imprisonment. The Cox case bears comparison with that of another doctor, Leonard Arthur, who was originally indicted in November 1981 for the murder of a 3-day-old baby manifesting Down's Syndrome. The jury found him not guilty of attempted murder on the direction of the trial judge, and not guilty to the charge of murder, which had earlier been withdrawn from the jury.

Public perceptions of different kinds of homicide, all of which may result in charges of murder, make it clear that while the received orthodoxy suggests that the mark of heinousness is uniformly dense and indelible, the social reality is otherwise. Indeed, the degree of public support for what is termed 'euthanasia' is probably substantial, although 'mercy killings' fall within the ambit of the law of murder, since they cannot in law be regarded as either justifiable or excusable instances of homicide. But even among those killings which are recognised as unacceptable, there is still considerable variation in the degree to which they are regarded as heinous. Is it seriously to be believed that the general public would greet the death of one drug dealer at the hand of another, albeit by being gunned down, with the same degree of anguish and outrage which would accompany the death of a child at the hands of a paedophile? Yet the law, presently, can make no distinction as far as the sentence of life imprisonment is concerned, and the provisions of Schedule 21 of the Criminal Justice Act 2003 do no more than to prescribe guidelines applicable to particular kinds of murder that establish the minimum terms normally to be stated judicially, none of which is particularly short.

If an offence is to be statutorily defined—and we have, as yet, no such definition for murder—it is still accepted as appropriate that there should be a degree of flexibility in sentencing. Take, for example, the offence of robbery. Section 8 of the Theft Act 1968 defines a person as guilty of robbery, thus:
A person is guilty of robbery if he steals, and immediately before or at the time of doing so, and in order to do so, he uses force on any person or puts or seeks to put any person in fear of being then and there subjected to force.

The same section provides that a person guilty of robbery, or of an assault with intent to rob, shall on conviction on indictment be liable to imprisonment for life. There can be no doubt that the law expresses a view which will be widely held, that to steal in such circumstances is a very grave offence indeed. Instances that come readily to mind are such things as the so-called 'Great Train Robbery' (which was marked by 30 year sentences for the ringleaders) as well as less-well identified crimes involving the robbery of banks, the hold-up of vans carrying valuables, and the like. Armed robbery, even if firearms are only employed as threats, or discharged against the ceilings of banks and building societies, is considered to be particularly serious. For such crimes, very long determinate sentences of imprisonment and discretionary life sentences appear as entirely appropriate, both as punishment for the crime and for the protection of the community.

Yet not all robberies involve the use of firearms; nor are their targets banks, building society offices, or high value goods in transit. Some involve interchanges between offender and victim on the street in a face-to-face, sometimes random or opportunistic fashion. Among the most commonly reported instances of robbery are those street robberies which involve the theft of goods such as mobile telephones, bicycles or even 'trainer' shoes. In many of these instances, both victim and offender are children or young persons. It is not, however, the case that when a 16-year-old threatens a 14-year-old to compel him to hand over a mobile telephone, a bicycle, or his footwear, that it crosses the mind of a court to consider a sentence of detention at Her Majesty's Pleasure (the juvenile equivalent of life imprisonment). But that is precisely the course that a court is obliged to take if the teenage offender is found to have murdered, as opposed to robbed, his victim. The example illustrates two things. First, that even a crime clearly defined by statute is inevitably a relatively heterogeneous rather than a homogenous category; and secondly, that being so, rational sentencing demands that the penalty be appropriate to all the circumstances of the case, including the circumstances of the crime, the effect on the victim and what future general threat there may be to society which may be moderated by the choice of a particular sentence.

UNTANGLING THE TWIN THREADS: THE CRIME AND THE PENALTY

That there is now a substantial body of opinion that considers the present common law offence of murder to be in urgent need of reform is undeniable. The Law Commission has said so.[20] It is our unequivocal view that the unsatisfactory state of the law of murder, *per se*, is beyond cure, whether by statute or judicial development. It is an anachronistic legacy from a bygone age that serves only as an impediment to justice. Yet it has remained, virtually intact for 400 years. Any change has largely related to the penalty. Normally a statute defines the crime and establishes the sanction; the two go hand in glove.

Our view, held no less unequivocally, is that the one cannot be reformed without reference to the other; they are inextricably linked. Apart from the abolition of the death penalty, every other change in the penalty for murder has brought in its train a whole series of difficulties. Some, like the distinction between capital and non-capital murder, were doomed from the start; others, like the concept of diminished responsibility, have had chequered histories ever since their introduction. Diminished responsibility has in recent times been employed as a defence in circumstances that Parliament might well not have anticipated in 1957. The partial defences to murder, which have been recently reviewed by the Law Commission, present a ramshackle intellectual appearance in the light of modern clinical psychology and psychiatry. The jurisprudential skein, in which crime and penalty are jointly present, is tangled; the more vigorously one thread is pulled, the more obstinate becomes the other in its resistance to being unwound prior to being neatly re-ordered.

ESCAPING THE BOX

The resolution with which successive governments and Home Secretaries have resisted suggestions that the mandatory penalty of life imprisonment for murder should be abandoned in favour of judicial discretion, indicates the degree to which it is possible for politicians to become prisoners of orthodoxy. It is as if they endure some form of intellectual imprisonment that to think 'outside the box' would spell some form of cataclysmic disaster that would not merely have dire electoral consequences, but which would in some way fatally damage public confidence in the criminal justice system and indeed, the very system of justice itself. In a symbolic way, the Criminal Justice Act 2003, in which the mandatory penalty was so stoutly defended, appears in this context like some great defensive stockade designed to repel any intellectual attack upon its orthodoxy. The precision with which the penalty for murder is addressed in the Act,

---

[20] *Partial Defences to Murder:* Law Commission, No 290 Cm 6301. August 2004.

no eventuality apparently unconsidered, is suggestive of an inward-looking defensiveness rather than an adventurous, outward-looking foray into the territory of reform. Positively, it may be recognised that Acts of Parliament, unlike perhaps some aspects of the common law, may be as readily deconstructed as they are constructed. Having regard both to the Homicide Act 1957 and the Murder (Abolition of Death Penalty) Act 1965, neither recent Conservative nor New Labour administrations appear to have had the courage of their predecessors in venturing upon what, at the time, were widely regarded as highly radical reforms.

LETTING THEM LOOSE OR KEEPING THEM CONFINED

At the heart of the stubborn opposition to change in either the penalty or indeed the law of homicide, there is undoubtedly a fear that giving the judges complete discretion in sentencing, the seriousness of the crime will not be reflected in the penalty. The provisions of Schedule 21 of the 2003 Criminal Justice Act, though they by no means eliminate juridical discretion, at least with regards the determination of the tariff period, embody the view that since murder is the most heinous of offences, it must be visited by a penalty that is both mandatory and substantial. The unspoken assumption is that the end of the mandatory penalty would result inevitably, in a reduction in the severity of the penalty for murder and a consequent loss of public confidence in the criminal justice system. Not so. Let it be said, and plainly, that if the judges were to have complete discretion in sentencing, we have not the least doubt that in appropriate circumstances the penalties imposed would seek to reflect the character of the criminal event, and have regard to a wide range of factors, including the effect upon the family and friends of the victim, the impact of the crime in the community, and the extent to which the offender would constitute a threat to society if he were to be released back into it. There would be circumstances in which a judge would consider it proper to impose a discretionary sentence of life imprisonment, as is presently the case in manslaughter and other serious crimes such as robbery and rape. What evidence is there to suggest that the judiciary would do otherwise in cases of criminal homicide when the occasion demanded? It must be for the opponents of change to say on what grounds, other than diffuse distrust, they cannot 'trust the judges'.

The idea that the contemporary judiciary is somehow afflicted with a condition of mind that compels them to impose sentences of increasing leniency in serious cases, while absurd and unsubstantiated, appears to have become embedded in the psyche of unbridled populism, notwithstanding that the prison population—a crude index of judicial activity and decision-making—is higher than at any point in history, and that sentence length of serious offences has been increasing in recent years, with a consequent effect upon the size of the prison population.

In the most serious cases, such as serial killings, killings with a racial or sexual motive, or the killing of children by strangers, there is no reason to suppose that the effect of the sentence would be substantially different from what it is at present. A life term might be considered appropriate with a correspondingly substantial indication of the minimum term to be served. The life sentence might likewise be employed in dealing with those offenders whose evident dangerousness is such that no one could be certain when it would be safe to release them, if at all. In those cases the life sentence would not be deliberately intended to be one of natural life; rather, the prisoner's case would be reviewed judicially at regular intervals to assess both progress towards rehabilitation and continued danger. Where the latter was identified, it might be that each periodic review would result in a negative assessment, with the result that the prisoner would, indeed, be incarcerated until his life's end. But the justification for such a result would be, and in justice could only be, that there remained a danger to the public. There are patients in Special Hospitals who are in that situation under mental health legislation. For it to be otherwise would be a retributive punishment of entombment for life, and to deny any offender, no matter how unspeakable their criminal behaviour, the opportunity of all hope of rehabilitation would constitute a cruel and inhuman response.

With offences of lesser gravity there is, similarly, no reason to believe that sentencing would present difficulties greater than those at present experienced by courts when attempting to impose the appropriate penalty. Not every assault, nor every sexual offence presents difficulties that cannot be overcome; there is an evident gradient of seriousness that can be identified in a variety of ways, not least by the experience of senior judges. There is no reason to doubt that judges would be able to distinguish a killing that arose from some drunken brawl from one involving premeditated assault; or one arising from a domestic argument, or quarrel between friends or acquaintances from a gangland or contract killing. The assumption that, given their heads, the judges would become a byword for lenient sentencing is a fantasy. The Attorney General already has the power to refer sentences that he considers to be unduly lenient to the Court of Appeal (Criminal Division) for its consideration and review. In the context of determinate sentences for criminal homicide the concept of 'undue leniency' is entirely apt and readily applied. For those sentenced indeterminately, however some judicial adaptation of 'undue leniency' may be necessary.

The notion that public confidence in the criminal justice system would disastrously evaporate is a fear for which there is little by way of solid evidence. In fact, it is likely that the general public, when asked well thought-out questions rather than being invited to make instant comments after some criminal event, is given to a more sober approach to identifying the relevant issues and social sentiments. Homicide, in the context of road traffic incidents, is widely considered to be inappropriately provided for by the law. On the other hand, a society that has accepted abortion is less troubled by euthanasia. Had either Dr Cox or Dr Arthur been convicted of murder, it is interesting to speculate upon the magnitude of the public dissatisfaction with such an outcome, if it had involved a sentence imprisonment for life, with a tariff that closely followed the guidelines of Schedule 21.

A SKETCH FOR LAW REFORM

As authors, we must readily admit to having once been inmates of the box from which we now invite others to escape. Forty years ago, when our more youthful eyes were fixed upon the objective of the abolition of capital punishment, all else paled into insignificance. The Homicide Act 1957, admitted even by its proponents to be regarded later as 'entirely friendless',[21] with all it manifest and immediate shortcomings, was a small crumb, not to be disdained, since it meant that the numbers of people facing death on the gallows would be fewer. Nor were we unduly troubled when, in 1965, the penalty of life imprisonment took the place of the penalty of death, not least since we could not envisage a situation in which any Home Secretary, and certainly no public official, would wish to set aside the practices developed over the years for the release of lifers. While they might well result in modification, such that the most serious offenders served much longer, there seemed no question of any prisoner, following a decision made in private, having hope extinguished, perhaps in advance of his or her knowledge, despondent in the realisation that, like Myra Hindley, they were destined to be entombed for life.

We also acknowledged, in discussing the trial of James Hanratty, that murder, when it was attended by capital punishment, was a 'crime apart'.[22]

Our case falls into two interrelated parts, the crime and the penalty. Neither of us remotely possesses the skills of a Parliamentary draftsman who might be asked to translate our proposals into statutory language, but we should, nevertheless give an indication of what those proposals are.

First, it will be necessary to abolish the separate crimes of murder and manslaughter, which will include the remaining effective parts of the ill-conceived and judicially discredited Homicide Act 1957. Abolition of the crime of murder will mean the consequential demise of all the partial defences which, if successfully pleaded, currently reduce the charge of murder to manslaughter. They will re-appear in the guise of mitigating circumstances in the single offence of criminal homicide as they do, curiously enough, in Schedule 21 of the Criminal Justice Act 2003. We think that it is unnecessary to repeal the Murder (Abolition of Death Penalty) Act 1965 once the crime of murder disappears from the criminal calendar; strictly the penalty becomes obsolete. The retention of the

---

[21] Lord Brooke of Cumnor speaking in the House of Lords in the debate in 1969 when abolition was finally confirmed. As Mr Henry Brooke he had been Home Secretary in 1961–64.

[22] Terence Morris and Louis Blom-Cooper, *A Calendar of Murder* (London, Michael Joseph, 1964).

1965 Act on the Statute Book might, however, alongside the Sixth Protocol to the Europen Convention on Human Rights, incorporated in Schedule 1 Part III to the Human Rights Act 1998, serve as a legislative monument to the unassertive sanity that capital punishment forms no part of the customs of a civilised society.

Our Criminal Homicide Act—perhaps of 2007—since a period of three years' gestation for the new statute ought to provide sufficient time for politicians and Parliamentarians to get their act together—would look something like this.

Clause 1

(1) A person* who, by any act or omission, intends to cause, or by behaviour manifesting recklessness, gross negligence or by reason of serious failure of corporate management, causes serious physical harm to another person resulting in that person's death, commits the offence of criminal homicide.

* By virtue of the Interpretation Act 1978 S 5. Schedule 1, unless the contrary intention appears, 'person' shall include a body of persons corporate or incorporate.

(2) A person convicted of criminal homicide shall be liable to a sentence of life imprisonment, or a fine, unlimited in amount, or both, or such other non-custodial penalty including a hospital order as the court might deem appropriate.

(3) Life imprisonment shall constitute the maximum penalty and all custodial sentences of determinate length shall be equally available to the court.

(4) Life imprisonment shall mean liability to incarceration for the period of the natural life of the offender so sentenced and not a sentence of incarceration determinable upon the life of the offender.

(5) In the case of a Child or Young Person convicted of criminal homicide the same penalties shall be available to the court, save that the maximum penalty shall be an order of detention at Her Majesty's Pleasure substituted for a sentence of life imprisonment.

Since the penalty of life imprisonment would become the maximum, the courts will be free to pass sentences of determinate length or alternatively impose a non-custodial sanction where immediate imprisonment would be inappropriate. Suspended sentences, whole or partial, might become a useful tool of social control over the less heinous killings. Where the court opts for the life sentence, because it cannot gauge the moment when it will be safe to release the convicted killer, we think the approach to discharge from custody should be along the lines of the current indeterminacy available in cases of manslaughter, save for the question of tariff fixing under Section 34 of the Criminal Justice Act 1991, which we would not wish to replicate for reasons which we now give.

INSIDE OUT, UPSIDE DOWN (OR, BACK TO FRONT)

If, at the time of conviction for murder or manslaughter (*criminal homicide*, if you have ingested the thrust of this book) the sentence of the trial court is life imprisonment, whether imposed mandatorily or selected judicially, the presumption must be that the judge feels uncertain when it would be safe to release on licence the convicted person from prison for the rest of his or her natural life. Only if the life sentence can be properly interpreted as 'whole life' which we seriously doubt is compatible with the ECHR,[23] is the risk of discharge back into the community not addressed. It must be contemplated that all lifers will become eligible for discharge from custody at some point in their penal career; the question is 'when'? The prison authorities, in association with the Parole Board, will be required, on the prisoner's reception into prison, to plan the lifer's sentence.

The longer life sentence prisoners remain in custody, the more difficult it becomes (a) to predict how the individual lifer will behave, as and when released into the community; and (b) for the lifer to be restored to familial and social relationships. Prediction of future risk of harm is of course, primarily dependant on the past record of violent behaviour, and that much is ascertainable at the time of reception. What is less predictable is how much removal from society further handicaps the lifer in adjusting to life outside the restricted regime of prison. Given an assessment on past performance and the lifer's response to prison conditions, the time lag of incarceration provides an imponderable which can be diminished by earlier rather than later release. In a sense, every day excluded from society increases the inability to adjust. Restoration to familial and social relationships—assuming that they existed in some way at the time of imprisonment—are vital to the expectation of compliance with parole licence. Again, any delays in establishing (or re-establishing) normal interaction in society will tend to militate against successful rehabilitation.

The answer to these concerns must be that penal policy should reflect social desire to contemplate loss of liberty for the shortest possible time consistent both with an acceptable level of risk of harm, based on a rigorous assessment of dangerousness and restrictive sense of penalty for the criminal event. If the lifer exhibits to the prison authorities his or her candidature for release, the moment of discharge ought not to be postponed beyond what might be regarded as an appropriate term of imprisonment. Otherwise the optimum for rehabilitation may be lost, even irretrievably. The contemporary jurisprudence of human rights in this respect is as follows:

> It is not apparent how public confidence in the system of criminal justice could be legitimately require the continued incarceration of a prisoner who had served the term required for punishment and no longer a risk to the public.[24]

---

[23] That is, if such a sentence were imposed for the purposes of retribution and deterrence. If a prisoner should experience what eventually proved to be a lifetime of incarceration arising from the continuous periodic estimation of the risk to the community, should he be released on licence, that is not a 'whole life' sentence, since it will not have been imposed *ab initio*.

[24] ECHR in *Stafford v UK* (2002) 35 EHRR 1121, at para 80. Cited *verbatim* by Brown and Buxton LJJ in *Anderson and Taylor* [2002] 2 WLR 1143, paras 57 and 82, and further cited by the House of Lords in *Anderson* [2003] 1 Cr App Rep 32.

Yet the criminal justice system currently proceeds to engage in a thoroughly illogical exercise. It instantaneously fixes the tariff—the minimum period the prisoner must serve in custody, for the purpose of reflecting punishment and deterrence for the crime, before consideration can be given to the question of parole. The court seeks to measure how long life will be without at that stage seeking any answer to the question: for how long will the prisoner not be safe to be released?

Since the tariff is only a milestone on the road to release we are unnecessarily playing with the prisoner's liberty, that most precious commodity in a civilised society. If we are serious about the future safety of all those who may come into contact with the lifer on licence, the assessment of dangerousness should be the priority in determining discharge. At that point the time actually spent in custody should be weighed against the measurement of punishment for the criminal event. And that assessment should be made either judicially in court or by the independent Parole Board subject to judicial review. If, for sound reasons of uncertainty about the length of time the prisoner should be kept out of society, the sentence of the court is considered to be indeterminate—i.e., life imprisonment—then the question, how long is 'life', should be deferred until such time as the demands of safety can be met.

There is nothing new in this analysis of the status of indeterminate sentencing. It was precisely what took place at the time of the abolition of the death penalty. The question, how long is 'life' was first raised in 1959 in an exchange of letters[25] between the Home Secretary (then R A Butler) and Sir (then Mr) Edward Gardner QC MP, to which the answer was, broadly speaking, that (at that time) a lifer would serve an average nine years. That lifer population was considerably different from the lifer population of today. It contained both those who had been reprieved from the gallows, prior to the 1957 Homicide Act and included the first tranche of those sentenced to non-capital murder, post-1957. The nine year average is now probably 15 years[26] and will tend to grow incrementally. Discounting the small minority of 'lifers' today who might have been candidates for the hangman's rope (in 1960, of the 26 persons charged with capital murder only 7 were hanged) the only rational explanation for the doubling in time of the period of custody of a 'lifer' is the heightened perception of society's punitiveness, no doubt sharply accentuated by a handful of high profile cases of particular gravity and even horror—the 'Moors' murderers Ian Brady and Myra Hindley (1965), Peter Sutcliffe (1979), Dennis Nilsen(1983)), Jon Venables and Robert Thompson (1993), Harold Shipman (2000) and Ian Huntley (2003).

'What ranks as a long sentence . . . is largely a matter of convention . . . these conventions are seen to be ultimately based on public opinion and that opinion

---

[25] This correspondence we reproduce in Annex 2.
[26] Schedule 21 of the CJA 2003 says so in respect of the ordinary conviction of murder. The starting points may subsequently be varied by ministerial order.

may itself be, and indeed has been, in its turn modified by changes in sentencing practice'.[27] A tolerant society should accommodate a minimalist approach in determining how long a person should be deprived of his liberty: short sentences can be as effective as long ones.

We do not know how the lifer system worked in practice before 1967 (the year in which the Parole Board was established). But generally speaking, informed opinion was that life sentence prisoners got their discharge much more readily in the days when release mechanisms were shrouded in Home Office secrecy. Formalisation has led to lifers spending longer times in prison. The defect in the system was the lack of transparency and the absence of judicial oversight of a lifer's time spent in custody. Both defects have been to some extent remedied. Most 'lifers' (and the public) will know, roughly speaking, at the time of reception into prison how many years stretch ahead before they can contemplate any release. The Home Secretary's legislative device of fixing high tariffs has at least produced that degree of serendipity. The judicialisation of the tariff itself is now impermissibly strait-jacketed. Given our recommendations, the provision for mandatory tariffs provided in Section 269 and set out in Schedule 21[28] of the Criminal Justice Act 2003 should be repealed, in favour of a system which we have described.

CONCLUSION

The system which we propose for the release of lifers is as follows. As soon as the prisoner comes into the lifer system, there should be an immediate and ongoing, rigorous risk assessment. This would mean that some of the 'one-off' domestic killers would have the optimum chance of early release. Others would know that their state of mental health would be constantly assessed, with the prospect of appropriate treatment. Once the prediction of safety is reached, and it is considered that the lifer's discharge would constitute minimal risk to the community to which he or she is returning on licence, the question of 'time-inside' should be assessed, either by or reference to a court of trial, or by the Parole Board subject to judicial review. (This would equate approximately with the position of a person subject to a hospital order unlimited in time.) The presumption would be that the time spent in custody while considered dangerous if released, would suffice to reflect the element of punishment for the criminal event that led to the life sentence. Any extension beyond the moment of a safe discharge would represent the need for more punishment than represented by incarceration so far.

In short, at the present time, we have got things the wrong way round—penalty for the crime first, dangerousness a matter for consideration only when the punishment has expired. The question of how long a lifer should spend inside should be determined only after the propriety of his safe release back into society has been established.

---

[27] Barbara Wootton, *Crime and Penal Policy* (London, George Allen and Unwin, 1978) at 65.
[28] The substantive periods set out in Sched 21 may be modified by ministerial Order.

Annex 1

Membership of the Royal Commission on Capital Punishment
1949 –1953
Appointed by Royal Warrant 4th May 1949

Sir Ernest Gowers (Chairman)
The Earl Peel
Sir Alexander Maxwell
Sir William Jones
Dame Florence Hancock
Elizabeth Cameron
John Mann
Norman Fox-Andrews KC
Horace Macdonald
Professor George Montgomery KC
Leon Radzinowicz
Dr Eliot Slater

Annex 2

Extracts from the Homicide Act 1957

An Act to make for England and Wales and for courts-martial (wherever sitting) amendments of the law relating to homicide and the trial and punishment of murder, and for Scotland amendments of the law relating to the trial and punishment of murder and attempts to murder. [21st March, 1957]

PART 1

AMENDMENTS OF LAW OF ENGLAND AND WALES AS TO THE FACT OF MURDER

Abolition of 'constructive malice'

1. (1) Where a person kills another in the course or furtherance of some other offence, the killing shall not amount to murder unless done with the same malice aforethought (express or implied) as required for the killing to amount to murder when not done in the course or furtherance of another offence.

   (2) For the purposes of the foregoing subsection, a killing done in the course or for the purpose of resisting an officer of justice, or of resisting or avoiding or preventing a lawful arrest, or of effecting or assisting an escape or rescue from legal custody, shall be treated as a killing in the course or furtherance of an offence.

2. (1) Where a person kills or is party to the killing of another, he shall not be convicted of murder if he was suffering from such abnormality of mind (whether arising from a condition of arrested or retarded development of mind or any inherent causes or induced by disease or injury) as substantially impaired his mental responsibility for his acts and omissions in doing or being a party to the killing.

   (2) On a charge of murder, it shall be for the defence to prove that the person charged is by virtue of this section not liable to be convicted of murder.

   (3) A person who but for this section would be liable, whether as principal or accessory, to be convicted of murder shall be liable instead to be convicted of manslaughter.

   (4) The fact that one party to a killing is by virtue of this section not liable to be convicted of murder shall not affect the question of whether the killing amounted to murder in the case of any other party to it.

Provocation

3. Where on a charge of murder there is evidence on which the jury can find that the person charged was provoked (whether by things done or by things said or by both together) to lose his self-control, the question whether the provocation was enough to make a reasonable man do as he did shall be left to be determined by the jury; and in determining that question the jury shall take into account everything both done and said according to the effect which, in their opinion, it would have on a reasonable man.

Suicide pacts

4. (1) It shall be manslaughter and shall not be murder, for a person acting in pursuance of a suicide pact between him and another to kill the other or be a party to the other [*killing himself or*][1] being killed by a third person.

(2) Where it is shown that a person charged with the murder of another killed the other, or was a party to his [*killing himself or*][2] being killed, it shall be for the defence to prove that the person charged was acting in pursuance of a suicide pact between him and the other.

(3) For the purposes of this section 'suicide pact' means a common agreement between two or more persons having for its object the death of all of them, whether or not each is to take his own life, but nothing done by a person who enters into a suicide pact shall be treated as done by him in pursuance of the pact unless it is done while he has he settled intention of dying in pursuance of the pact.

PART II

LIABILITY TO DEATH PENALTY

Death penalty for certain murders

5. (1) Subject to subsection (2) of this section, the following murders shall be capital murders, that is to say,—

    (a) any murder done in the course or furtherance of theft;

    (b) any murder done by shooting or causing an explosion;

    (c) any murder done in the course or for the purpose of resisting or avoiding or preventing a lawful arrest, or of effecting or assisting an escape or rescue from legal custody;

    (d) any murder of a police officer acting in the execution of his duty or of a person assisting a police officer so acting;

    (e) in the case of a person who was a prisoner at the time when he did or was party to the murder, any murder of a prison officer acting in the execution of his duty or a person assisting a prison officer so acting.

---

[1] These words were removed by their repeal in the Second Schedule to the Suicide Act 1961.
[2] *Ditto.*

(2) If, in the case of any murder falling within the foregoing subsection, two or more persons are guilty of the murder, it shall be capital murder in the case of any of them who by his own act caused the death of, or inflicted or attempted to inflict grievous bodily harm on, the person murdered, or who himself used force on that person in the course or furtherance of an attack on him; but the murder shall not be capital murder in the case of any other persons guilty of it.

(3) Where it is alleged that a person accused of murder is guilty of capital murder, the offence shall be charged as capital murder in the indictment, and if a person charged with capital murder is convicted thereof, he shall be liable to the same punishment for the murder as heretofore.

(4) In this Act 'capital murder' means capital murder within subsections (1) and (2) of this section.

Death penalty for repeated murders

6. (1) A person convicted of murder shall be liable to the same punishment as heretofore, if before conviction of that murder he has, whether before or after the commencement of this Act, been convicted of another murder done on a different occasion (both murders having been done in Great Britain).

(1) Where a person is charged with the murder of two or more persons, no rule of practice shall prevent the murders being charged in the same indictment or (unless separate trials are desirable in the interests of justice) prevent them from being tried together: and where a person is convicted of two murders tried together (but done on different occasions), subsection (1) of this section shall apply as if one conviction had preceded the other.

Annex 3

Life sentences for Murder

AN EXCHANGE OF CORRESPONDENCE BETWEEN MR RA BUTLER, SECRETARY OF STATE
FOR THE HOME DEPARTMENT AND MR (LATER SIR) EDWARD GARDNER, QC, MP

*While by the late 1950s many Conservative Members of Parliament had, though
some with reluctance, come to accept that some reform of the law relating to the
punishment for murder was required, not all of them had been content with the
changes brought about by the Homicide Act. Many felt that certain non-capital
murders ought to have been included in the capital category, for example those
of a sexual or sadistic nature. That not having been the case, it was felt that the
imprisonment of those sentenced following such offences ought to be substantial. It is possible to discern in the Gardner letter a pre-echo both of the policy
to be introduced by Leon Brittan as Home Secretary twenty years later and of
the approach to the 'life' sentence enshrined in Criminal Justice Act 2003 by
New Labour's David Blunkett and its Schedule 21. Butler's reply is characteristic of the careful approach for which he is generally regarded as having been one
of the most outstanding incumbents of the office of Secretary of State for the
Home Department.*

*Edward Gardner continued doggedly in his support of capital punishment,
albeit limited, for more than twenty years, being actively involved in the several
attempts during the Thatcher era to re-introduce it by means of 'piggy-back'
clauses attached to other criminal justice legislation. All were defeated and later,
in a private conversation with one of us [TM], he finally admitted defeat, reflecting sadly: "I'm giving up. It's hopeless".*

JUNE 12TH 1961

Dear Home Secretary,
May I invite your urgent attention to the motion No. 121, on the Order Paper,
which has now been signed by more than fifty Conservative Members of
Parliament? This, I believe, reflects the loss of confidence by most people in the
country in the present punishment of 'life imprisonment' for non-capital murder and shows a strong desire that the government should "take immediate steps
to introduce legislation to ensure that a sentence of life imprisonment for this
crime shall be for a period of not less than twenty-five years, unless a court in its
discretion orders otherwise".

The Homicide Act of 1957 distinguished non-capital murder from all
other crimes by expressly limiting punishment to an indeterminate sentence

'imprisonment for life'. In theory this is 'the most rigorous sentence of imprison-ment known to the law; in practice it is an empty formula. This dangerously debases both the deterrent and punitive value of the only sentence upon which the community can now rely for protection from sadistic, sexual and other murder-ers. Under the Homicide Act their methods of killing allow them to escape the death sentence.

The average term of imprisonment served by a prisoner sentenced to life imprisonment has recently been about nine years (for murders committed before 1957). In future, one understands 'life imprisonment' is likely to be pro-longed to an average of about twelve years. It may be argued that the average includes longer (and shorter) periods of imprisonment but the weakness of an indeterminate sentence is not its ultimate length or brevity but its *uncertainty*. What has a killer to fear if he can kill believing that if he is caught and convicted he may spend less time in prison than a thief?

Among the reasons for the present dissatisfaction with the working of the Homicide Act are:

(i)   It seems incredible that, when Parliament replaced the death penalty by life imprisonment in 1957, it can have intended to bring about the pre-sent illogical consequences.

(ii)   Murder has always been the 'gravest of all crimes' for which the com-munity has always exacted 'the severest of all penalties'.

(iii) Though the deterrent effect of the death penalty may be debateable, no one can doubt the deterrent of a long term of imprisonment.

(iv)   There is a strong and growing anxiety in the country that the Homicide Act does not give the community the protection which it has the right to expect.

(v)   But where a murderer may deserve compassion, for instance in the case of a mercy killing, a trial Court should have discretion to impose a lenient sentence.

I know that I write expressing views that are widely held and that there are many people who would be grateful for your answer.

Yours sincerely
(Sgd.) Edward Gardner

4TH JULY 1961
Dear Gardner
You wrote on 12th June drawing my attention to the motion on the Order Paper on the subject of life imprisonment for murder and seeking my views. You will not expect me to deal in detail with the proposals for legislation contained in the motion. It may, however, be helpful if I say something about the existing policy in relation to the release of prisoners serving life sentences, since the terms of the motion suggest that there may be some misunderstanding on this matter.

Dealing first with the pre-Homicide Act cases, it is true that for life sentence prisoners released in recent years the period of detention served in an average case has been about nine years. This is not a mathematical average. It is the period served in a case in which there were some mitigating features which justified a reprieve, where there were no compassionate circumstances calling for specially early release and where the Home Secretary has been satisfied, on the basis of full reports on the circumstances of the offence and on the prisoner, including reports on his conduct in prison and his mental condition, that he could be released without danger to the public at the end of that period. Where there have been specially mitigating or compassionate circumstances the period of detention has been shorter. On the other hand, there have been many cases in which it has been thought right to detain a prisoner for more than nine years. The important point is that no prisoner serving a life sentence is released unless the Home Secretary is satisfied that there is unlikely to be a risk of his repeating his offence or being a danger to the public. One person released during the last five years had been detained for 20 years, and among the life sentence prisoners now detained are two who have served 16 years and two who have served 13 years. A further point I should like to make is that life sentence prisoners are always released on licence and can be recalled to prison at any time if this is thought to be desirable. Successive Home Secretaries have not hesitated to use this power in the interests of public safety.

The passing of the Homicide Act created a new situation. Prisoners who are now sentenced to life imprisonment for non-capital murder include some whose crimes present no mitigating features, and who, before the Act, would have been executed. It is to be expected that many of these prisoners will have to be detained for periods much longer than has been found necessary, save in the most exceptional circumstances, in the past, where there have usually been extenuating circumstances to justify a reprieve. In an extreme case it may be necessary to detain a prisoner until he dies. It is obviously quite impossible, when the Act has been in operation for only just over four years and the only prisoners released have been those for whom some exceptional compassionate grounds for early release existed, to predict what the average period of detention will be in the future. I do not know the origin of the figure of twelve years to which you refer; it certainly does not derive from anything I have said on this subject.

You say that the weakness of an indeterminate sentence is its uncertainty. I do not believe that this is so. Prisoners do not know until about a year before they are due to be discharged how long they will have to serve, and experience has shown that this uncertainty is, for most prisoners, the worst feature of their detention. As regards deterrence, the Royal Commission on Capital Punishment saw no reason to conclude that any general increase in the periods served was necessary to ensure the deterrent effect of the life sentence. Nine years—the period recently served, in an average case, by a man whose sentence was commuted to life imprisonment before the Homicide Act—is the equivalent, with one third remission of a sentence of imprisonment of nearly fourteen years. Moreover, as I have already said, many prisoners sentenced to life imprisonment under the Homicide Act are likely to be detained for more—some for much more—than nine years. It is therefore not correct to say that a man who commits murder will spend less time in prison than a thief. Indeed, it is clear that the period of detention served by murderers in recent years, and still more the period which they are likely to serve in the future, is very much longer that that served for any offence of theft, or indeed, save in the most exceptional cases, for any offence not involving homicide. (In 1959, for example, apart from 44 sentences of life imprisonment for murder or manslaughter, only six sentences of imprisonment for more than 10 years were imposed—one for manslaughter, one for felonious wounding, one for burglary and three for robbery. Two of these were life sentences; the other four were determinate sentences (on which remission can be earned).

As regards your proposal to make a life sentence one of not less than twenty-five years, unless a court in its discretion orders otherwise, it seems likely that in practice the twenty five years' sentence would become the exception rather than the rule, since the great majority of murders are not of the kind which understandably give rise to especial public anxiety and concern, and which have no doubt prompted your motion, but are murders committed by relatives, often in circumstances which allow a compassionate view to be taken.

I should have no objection to our arranging for this letter to be published. Indeed I would welcome any steps which might help to remove some of the misapprehensions which I believe to exist on the subject.

I am sending a copy of this letter to Bingham,[3] who has also written to me about the motion.

Yours ever
(Sgd) RA Butler

---

[3] Richard Bingham, QC, was Conservative MP for the Garston Division of Liverpool 1957–1966

Annex 4

Law Lords voting for the Parker Amendment on 27 July 1965

The Lord Chief Justice, Lord Parker of Waddington, described the object of his amendment as very simple:

> to abolish once and for all a fixed penalty for murder; in other words, to prevent life imprisonment from being the only sentence which can be passed. Subsection (1) will read: " . . . a person convicted of murder shall be liable at the discretion of the court to imprisonment for life."[4]

The Lord Chancellor, Lord Gardiner, was opposed. While recognising that it was a debateable matter, he argued that the Amendment was

> . . . seeking, it may be rightly, to take for the judiciary a power which in murder cases they have never had.
> Murder, I suggest, is a crime apart. . . because there is no other crime which is so largely a product of the disordered mind.[5]

In his view, the life sentence provided the element of indeterminacy that was essential if murderers, who manifested so often this degree of abnormality, were to be safely released at some future date.

But perhaps the most important point was to emerge in Lord Parker's summing up at the end of the debate.

> The noble Lord, Lord Stonham, held up his hands in horror at the fact that I was tending and intending to merge manslaughter and murder. Let me make it clear. Of course, as a matter of law murder is a separate offence, and it is also perhaps the most serious offence. But . . . I dislike fine lines and technical distinctions. I think that there is one offence of homicide, varying infinitely from the lowest degree of manslaughter up to the most intentional, deliberate and calculated true murder. Therefore, I think that my argument, as was that of the noble Lord, Lord Reid, is based on the anomaly which has been produced by the abolition of the death penalty.[6]

[4] Hansard HL Vol 268 Cols 1211–1212.
[5] *Ibid* Col. 1239.
[6] *Ibid* Col. 1241.

Apart from the Lord Chancellor, Lord Gardiner, every other Law Lord voted for the Amendment, the list being as follows:[7]

DENNING *[Teller]*

DILHORNE

GUEST

HODSON

MORRIS OF BORTH-Y-GEST

PARKER OF WADDINGTON

PEARSON

REID *[Teller]*

WILBERFORCE

---

[7] *Ibid* Cols 1243–1244.

Annex 5

Extracts from the Murder (Abolition of Death Penalty) Act 1965

An Act to abolish capital punishment in the case of persons convicted in Great Britain of murder or convicted of murder or a corresponding offence by court-martial and, in connection therewith, to make further provision for the punishment of persons so convicted [8th November 1965]

1. (1) No person shall suffer death for murder, and a person convicted or murder shall, subject to subsection (5) below,[8] be sentenced to imprisonment for life.
2. (2) On sentencing any person convicted of murder to imprisonment for life the Court may at the same time declare the minimum period which in its view should elapse before the Secretary of State orders the release of that person on licence under section 27 of the Prison Act 1952 or section 21 of the Prisons (Scotland) Act 1952.
3. No person convicted of murder shall be released by the Secretary of State on licence under section 27 of the Prison Act 1952 or section 21 of the Prisons (Scotland) Act 1952 unless the Secretary of State has consulted the Lord Chief Justice of England or the Lord Justice General as the case may be together with the trial judge if available.

Section 4 of the Act provided that it should continue in force until the 31st of July 1970 and should then expire unless Parliament by affirmative resolutions of both Houses should otherwise determine. That is what happened in 1969, and capital punishment for murder was finally abolished.

---

[8] This relates to section 53 of the Children and Young Persons Act 1933 and the corresponding legislation for Scotland whereby those under 18 who are convicted of murder are subject to be detained during Her Majesty's pleasure and are not subject to the sentence of life imprisonment.

Annex 6

Life sentences for Murder

THE VIEWS OF MR JACK STRAW WHEN SECRETARY OF STATE FOR THE HOME DEPARTMENT

When the Lane Committee reported in 1993, the response of the then Home Secretary, Mr Michael Howard was unambiguous. He was not prepared to entertain any change respecting the mandatory nature of the life sentence for murder. On 30 May 2000 The Times published an article by one of the present authors [L B-C] who shortly beforehand wrote to Jack Straw seeking his views. His substantially argued and extensive reply came to the same conclusion. He did not persuade us to abandon our position. In line with our view that it is important that the matter be resolved by reasoned argument, which includes considering opposing arguments, we publish, with his agreement, the text of his reply.

It must be borne in mind that the letter was written before the question of the Home Secretary's role in tariff setting had been considered in by the case of Anderson[9] and before even the conception of the Criminal Justice Act 2003 by which Jack Straw's successor in office, David Blunkett, sought to re-establish the status quo ante.

23 June 2000

Dear Louis

Thank you for your letter of 24 May 2000 seeking my views on the mandatory nature of the penalty for murder.

I read your article in *The Times* (Tuesday 30 May) on this subject with interest but, although many of the arguments are well made, they are insufficient to persuade me that the mandatory penalty for murder should be removed.

You ask to what extent I advance the arguments set out by Michael Howard in his response to the Lane Committee's report of 1993. I agree entirely with the view that murder occupies a very special place in our criminal law. The special status of the offence arises not only from the tragedy of the loss of life but also from the murderer's intention that the victim should die or at least suffer serious harm. These characteristics of the offence obtain whatever the circumstances in which it occurred. The sentence of mandatory life imprisonment reflects this unique nature of the offence and the fact that the public rightly regards it as a particularly abhorrent crime. In my view the arguments advanced by Mr Howard comprised all of the major points that need to be made in favour of retention of the mandatory penalty and the setting of tariffs by the Home Secretary. There are, however, a few points I would like to add.

[9] [2003] 1 AC 387.

There is a clear distinction between the mandatory life imprisonment for murder by adults and discretionary life. The former is characterised as a mandatory sentence automatically imposed by law as a punishment for life reflecting the unique gravity of the offence. The discretionary life sentences, on the other hand, are justified primarily by considerations of the offender's character, mental state or age, and their resulting dangerousness and consequently are not complete until the court has determined the relevant part. This distinction between the mandatory and discretionary sentences has been recognised and confirmed in a number of cases by the Commission and European Court of Human Rights notably in the cases of Wynne; Ryan; Thynne, Wilson and Gunnell; and most recently in Thompson and Venables. The distinction raises issues about the role of the discretionary life sentence if the mandatory life sentence was removed. Would the discretionary life sentence continue to have the same role when applied to murder or would judges simply use it as a substitute for long-term determinate sentences? What would be the relationship of the discretionary life sentence to the determinate sentence of imprisonment? An element of uncertainty would be introduced which I believe would undermine public confidence in the criminal justice system's ability to deal effectively with murderers. One could legislate to provide some kind of safeguard, as your article suggests, but such a course concedes the special place murder occupies

The Human Rights Act, when it comes into force, will require our courts to take into account the reasoning in the decisions referred to above and, whilst it is true that they do not have to be followed, I believe that they are persuasive evidence that the current arrangements do not amount to a breach of the Convention. Moreover, the House of Lords in the judgment in the Hindley case on 30 March stressed the unique position of murder and the mandatory sentence in our criminal justice system and unanimously endorsed as both lawful and proportionate the decision of successive Home Secretaries to set a whole life tariff in that case.

The current arrangements work well in practice and have a number of advantages for victims' families, the public, judiciary and offenders. The mandatory life sentence for murder provides vital safeguards against re-offending by ensuring that murderers are released after only the most careful thought. It would be wrong to abolish such a sentence if we were not sure that an alternative would meet all of these important requirements. The mandatory life sentence ensures that a thorough assessment of the risk involved in releasing a prisoner occurs over a suitably long period and is finally determined only when a possible release date approaches. In the absence of a mandatory sentence this important safeguard would be lost. A court would be required to assess this risk at the time of sentencing. A prisoner sentenced to a determinate sentence would have to be released at a certain date even though there were concerns about the risk of re-offending. Even the extended licence period of an extended sentence under the Crime and Disorder Act 1998 is finite. Moreover, the mandatory penalty also ensures that those convicted of murder are released on a life licence. These provisions are a necessary and powerful tool for the supervision of lifers. They provide the powerful and immediate sanction of recall to prison for the lifer whose behaviour gives cause for concern, reassurance for the families of victims, and an important element in maintaining public confidence in the arrangements for the conditional release of convicted murderers. The risk of re-offending by released determinate prisoners currently causes concern; the stakes are likely to be unacceptably high in the case of murder.

You refer in the letter and the article to my view that removal of the mandatory element in the penalty would result in short sentences for murderers. It seems to me that the view that in the absence of mandatory life imprisonment judges may sentence murderers to determinate sentences under which they would spend less time in custody than they would have done if they had been subject to an appropriate tariff is entirely supportable. The role of the discretionary life sentence, as I suggest above, is an issue in itself but it must be that some of those convicted of murder would, in the absence of the mandatory penalty, receive determinate sentences. Judges may be reluctant to impose a determinate sentence of the length that would be required to ensure a prisoner spends the same time as he or she would spend in custody under a tariff. Such a sentence may appear to be disproportionately long. A prisoner who would have been subject to an eight year tariff, for example, would, under current release arrangements, have to receive a sentence of sixteen years imprisonment in order to ensure that he or she would spend the same period in custody.

The present system has the benefit of finality and clarity. Imposition of the mandatory life sentence immediately on conviction meets in most cases the needs of the family of the victim and public to see justice done straight away at the end of what has often been a harrowing ordeal. That feeling of relief is commonly expressed through the media in the aftermath of a trial. The arrangements allow the trial judge to reflect on the whole circumstances of the offence including any mitigating or aggravating circumstances before making a recommendation on tariff through the Lord Chief Justice. It is striking how few judges avail themselves of the statutory power to make a recommendation for a minimum period when they pass sentence (only 5 out of more than 200 in the recent 12 month period). There is no need to reconvene the Court some weeks later, with consequent further distress and inconvenience to the victim's family (and considerable extra cost), to consider reports and set publicly a determinate tariff which in many cases will not satisfy the family and will be open to lengthy appeal procedures.

The current tariff setting system is open and seen to be fair so far as the prisoner is concerned. Tariff recommendations are all seen by the LCJ who applies a common judicial approach. They are disclosed to the prisoner who can make representations before the tariff is set. The consideration of all cases by a single senior official and Minister ensures a high degree of consistency in tariff setting. Unlike 'relevant parts' set by the courts Ministerial tariffs can be reviewed at any time and can be reduced on grounds of exceptional circumstances including exceptional progress in prison (5 have been so reduced since the 10 November 1997 statement). This wide discretion enables the punitive periods to be reviewed and, exceptionally, reduced, long after the judiciary and Ministers concerned may have left the scene.

For all these reasons the current mandatory sentence for murder and the tariff setting arrangements attract public and Parliamentary support. The Secretary of State's role in tariff setting in murder cases is perceived by many as falling within the government's responsibility to provide adequate public protection and does, in some good measure, contribute to public confidence in the criminal justice system.

Accordingly, I remain unconvinced that change to the current system is either necessary or appropriate.

Yours ever
(SGD) Jack

JACK STRAW

Annex 7

Practice Direction (Crime: Mandatory Life Sentences) (No 2)
29 July 2004

It should not be assumed that Parliament, in enacting the Criminal Justice Act 2003, intended to raise to 15 years all mandatory life sentence minimum terms that would previously have had a lower starting point.

Lord Woolf CJ so stated in the Supreme Court when handing down an amendment to Practice Direction (Criminal Proceedings: Consolidation) [2002] 1 WLR 2870 ("the consolidated criminal practice direction").

LORD WOOLF CJ said that this practice direction amends the consolidated criminal practice direction handed down by his Lordship on 8 July 2002.

IV.49 Life sentences

IV.49.1 This direction replaces Practice Direction (Crime: Mandatory Life Sentences) [2004] 1 WLR 1874 handed down on 18 May 2004 (previously inserted at paras IV.49.1 to IV.49.25 of the consolidated criminal practice direction). Its purpose is to give practical guidance as to the procedure for passing a mandatory life sentence under s 269 of and Sch 21 to the Criminal Justice Act 2003 ("the Act"). This direction also gives guidance as to the transitional arrangements under s 276 of and Sch 22 to the Act. It clarifies the correct approach to looking at the practice of the Secretary of State prior to December 2002 for the purposes of Sch 22 to the Act, in the light of the Judgment in R v Sullivan [2004] EWCA Crim 1762; The Times, 14 July 2004.

IV.49.2 S 269 of the Act came into force on 18 December 2003. Under s 269 all courts passing a mandatory life sentence must either announce in open court the minimum term the prisoner must serve before the Parole Board can consider release on licence under the provisions of s 28 of the Crime (Sentences) Act 1997 (as amended by s 275 of the Act) or announce that the seriousness of the offence is so exceptionally high that the early release provisions should not apply at all (a "whole life order").

IV.49.3 In setting the minimum term the court must set the term it considers appropriate taking into account the seriousness of the offence. In considering the seriousness of the offence the court must have regard to the general principles set out in Sch 21 to the Act and any other guidelines issued by the Sentencing Guidelines Council which are relevant to the case and not incompatible with the provisions of Sch 21. Although it is necessary to have regard to the guidance, it is always permissible not to apply the guidance if a judge considers there are reasons for not following it. It is always necessary to have regard to the need to do justice in the particular case. However, if a court departs from any of the starting points given in Sch 21 the court is under a duty to state its reasons for doing so.

IV.49.4 The guidance states that where the offender is 21 or over, the first step is to choose one of three starting points: "whole life", 30 years or 15 years. Where the 15-year starting point has been chosen, judges should have in mind that this starting point encompasses a very broad range of murders. At para 35 of Sullivan the court found that it should not be assumed that Parliament intended to raise all minimum terms that would previously have had a lower starting point to 15 years.

IV.49.5 Where the offender was 21 or over at the time of the offence, and the court takes the view that the murder is so grave that the offender ought to spend the rest of his life in prison, the appropriate starting point is a "whole life order". The effect of such an order is that the early release provisions in s 28 of the Crime (Sentences) Act 1997 will not apply. Such an order should only be specified where the court considers that the seriousness of the offence (or the combination of the offence and one or more other offences associated with it) is exceptionally high. Para 4(2) of Sch 21 to the Act sets out examples of cases where it would normally be appropriate to take the "whole life order" as the appropriate starting point.

IV.49.6 Where the offender is aged 18 to 20 and commits a murder that is so serious that it would require a whole life order if committed by an offender aged 21 or over, the appropriate starting point will be 30 years.

IV.49.7 Where a case is not so serious as to require a "whole life order" but where the seriousness of the offence is particularly high and the offender was aged 18 or over when he committed the offence the appropriate starting point is 30 years. Para 5(2) of Sch 21 to the Act sets out examples of cases where a 30-year starting point would normally be appropriate (if they do not require a "whole life order").

IV.49.8 Where the offender was aged 18 or over when he committed the offence and the case does not fall within para 4(1) or 5(1) of Sch 21 the appropriate starting point is 15 years.

IV.49.9 18 to 20 year olds are only the subject of the 30-year and 15-year starting points.

IV.49.10 The appropriate starting point when setting a sentence of detention during Her Majesty's pleasure for offenders aged under 18 when they committed the offence is always 12 years.

IV.49.11 The second step after choosing a starting point is to take account of any aggravating or mitigating factors which would justify a departure from the starting point. Additional aggravating factors (other than those specified in paras 4(1) and 5(1)) are listed at para 10 of Sch 21. Examples of mitigating factors are listed at para 11 of Sch 21. Taking into account the aggravating and mitigating features the court may add to or subtract from the starting point to arrive at the appropriate punitive period.

IV.49.12 The third step is that the court should consider the effect of s 151(1) of the Powers of Criminal Courts (Sentencing) Act 2000 (or, when it is in force, s 143(2) of the Act) in relation to previous convictions and s 151(2) of the Powers of Criminal Courts (Sentencing) Act 2000 (or, when it is in force, s 143(3) of the Act) where the offence was committed whilst the offender was on bail. The court should also consider the effect of s 152 of the Powers of Criminal Courts (Sentencing) Act 2000 (or, when it is in force, s 144 of the Act) where the offender has pleaded guilty. The court should then take into account what credit the offender would have received for a remand in custody under s 240 of the Act, but for the fact that the mandatory sentence is one of life inprisonment. Where the offender has been remanded in custody in connection with the offence or a related offence, the court should have in mind that no credit will otherwise be given for this time when the prisoner is considered for early release. The appropriate time to take it into account is when setting the minimum term. The court should normally subtract the time for which the offender was remanded in custody in connection with the offence or a related offence from the punitive period it would otherwise impose in order to reach the minimum term.

IV.49.13 Following these calculations the court should have arrived at the appropriate minimum term to be announced in open court. As para 9 of Sch 21 makes clear, the judge retains ultimate discretion and the court may arrive at any minimum term from any starting point. The minimum term is subject to appeal by the offender under s 271 of the Act and subject to review on a reference by the Attorney General under s 272 of the Act.

Transitional arrangements for new sentences where the offence was committed before 18 December 2003

IV 49.14 Where the court is passing a sentence of mandatory life inprisonment for an offence committed before 18 December 2003, the court should take a fourth step in determining the minimum term in accordance with s 276 of and Sch 22 to the Act.

IV.49.15 The purpose of those provisions is to ensure that the sentence does not breach the principle of non-retroactivity by ensuring that a lower minimum term would not have been imposed for the offence when it was committed. Before setting the minimum term the court must check whether the proposed term is greater than that which the Secretary of State would probably have notified under the practice followed by the Secretary of State before December 2002.

IV.49.16 The decision in Sullivan [2004] EWCA Crim 1762; The Times, 14 July 2004 gives detailed guidance as to the correct approach to this practice and judges passing mandatory life sentences where the murder was committed prior to 18 December 2003 are well advised to read that judgment before proceeding.

IV.49.17 The practical result of that judgment is that in sentences where the murder was committed before 31 May 2002, the best guide to what would have been the practice of the Secretary of State is the letter sent to judges by Lord Bingham of Cornhill CJ on 10 February 1997, the relevant parts of which are set out at paras IV.49.18 to IV.49.21 below.

IV.49.18 The practice of Lord Bingham CJ, as set out in his letter of 10 February 1997 was to take 14 years as the period actually to be served for the "average", "normal" or "unexceptional" murder. Examples of factors he outlined as capable, in appropriate cases of mitigating the normal penalty were: (1) youth; (2) age (where relevant to physical capacity on release or the liklihood of the defendant dying in prison); (3) subnormality or mental abnormality; (4) provocation (in a non-technical sense), or an excessive response to a personal threat; (5) the absense of an intention to kill; (6) spontaneity and lack of premeditation (beyond that necessary to constitute the offence: eg a sudden response to family pressure or to prolonged and eventually insupportable stress; (7) mercy killing; (8) a plea of guilty, or hard evidence of remorse or contrition.

IV.49.19 Lord Bingham CJ then listed the following factors as likely to call for a sentence more severe than the norm: (1) evidence of a planned, professional, revenge or contract killing; (2) the killing of a child or a very old or otherwise vulnerable victim; (3) evidence of sadism, gratuitous violence, or sexual maltreatment humiliation or degradation before the killing; (4) killing for gain (in the course of burgulary, robbery, blackmail, insurance fraud, etc); (5) multiple killings; (6) the killing of a witness or potential witness to defeat the ends of justice; (7) the killing of those doing their public duty (policemen, prison officers, postmasters, firemen, judges, etc); (80 terrorist or politically motivated killings; (9) the use of firearms or other dangerous weapons, whether carried for defensive, or offensive reasons; (10) a substantial record of serious violence; (11) Macabre attempts to dismember or conceal the body.

IV.49.20 Lord Bingham CJ further stated that the fact that a defendant was under the influence of drink or drugs at the time of the killing is so common he would be inclined to treat it as neutral.But in the not unfamiliar case in which a married couple, or two derelicts, or two homosexuals, inflamed by drink, indulge in a violent quarrel in which one dies, often against a background of longstanding drunken violence, then he would tend to recommend a term somewhat below the norm.

IV.49.21 Lord Bingham CJ went on to say that given the intent necessary for proof of murder, the consequences of taking life and the understandable reaction of relative of the deceased, a substantial term will almost always be called for, save perhaps in a truly venial case of mercy killing. While a recommendation of a punitive term for longer than, say, 30 years will be very rare indeed, there should not be any upper limit. Some crimes will certainly call for terms very well in excess of the norm.

IV.49.22 For the purposes of sentences where the murder was committed after 31 May 2002 and before 18 December 2003, the judge should apply Practice Statement (Crime: Life Sentences) [2002] 1 WLR 1789 handed down on 31 May 2002 reproduced at paras 49.23 to 49.33 below.

IV.49.23 This statement replaces the previous single normal tariff of 14 years by substituting; a higher and a normal starting point of respectively 16 (comparable to 32 years) and 12 years (comparable to 24 years). These staring points have then to be increased or reduced because of aggravating or mitigating factors such as those referred to below. It is emphasised that they are no more than starting points.

The normal starting point of 12 years

IV.49.24 Cases falling within this starting point will normally involve the killing of an adult victim, arising from a quarrel or loss of temper between two people known to each other. It will not have the characteristics referred to in para 49.26. Exceptionally, the starting point may be reduced because of the sort of circumstances described in the next paragraph.

IV.49.25 The normal starting point can be reduced becuase the murder is one where the offender's culpability is significantly reduced, for example, because: (a) the case came close to the borderline between murder and manslaughter; or (b) the offender suffered from mental disorder, or from a mental disability which lowered the degree of his criminal responsibility for the killing, although not affording a defence of diminished responsibility; or (c) the offender was provoked (in a non-technical sense), such as by prolonged and eventually unsupportable stress; or (d) the case involved an over reaction in self-defence or (e) the offence was a mercy killing. These factors could justify a reduction to 8/9 years (equivalent to 16/18 years).

The higher starting point of 15/16 years

IV.49.26 The higher starting point will apply to cases where the offender's culpability was exceptionally high or the victim was in a particularly vulnerable position. Such cases will be characterised by a feature which makes the crime especially serious, such as (a) the killing was "professional" or a contract killing; (b) the killing was politically motivated; (c) the killing was done for gain (in the course of a burglary, robbery etc.); (d) the killing was intended to defeat the ends of justice (as in the killing of a witness or potential witness); (e) the victim was providing a public service; (f) the victim was a child or was otherwise vulnerable; (g) the killing was racially aggravated: (h) the victim was deliberately targeted because of his or her religion or sexual orientation; (i) there was evidence of sadism, gratuitous violence or sexual maltreatment, humiliation or degradation of the victim before the killing; (j) extensive and/or multiple injuries were inflicted on the victim before death; (k) the offender committed multiple murders.

Variation of the starting point

IV.49.27 Whichever starting point is selected in a particular case, it may be appropriate for the trial judge to vary the starting point upwards or downwards, to take account of aggravating or mitigating factors, which relate to either the offence or the offender, in the particular case.

IV.49.28 Aggravating factors relating to the offence can include; (a) the fact that the killing was planned; (b) the use of a firearm; (c) arming with a weapon in advance; (d) concealment of the body, destruction of the crime scene and/or dismemberment of the body; (e) particularly in domestic violence cases, the fact that the murder was the culmination of cruel and violent behaviour by the offender over a period of time.

IV.49.29 Aggravating factors relating to the offender will include the offender's previous record and failures to respond to previous sentences, to the extent that this is relevant to culpability rather than to risk.

IV.49.30 Mitigating factors relating to the offence will include: (a) an intention to cause grievous bodily harm, rather than to kill; (b) spontaneity and lack of premeditation.

IV.49.31 Mitigating factors relating to the offender may include: (a) the offender's age: (b) clear evidence of remorse or contrition; (c) a timely plea of guilty. Very serious cases

IV.49.32 A substantial upward adjustment may be appropriate in the most serious cases, for example, those involving a substantial number of murders, or if there are several factors identified as attracting the higher starting point present. In suitable cases, the result might even be a minimum term of 30 years (equivalent to 60 years) which would offer little or no hope of the offender's eventual release. In cases of exceptional gravity, the judge, rather than setting a whole life minimum term, can state that there is no minimum period which could properly be set in that particular case.

IV.49.33 Among the categories of case referred to in para IV.49.26 some offences may be especially grave. These include cases in which the victim was performing his duties as a prison officer at the time of the crime or the offence was a terrorist or sexual or sadistic murder or involved a young child. In such a case, a term of 20 years and upwards could be appropriate.

IV.49.34 In following this guidance, judges should bear in mind the conclusion of the court in Sullivan that the general effect of both these statements is the same. While Lord Bingham CJ does not identify as many starting points, it is open to the judge to come to exactly the same decision irrespective of which was followed. Both pieces of guidance give the judge a considerable degree of discretion.

Procedure for announcing the minimum term in open court

IV.49.35 Having gone through the three or four steps outlined above, the court is then under a duty under s 270 of the Act, to state in open court in ordinary language, its reasons for deciding on the minimum term or for passing a whole life order.

IV.49.36 In order to comply with this duty the court should state clearly the minimum term it has determined. In doing so, it should state which of the starting points it has chosen and its reasons for doing so. Where the court has departed from that starting point due to mitigating or aggravating features it must state the reasons for that departure and any aggravating or mitigating features which have led to that departure. At that point the court should also declare how much, if any, time is being deducted for time spent in custody. The court must then explain that the minimum term is the minimum amount of time the prisoner will spend in prison, from the date of sentence before the Parole Board can order early release. If it remains necessary for the protection of the public, the prisoner will continue to be detained after that date. The court should also state that where the prisoner has served the minimum term and the Parole Board has decided to direct release the prisoner will remain on licence for the rest of his life and may be recalled to prison at any time.

IV.49.37 Where the offender was 21 or over when he committed the offence and the court considers that the seriousness of the offence is so exceptionally high that a "whole life order" is appropriate, the court should state clearly its reasons for reaching this conclusion. It should also explain that the early release provisions will not apply.

Index

Notes are shown by *n* after the page number